GROWING UP PURE

Growing Up Pure

White Girls, Queer Teens, and the Racial Foundations of Purity Culture

Lauren D. Sawyer

NEW YORK UNIVERSITY PRESS
New York

NEW YORK UNIVERSITY PRESS
New York
www.nyupress.org

Please contact the Library of Congress for Cataloging-in-Publication data.

ISBN: 9781479838448 (hardback)
ISBN: 9781479838455 (paperback)
ISBN: 9781479838479 (library ebook)
ISBN: 9781479838486 (consumer ebook)

This book is printed on acid-free paper, and its binding materials are chosen for strength and durability. We strive to use environmentally responsible suppliers and materials to the greatest extent possible in publishing our books.

The manufacturer's authorized representative in the EU for product safety is Mare Nostrum Group B.V., Mauritskade 21D, 1091 GC Amsterdam, The Netherlands.
Email: gpsr@mare-nostrum.co.uk.

Manufactured in the United States of America

10 9 8 7 6 5 4 3 2 1

Also available as an ebook

For Davy

CONTENTS

Introduction

Here is a story I have told many times, about the afternoon I drove from my parents' house to the Starbucks across from Glenbrook Mall, where my best friend came out to me as queer. I have told the story of sitting in my car, Blake in the passenger seat, us with frothy Frappuccinos between our knees, and the "I'm gay—well, bi" coming out of my best friend's mouth. The "I think that's why I was jealous of Luke"—my junior-year boyfriend—"'cause I liked you." And the adamant but shaky response I gave: "No."

No, you're not gay. No, you didn't like-like me. No, I do not accept this as true.

That one word, *no*, marked the end of our friendship and the beginning of Blake's rejection by our church community. Despite being a model churchgoer and a vital member of the youth group and worship team, that spring, Blake was kicked out of our evangelical church for being gay. As for us, Blake and I hardly spent time together after that fateful trip to Starbucks. We were certainly not laughing at inside jokes or whispering about our mutual crushes the way we had for years. Blake had to suffer rejection from friends, parental lockdown (no cell phone, no hanging out with friends after school), and a loss of a spiritual community, all for having a sexual identity that did not align with normative evangelical sexual ethics. And while this was heartbreaking to me as a teenager, I was also convinced that this was the way it ought to be.

At eighteen years old, I was steeped in what critics would later call *purity culture*, or "the constellation of beliefs, practices, and organizations that constitute the sexual values of most evangelical subcultures in the United States."[1] The central injunction of purity culture is to refrain from all sexual behavior and eschew all sexual desire until heterosexual marriage—a marriage reflecting the white American middle-class fantasy of two parents, "two children and a dog."[2] For its advocates, maintaining purity is understood as the primary responsibility of young white women, who are thought to not crave sex as men or women of color do. While other racial groups in the United States promote sexual purity in their churches, contemporary evangelical purity culture is a uniquely white construction that relies on a complex entanglement of race, gender, and economic structures and stereotypes. As Sophie Bjork-James argues in *The Divine Institution*, the family—particularly the white, patriarchal, and heteronormative family—is the center of evangelical lived religion. That is, for white American evangelicals, "defending the patriarchal family—particularly through opposition to LGBTQ rights—then, becomes a way to defend one's faith and one's understanding of God."[3] This particular construction of the family was birthed out of racial segregation, Bjork-James argues, which reinforces a color-blind, individualistic ethic of family values.[4]

As white suburban kids raised in purity culture, Blake's and my heterosexuality were a given. I believed we would eventually marry one of the cute, white, muscular boys we dated or had crushes on in high school. We would serve as missionaries abroad (India was my country of choice) or be pastors' wives and give birth to many children. And in the meantime, I knew it was our responsibility to keep the boys in line. I remember the summer at church camp when the middle-aged camp director motioned for me to pull the shoulder of my long-sleeved zip-up over the bra strap that was peeking out. It had been well established that a bra strap alone could lead a boy astray: he might be led to lust, masturbate, or interpret the bra strap as permission to rape the bra-wearer in question.[5] Despite the many ways I embodied the ideal "pure" girl—I was thin, white, and middle-class; I dutifully attended church and read my Bible every night; I only dated Christian boys whom I could imagine myself marrying one day—I still managed to stumble on this one important criterion. I was embarrassed that I had not been as modest (or performed modesty as well) as the other girls at camp.

It is easy to look at this time of my life through the lens of victimhood. As a teenager, I was a victim to the structures of purity culture and the powerful institutions that upheld its messaging. The Powers that Be patiently and lovingly explained that being impure led one to become like a chewed-up piece of gum, a "'trashable' Styrofoam cup," a used car, a licked lollipop.[6] Disgusting, unwantable, used, garbage. By the time I got to the Starbucks parking lot, I had attended youth group for four years and church camp for five. I had been gifted two teen Bibles with messages about purity embedded within the scriptural text.[7] I had received abstinence-only-until-marriage education in my public high school.[8] I had read dozens of Christian dating guides, books provocatively called *Dateable* and *Little Black Book on Sex and Dating*,[9] and had sung along to songs with the refrain "God's writing my love story."[10] I had internalized what it meant to be pure. I knew how to be the good Christian girl, even though I could never quite live up to it myself. What I did not know was how to respond to my friend in any way but with contempt and disbelief. For all the lessons my pastors, mentors, books, and favorite musicians had taught me, they failed in helping me see how flourishing might exist outside the structures of white, middle-class, heterosexual marriage.

As tempting as it is to give into this victim narrative wholesale, I have come to see how inadequate it is. Plenty of well-intentioned people have invited me to forgive myself and forget what happened at that Starbucks, to remember that I was just a kid and did not know then what I know now. They have reminded me of how I have made amends in my adulthood by teaching queer theologies and advocating for LGBTQ+ rights. While I know that harboring self-contempt and engaging in self-flagellation are equally unproductive responses, I also know that seeing my younger self as merely a victim of a culture does nothing for Blake or for my younger self, nor does it undo the damage that was done to our friendship that day. Understanding myself as merely a *victim* to purity culture misses the ways I was *agential*: I resisted the teachings that did not fit within my personal worldview, and I complied with the norms that asked me to reject Blake. More than merely being indoctrinated into its cause, I chose to participate in purity culture. I purchased books, music, and a purity ring with my hard-earned allowance. I was the one who begged my Jewish mother to drive me across town for youth group and Wednesday night Bible studies. I chose to date and kiss my boyfriends despite the popularity of Joshua Harris's book *I Kissed Dating Goodbye*.[11] And I chose to respond to my best friend quite cruelly in such a vulnerable moment. Understanding myself as merely a victim of purity culture obscures the fact that, even as a teenager, I was a moral agent. I made choices, however lacking in wisdom, based on what made sense in my social context—but I made choices nonetheless. As an adult looking back, it is important to me to empower my younger self and my contemporaries to own those choices and their consequences.

From Victim to Moral Agent

The aim of this book is to challenge adult-centric, normative views of adolescent participation in purity culture in order to imagine a post-purity sexual ethic that is both child-centric and queer. I argue that young people are not merely victims of purity culture but are uniquely vulnerable and complicit within it. This requires us to see young people as moral agents (choice-makers) and full sexual subjects, regardless of their age. This does not mean that young people are "agentic warriors" or more resilient to harm done to them than adults are.[12] Young people, like all humans, are contributors to their moral worlds and participate in ways commensurate to their age and positionality. Nor does this mean that purity culture is not as harmful as its critics suggest. In the early 2020s alone, we saw the unveiling of the Southern Baptist Convention's widespread sexual abuse and the role of purity teachings in a mass shooting in Atlanta, Georgia.[13] These two examples, though extreme, remind us that purity culture was and is a source of real harm to its constituents. However, only focusing on young people's victimhood—especially *white* youth's victimhood—can mask the ways in which they actively participated in the movement. Being perceived as innocent victims affords white youth the privilege of participating in harmful behaviors themselves, without accountability. At the same time, that perception of innocence prevents us from recognizing white youth's creative, agential acts of resistance.

As an inductive and intersectional project, this book centers the lived experiences of white youth *as* white youth. My intention here is not to center whiteness as the norm but rather to uncover what has been made invisible. Just as the white race was constructed only to distinguish itself from Black and Brown bodies, white "purity" exists only in opposition to Black/Brown "impurity" and heterosexual "normalcy" in opposition to queer "deviance."[14] I argue that contemporary evangelical purity culture is one iteration of many purity *cultures* that function to denigrate white women at the expense of people of color and for the conservation of white male power.[15] Purity culture is, then, a white supremacist project, something that both implicitly and explicitly teaches the superiority of white epistemologies, white values, and white family structures and recruits young people to do its bidding.[16] Purity culture is a *normalizing force*, for what has been deemed "normal" in modern U.S. culture had been "defined in large part through a powerfully racialized understanding of sexuality."[17]

Within contemporary evangelical purity culture (hereafter, purity culture), young white women are viewed as both emblems of innocence and harbingers of sin. From their conception, white girls raised in evangelicalism are considered vulnerable, the standard of innocence for whom campaigns against abortion and child trafficking exist. White girls are vulnerable to outside forces as well, thought to be easily duped into having sex with men or buying into secular beauty standards.[18] Therefore, these girls must rely on their fathers, pastors, or the state to protect them at all costs.[19] The stakes are particularly high when a white girl reaches adolescence, when she is typically developmentally ready for sex. Yet, under purity culture, white girls are taught that they do not desire sex.[20] When a young white woman expresses her sexual desires by engaging in sexual behavior or wearing immodest clothing, she is thought to be dangerous, capable of bringing good white men down with her. For it is white adolescent girls' and women's responsibility to keep men from crossing a line sexually (e.g., via premarital or extramarital sex).

White queer youth of all genders (that is, those who "may fall outside of heterosexuality and gendernormativity")[21] embody "deviant" sexuality, representing what happens when evangelical youth stray from the teachings of purity culture. They are viewed as either victims of predatory gay adults or merely confused Christian boys and girls who can be "cured" through repentance and by submitting to binary gender norms.[22] In purity culture, all youth are presumed to be heterosexual and receive teaching based on their sex assigned at birth. Girls, no matter their sexual identities, are taught that they need to protect their purity for their future husbands. Boys, no matter their sexual identities, are taught that their sexual desire for girls is nearly impossible to control yet pornography and masturbation are sinful ways to curb their raging hormones.[23]

As more scholars, memoirists, and documentarians have traced the harmful impact of purity culture on mostly white youth who were raised with its teachings, a common theme of victimhood has emerged.[24] Much like its advocates, some critics of purity culture treat youth as though they were unable to make moral and sexual choices for themselves due to age, gender (for young women), and sexual identity (for queer youth).[25] Young women are said to have been "forced" or "manipulated" into wearing purity rings gifted by their fathers[26]—they could not possibly have gladly received them. Queer teens are "recruited" by powerful evangelical organizations only to be banished later for being gay[27]—they would never dream of joining such organizations of their own volition. Even in their vulnerability, even within systems as harmful as purity culture, young people are capable of making choices about their sexual identities and behaviors, no matter how liberative or destructive those choices may be.

Uniquely targeted by purity culture's messaging, white girls and white queer youth have engaged in the culture for any number of reasons with different degrees of involvement and commitment. Some young people were all but forced to attend youth group as long as they lived in their parents' home. Some attended Sunday school with friends after a Saturday night sleepover, receiving purity teachings only occasionally. Some were introduced to purity culture through programs like Fellowship of Christian Athletes at their public high schools. And some, like me, willingly participated in youth group, read purity culture books, sang abstinence anthems, and internalized purity culture's antifeminist, antiqueer teachings. While much attention has been given to the *effects* of purity culture on young people, especially on young white women, few are asking how young people act as full moral agents and sexual subjects within the context of purity culture. In order to understand the impact of purity culture on white youth and understand how and why young people have participated in it, we must grapple with the social constructions and intersections of race, gender, religion, and age in U.S. history and the present context. But more than that, we must listen to the voices of youth themselves.

The Moral Insights of Girls and Queer Youth

For most of the Western philosophical tradition, children and adolescents were excluded from participating in the moral worlds of adults, as they were believed not to be developmentally fit to do so. But due to the contributions of feminist and childhood studies scholars in the late twentieth century, ethicists are beginning to recognize youth as moral agents who have unique perspectives to bear on ethical issues, including those related to sex. To borrow language from queer feminist Marvin Ellison, we have so much to learn about sex from young people.[28] Peeking into young people's moral worlds gives us a vision for sexualities that decenter adult experiences—especially the long-held standard of white cisgender male adult sexuality—as the norm.

This book considers white young women and queer youth valuable conversation partners, for not only do authorities of white evangelicalism—authors, speakers, musicians, pastors, and parents—shape purity culture, young people do as well, through the choices they make. Therefore, I begin with the experiences of young white women and white queer youth and then constellate other sources of knowledge (e.g., sociology, history, media, ethics, etc.) to analyze those experiences. I place ethics, social science, and historical scholarship in conversation with personal narratives in order to paint a robust portrait of young people's sexual agency within the oppressive system of contemporary evangelical purity culture.

My choice to privilege the lived experiences of young people is in line with my feminist commitment to reject the so-called "view from nowhere"[29]—the idea that "real" scholarship represents an objective neutrality. Feminist scholars have argued that this view from nowhere is actually an androcentric positionality, as all perspectives are embodied.[30] Just as my relationship to my research has not been formed in a vacuum but is shaped by my embodied experience as a cisgender white woman, the same is true for the youth I study. My feminist commitments lead me to be self-reflexive of my own embodiment. I recognize that my experience within purity culture does not encompass all human experiences, not even all cisgender, female, white, heterosexual experiences. While this book does not include autoethnography as a method, per se, I do recognize that my particular relationship to the subject of this book has a bearing on how it is written and the conclusions I make.[31] My perspective as someone who was committed to the ideologies of purity culture and who experienced, witnessed, and participated in the policing of sexuality allows me to approach my topic not just as an outsider looking in but as someone who has deftness with the rhetoric and norms of evangelicalism and a personal stake in the work. Who I am as an "embodied self-as-scholar" is, as Brent Smith writes, "never far from the surface."[32]

As a feminist committed to childism, or the "critical lens for deconstructing adultism across research and societies and reconstructing more age-inclusive scholarly and social imaginations,"[33] I prioritize the subjectivity of young people, specifically adolescent girls and queer youth who grew up within purity culture, while avoiding sentimentalizing, demonizing, or overly generalizing their experiences. I echo the sentiments of feminists Stevi Jackson and Sue Scott, who argue, "It is important . . . not to locate children and young people as cultural dopes, as passive recipients" of media or, in this case, purity culture rhetoric. "It is equally important in recognizing children's agency not to equate it with resistance. If we see girls as either 'brainwashed' by the media or as in rebellion against dominant discourses, we lose sight of the actualities of their everyday experiences and practices."[34] Affording youth epistemological privilege, I listen to their experiences to consider how they negotiated their agency within purity culture, despite the limitations placed on them because of their gender, their (however hidden) sexual identities, or the privileges of their race. This does not assume that youth always make well-reasoned or morally good decisions. But it also does not assume that they are inherently bad decisions.

Queer theory functions as a helpful, though perhaps surprising, companion to childism. Queer theory tugs from the margins what has been labeled non-normative, queer, odd, or unruly,[35] including the sexual deviance of evangelical queer youth and sexually active white girls. But it is not only about sexual behaviors and identities. Queer theory is a political, anti-capitalist project that critiques the very norms at the heart of white evangelicalism.[36] That is, while purity culture preaches a normative way for children and teens to grow up toward heterosexual love, marriage, and sex, "any and *every* child [is] queer."[37] As queer theorists like Kathryn Bond Stockton and Hannah Dyer argue, young people do not follow the scripts adults write for them in terms of how they behave, how they perform gender, or how they love or desire.[38] Children's and youth's desires and behaviors "frustrate the adult-centric, neo-liberal, white, heteropatriarchy construction of sexuality"[39] that suggests they must remain innocent until a certain age and then still eschew all desire (for girls) or channel their desires appropriately (for boys) toward heterosexual marriage. Alongside childist and feminist commitments, queer theory invites us to see youth as they are, not as we expect or hope for them to be.

In centering the subjectivities of adolescents, I consider written narrative as one way of crystallizing personal experience. In this book I rely on the multitude of already-published ethnography and personal essays written by white women and white queer folks of all genders, looking back at their adolescence. This methodological choice frees me to probe these narratives for examples of moral and sexual agency rather than replicating ethnographic work. Yet relying on already-constructed narratives has its limitations. For one, stories are always written within specific "narrative environments . . . assembled and told to someone, somewhere, at some time, with a variety of consequences for those concerned."[40] The narratives analyzed in this book are written by adults reflecting on their adolescent experiences, for some many years later; these are not diary entries, nor are they attempting to address my specific research questions. The truths that I extract from these stories, therefore, may not reflect adolescent experience as much as they reflect the adult perspective interpreting the adolescent experience. I mitigate this issue by drawing on social science research that includes adolescent voices and by using a broad set of sources that suggests a level of consistency among different people writing or responding to interviews in strikingly similar ways.

All of this descriptive work (both personal experience and scholarship) provides grounding for my constructive argument that despite the restrictive nature of purity culture—especially to young women who are thought to *not* have sexual desire and queer youth who have *deviant* sexual desire—adolescents find paths to negotiate and develop their own sense of moral agency and sexual subjectivity within those strict boundaries. To argue this, I borrow language from ethicists including Cristina L. H. Traina, Kate Ott, and John Wall, who understand moral agency as generative, not just belonging to adulthood or precluding vulnerability. These feminist and childist voices again challenge the sentimentalization or demonization of youth sexual experiences apparent in evangelical texts as well as in some social science and historical research.

At the same time, I bring in the needed critique of Black feminists and scholars in the field of critical whiteness studies who help locate youth within their racial environments or their "social greenhouses," as anthropologist Marilyn Strathern puts it.[41]

Ultimately, I draw on multiple disciplines and sources of knowledge that reflect my feminist, childist, and queer commitments to centering the experiences of young women and queer youth while also giving attention to issues of white supremacist ideology inherent within purity culture. At one level, this book points toward a more inclusive and complex understanding of young people's sexual and moral agency within the context of purity culture. Even more so, this project invites us to envision a more expansive moral universe, one that includes both adults and youth, by attending to the questions: How do we understand youth agency and choice when they are constrained by the limits of their experience and rely on adults for much of their well-being? How do those of us who are white hold ourselves accountable for participating in white supremacist structures, even when we cannot see a world beyond them? How can we expand our understanding of sex and sexuality that decenters the adult white male experience?

In understanding young people as both vulnerable to purity culture but complicit in it as full sexual subjects and agents, we can begin to uncover the extent of the harm done to them without overlooking the harm they have perpetuated against others. Healing does not become pigeonholed to just the white girls who were infantilized and desexualized by purity culture, but it extends to the queer kids, the Black and Brown boys and girls, and the nonbinary young people (among others) upon whom harm was inflicted. It takes seriously all the ways young people have been hurt by purity culture as a mechanism of normative white supremacy while acknowledging that young people have always had choices in how to act, even if those choices were constrained. While this book does not offer a specific prescriptive or proscriptive sexual ethic, it does offer ethical interventions, namely, through virtue ethics ("burdened virtues") and creative queer failure ("orgasmic failure") as ways of recognizing young people's subjectivity, agency, and ultimately dignity as part of the human race. I argue for a post-purity sexual ethic that expands our understanding of adolescent sex beyond the framework of risk, invites young people to see how their social location shapes how they engage in their sexual/moral universes, and asks adults to take young people's sexual behaviors and expressions seriously.

Organization of This Book

This book moves toward understanding young people as both interdependent agents and complex subjects within the context of purity culture. Chapter 1 begins by introducing purity culture in light of its fraught historical foundations and connection to white American evangelicalism. I argue that the discourse surrounding purity culture, including critique against it, sets up an unhelpful binary between perpetrating adults and victimized youth. This binary thinking, I argue, reinforces the inherent whiteness of purity culture discourse rather than offering a true counternarrative.

From that foundation, the next three chapters uncover centuries-long understandings of childhood and adolescence as unformed, innocent, deviant, or precocious. Children and Adolescents as bourgeois constructions—not living, breathing persons—are overwhelmingly configured as heterosexual and white. The Child and Adolescent, understood in these ways, have been used as political props by adults to quell their anxieties about changing mores and power structures. In moral/sex panics, the Child and Adolescent are deemed those who need protecting from the racialized other or from social freedoms run amok. Along with queer theorists and childist scholars, I ask, what if we understood youth on their own terms, as agents and subjects, not merely vessels of adult anxieties?

Chapter 5 turns to the lived experiences of young people as valid sources of knowledge. As the heart of this book, this chapter locates moments of moral and sexual agency within young people's narratives. It draws attention to how whiteness—though often made invisible—alongside heteronormative and middle-class values functions within a young person's gender and sexual development. This chapter reveals young people's inherent agency, even as they are vulnerable to the structures they participate in.

Finally, in chapter 6, I argue that in order to develop a post-purity sexual ethic, we must address purity culture as a product of normative whiteness in the United States. In that, we must recognize young white women and white queer youth as both complicit participants in and vulnerable victim-survivors of its teachings, materials, and norms. This book furthers the work of feminist ethics, locates childist ethics in an arena it has yet to enter (post-purity), and offers a novel perspective on how to respond to purity culture that does not recapitulate its same white supremacist problems. By returning to the categories of "orgasmic failure" and "burdened virtues," both introduced in chapter 4, I offer a view of white adolescence that rejects the binaries of *complicit* and *vulnerable* and invites young people into the moral world usually restricted to adults.

Meanwhile, in the Starbucks Parking Lot

When I tell the story about Starbucks and the Frappuccinos, I rarely mention all that was leading up to that moment. For months, my best friend had been pulling away, finding friendship in a girl with a gap-toothed smile. To say I was jealous of the new girl was an understatement. I was desperate for Blake. I had confided in two of my guy friends, two of Blake's ex-boyfriends no less, trying to figure out what to do. In adolescent fashion, my guy friends divulged the rumors they had heard, that Blake and the gap-toothed girl were sending each other sexual text messages. I laughed it off, not even entertaining the idea, as I had known from experience that when two girls were best friends, people were bound to suspect they were lesbians.

But then, a few days later, I was on my way to Starbucks. I remember being at the intersection of Coldwater and Collins Road when it hit me. *Maybe the rumors were true.* This was quite literally a crossroads moment for me. I had a choice in that moment in how I would respond to Blake if the rumors were true (as they were). The choice I made in that moment, and again in the Starbucks parking lot, was to let my culture; my own adolescent sexual ethic; my gender, sexuality, and race; and my understanding of the Bible and theology have the final say about what it meant to be in relationship with Blake. I knew in that moment that I could have chosen a different way—and, in fact, I did choose differently in the weeks, months, and years that followed.

As soon as word got around about Blake and the gap-toothed girl, parents and church leaders were mobilized and began making rules about who could see whom when and who could attend church. My youth pastor's wife sat with me, again at the Starbucks across from the mall, and reminded me that what Blake was doing—or who Blake claimed to be—was sinful.

And yet, not in any streamlined way and certainly not with a particular future in mind, I started asking questions. I started questioning the sexual norms that I had come to take for granted. Those norms had truly served me so well at this point in my life: with three high school boyfriends and plenty of chaste kissing, I allowed myself to explore while still feeling relatively comfortable within the range of what was considered by those around me to be *pure enough*. As Lorraine Delia Kenny writes, "The moment one calls attention to privilege it begins to unravel."[42] Slowly, the norms of purity culture began to unravel for me. Although kissing is not universally accepted within purity culture, I was at least kissing *boys*. It became clear to me that, next to Blake, I was the Good Girl. My first awareness of heterosexual privilege began to take shape.

About a year later, after Blake had "successfully" gone through a church camp conversion—as proven by a heterosexual relationship—and then come back out as queer, Blake called me in a crisis, the details of which were as blurry then as they are now. I was at my evangelical college then, and we were not allowed to stay over at anyone's house—even a best friend's—without being granted permission. I told my R.A. the gist of what I knew. With her blessing, I drove through snowy Indiana to Blake's parents' house, a place I had spent so many hours of my adolescence. Blake was OK. Whatever the crisis was, it was over. I felt like the best friend once again, Blake's savior, the beloved.

It was late, maybe midnight, and we discussed sleeping arrangements. Did I want to share a bed with Blake—as I had for years—or sleep in the guest room? Another crossroads. I remembered what I had learned about sexual temptation and lust. I chose the guest room.

I tell this story in full because it illustrates how recognizing a young person's sexual and moral agency—in this case my own—is important in cultivating a sexual ethic that does not recapitulate the same problems of white supremacist purity culture. Merely decrying the harmful choices I made in my youth is not enough, but neither is forgiving and forgetting them without deeper reflection. My own sexual subjectivity and agency grew "poorly, barely, slowly"[43] through my adolescence and are still growing in such a haphazard, awkward way in my thirties. The choices I made, and make, are not always products of my purity culture upbringing. There were minor moments of questioning and disagreeing that, though small, led to bigger questions and the more momentous choice to, eventually, leave behind evangelical views on homosexuality altogether. There were other moments, too, in which I slid—and slide—back into those encultured ways of thinking that lead to harm to myself and others. But failure is part of the messy work of being human, and if we deny our failures, we deny our own humanity, in all of its flawed complexity.

1

What We Talk About When We Talk About Purity Culture

"Ready to get your blood pressure up?"

Stephanie Drury, a public critic of American evangelicalism, tweeted a screenshot of a Facebook post with this added caption. The original poster, a mom of twin teenage girls, had shared about the "very special gift" her husband was giving each daughter for her fifteenth birthday: three rings, each representing different aspects of the girl's sexual purity prior to marriage. The first kiss. The first I love you. The loss of her virginity. The girls' mother wrote: "Each time the girls [Ariana and Ariah] reach one of those milestones they must remove one of their rings and give it to the young man signifying that they understand that they are giving a piece of themselves away. The goal is that their husbands will have collected all three rings and can return them to [the girls] after their wedding night to be worn on their right ring finger." The mother celebrates "the fact that both girls accepted these gifts and agreed to enter into covenant with us as we wait for the Lord to bring the men into their worlds that we have been praying for their entire lives."[1]

Drury's Twitter followers, many of whom self-identify as ex-evangelicals or "exvangelicals,"[2] expressed outrage at the mother's Facebook post, responding to Drury's tweet with "gross" or "disgusting" or by expressing disapproval in gifs, memes, and vomiting emojis.[3] Some respondents darkly predicted abusive marriages in Ariana's and Ariah's futures.[4] One poster, @AlsoNamedSara, wrote what the other reactions seem to imply: "I'm guessing these girls didn't actually 'agree to enter this covenant' as much as they were forced and manipulated into accepting this 'gift.'"[5]

What these responses miss is Ariana and Ariah themselves. How do we know what they desire? Their mom states that both girls accepted these rings and agreed to enter into a covenant with their parents. Can we believe that these girls chose this for themselves? Can we take them at their word? The respondents to Drury's post seem quick to say no. The girls must be either brainwashed or lying about their commitment to purity.

These exvangelical responses reflect much of the growing literature on purity culture, which views girls like Ariana and Ariah as helpless victims to their parents and their conservative churches. But this thinking only reinforces the messages of the movement they purport to critique: that young white women cannot think for themselves and therefore must be protected from dangerous ideologies. As this social media exchange suggests, the dilemmas of purity culture provide an occasion to discuss, critique, theorize, and make assumptions about adolescent sexuality and agency. The discourse tends to rehearse a victimological view of white girls and white queer youth and fails to see the broader historical, systemic, and racialized origins and commitments of evangelicalism. A more holistic understanding of purity culture and its origins and discourses can help us make sense of what is at stake and orient us toward a different way of understanding youth sexualities and agency.

As the title of this chapter suggests, a discourse exists beyond our mere definitional understanding of purity culture. The "we" in this case suggests a consistent narrative around purity culture, especially by those who identify as formerly evangelical, post-evangelical, or exvangelical. As Sarah McCammon argues in her book *The Exvangelicals*, *exvangelical* is a capacious category, which includes those like Drury and her followers who actively and publicly critique evangelicalism on social media as well as those who have quietly left evangelicalism for progressive mainline denominations.[6] Whether identifying as exvangelical or otherwise, we may have common language for talking about purity culture, but we often speak past each other.

In light of this and in service to the broader project at hand—understanding youth on their own terms—I make three major moves here. First, I define purity culture *as a culture* with its own language, rituals, and beliefs. Then, I locate purity culture within its historical context within conservative white evangelicalism. Finally, I look at the present-day discourse around purity culture and what it misses, particularly around understanding purity as a racial category and a system of harm.

A Purity "Toolkit"

Defining a culture is a notoriously difficult task. For our purposes, we can understand culture as consisting of "such symbolic vehicles of meaning, including beliefs, ritual practices, art forms, and ceremonies, as well as informal cultural practices such as language, gossip, stories, and rituals of daily life."[7] These "vehicles of meaning" are used as "tools" with which individuals and communities act. Culture is not determinative or causal per se; rather as a "toolkit," it shapes or influences how and what actions take place by giving people the tools to use.[8] What, then, is a purity culture, and how do its community members act?

At the heart of contemporary evangelical purity culture is the belief in the sacredness and salvific (power-to-save) nature of sex, as ordained by the Christian God.[9] For its members, this core belief necessitates an adherence to the sex-gender binary: that there are only two sexes (male, female) that are to be performed in only two legitimate ways (masculine, feminine). This belief is ritualized through the practice of heterosexual marriage for adults and abstinence for teenagers.[10] Ceremonies exist for both parties: the wedding and the purity ball,[11] where rings are exchanged and promises of fidelity and submission are made to men (husbands and fathers, respectively). Purity culture has its own language of *secondary virginity*, *saving oneself for marriage*, or *dating Jesus* for teens. For adults, the language of *bouncing the eyes*,[12] *biblical marriage*, or *helpmeet* is used to reinscribe the values of the culture. The stories of purity culture, and its gossip, center on the "prosperity gospel" of penile-vaginal intercourse (PVI) within heterosexual marriage[13]—especially if both husband and wife are virgins—and the "physically and psychologically dangerous" nature of PVI outside it.[14]

What I am describing here is mainstream purity culture. Much more extreme or high-control versions of purity culture exist in the form of, for example, the Quiverfull movement. Quiverfull families have the same "toolkits" as mainstream adherents, but they use their tools toward different ends. Like those in the mainstream, Quiverfull members believe in the sacredness and salvific nature of sex, emphasize the gender and sex binary (perhaps more so than what is mainstream), and believe sex only belongs within heterosexual marriage. What makes them a more extreme version of purity culture, however, or at least outside the mainstream, is their belief that birth control "interferes with God's authority and constitutes a form of abortion."[15] The Quiverfull movement[16] is named for Psalm 127:3–5: "Like arrows in the hands of a warrior are children born in one's youth. Blessed is the man whose quiver is full of them." Quiverfull families believe that "Christian parents who limit the number of children they have are, whether they know it or not, helping Satan."[17] On the other hand, mainstream adherents of purity culture are much more apt to use birth control within heterosexual marriage—and more significantly, they treat PVI not merely as a means to procreate but as a form of union and connection with one's spouse.[18]

Mainstream purity culture established its presence in the popular imagination in July 1994 when 25,000 conservative evangelical teens and young adults declared their commitment to sexual purity by gathering in the nation's capital and thrusting signed abstinence pledges into the lawn by the Washington Monument. "I make a commitment to God, myself, my family, my friends, my future mate, and my future children to be sexually abstinent from this date until the day I enter a Biblical marriage relationship," the pledge cards read.[19] Between 1994 and the mid-2010s, millions of primarily white evangelical teenagers and young adults across North America[20] would participate in purity culture by gathering at rallies, signing abstinence pledges, and wearing purity rings.

True Love Waits, the Southern Baptist organization behind the Washington event, saw this new purity movement as countercultural, an antidote to the sexual revolution of the 1960s. Teens were encouraged to talk about their commitment to purity in the language of empowerment and as a form of "coming out" (as a virgin), warping the language of women's and gay liberation. In suggesting a contested relationship with liberation movements, these evangelical leaders saw sexual purity as "transformative—even prophetic, to use theological language—in that it is a sexual orientation that witnesses to a new way of being that has the ability to transform the world."[21] Indeed transformative, Silver Ring Thing, a purity organization with a similar vision as True Love Waits, joined forces with the federal government to provide abstinence-only-until-marriage education in public schools.[22] Such education still thrives in certain states that have chosen to tap into governmental resources.[23]

Contemporary evangelical purity culture has certainly lost its cultural force since its heyday in the '90s and '00s,[24] perhaps due to the growing scholarship on how psychologically and physiologically damaging its teachings are, especially to young women.[25] However, there appears to be a reemergence of purity culture—"purity culture 2.0"—through Generation Z–saturated media like TikTok and YouTube.[26] Still today, the tenants of purity culture have been reinforced through institutions including churches, the U.S. government, conservative political organizations and politicians,[27] Disney,[28] and crisis pregnancy centers.[29] Even so, its primary disseminator was and is white American evangelicalism.

The Moral and Social Structures of Evangelicalism

Like the term *culture, evangelicalism* is not easily definable. When explained theologically, scholars often draw on David Bebbington's quadrilateral, which describes evangelicals in the United States and abroad as those who believe in the necessity of evangelism, personal conversion, the inerrancy of the Bible, and the saving power of the Cross. Historically, in the United States, evangelicalism is a branch of American Protestantism that was "broadly orthodox and active in social and missionary outreach,"[30] with its roots in the Second Great Awakening (1790s–1840s) and its subsequent reform movements. Undergoing shifts throughout the next century, evangelicalism reemerged powerfully in the 1940s as neo-evangelicalism, a politically and socially conservative form of Protestantism that clung to the fundamentals of the faith, akin to Bebbington's quadrilateral,[31] while attempting to engage broader culture through mass media, popular culture, and politics.[32]

Stepping beyond its theological origins, others have named evangelicalism a subculture of U.S. Protestantism with its own common language and material goods,[33] like, as Barbara Wheeler writes: "thousands of Christian recordings, even more books . . . magazines, pamphlets, newspapers, broadsides, leaflets, plaques, posters, greeting and note cards, bumper stickers, ceramics, jewelry."[34] Like Justice Stewart's infamous statement on pornography, many scholars and thinkers suggest that they know evangelicalism when they see it.[35] Thus, *evangelical* has come to describe people from a variety of different denominational affiliations, even those from non-Protestant traditions like Catholicism and Mormonism, who consume similar products and espouse similar values.[36]

As a subculture, evangelicalism grew rapidly within postwar suburbanization. The suburbs had everything: malls, grocery stores, neighborhoods—and churches. Christian media, through the proliferation of, say, Family Christian bookstores,[37] thrived in the suburbs, peddling a homogeneous and normative message about what it means to be an evangelical Christian. This is what scholar Heather Hendershot calls the "Christian lifestyle" market.[38] That is, within the isolation of the suburbs, normative beliefs about family life (as nuclear, heterosexual, white) and the Protestant work ethic thrived, as there were no visible alternatives to challenge them.[39] This was mutually reinforcing. The Christian lifestyle market "reproduce[d]" evangelicalism just as much as evangelicalism produced its media and business empires.[40]

Arguing cheekily in the introduction to his book *The Other Evangelicals*, Isaac B. Sharp states that "if twentieth-century American evangelicals could humorously (and not inaccurately) be defined as 'those who liked Billy Graham,' they might also be described as 'those who *were like* Billy Graham'—or, if not Graham, someone who believed, thought, acted, voted, and looked an awful lot like him."[41] Of course, not all evangelicals in the twentieth and twenty-first centuries were conservative, straight, and white like Billy Graham, Sharp argues. Evangelicalism, for instance, is growing rapidly in Central and South America[42] and among Latinos in the United States.[43] There are Black, Asian, Latino, feminist, and queer evangelicalisms that are often subjugated within this broad definition of evangelicalism as a religious movement or subculture.[44] These "other evangelicals" are, indeed, worthy of our scholarly attention. They are not at the center of this project, which is concerned with the mainstream white American evangelicalism, very much *because* of its power in determining who is "in bounds."[45]

Whether understood historically, theologically, or socially in our present consciousness, evangelicalism has become associated with conservative politics, the policing of women's and people of color's bodies, and white supremacy. Since its roots in the Second Great Awakening, evangelicalism has been at the forefront of present and historical purity cultures focused on regulating sexual desire, particularly white women's desire. In the early 1900s, white women were deemed "insane" for falling in love with Asian men.[46] In the 1910s, women were discouraged from socializing in coed spaces like dance halls, ice cream parlors, and theaters, especially where non-white immigrant men might also be present.[47] Up until 1967, white women in parts of the South (and elsewhere in the country) were forbidden to marry Black men.[48] That is, *purity* in the United States has always suggested *racial purity*.[49] A white woman's sexuality had to be controlled to ensure she mated with a suitable white companion and reproduced suitable white children. This is not to mention the severe consequences the non-white men in the preceding scenarios suffered for "tainting" white women's purity: ostracism, imprisonment, lynching. In all of these cases, evangelical leaders were among those who opposed so-called racial mixing.[50]

By the 1980s, the language of "family values" became a much more palatable way of speaking of this fundamentally white supremacist idea. That is, conservative political leaders and their evangelical voting bloc rolled back welfare reform, imposed greater abortion restrictions (both of which disproportionately affected poor Black women), and incited fear campaigns against gay schoolteachers—all under the guise of protecting the family.[51] In his 1980 book *Listen, America!*, Jerry Falwell, founder of the Moral Majority, called on evangelicals to "face" the moral failings of America—one major failing being "the fractured family." "With a skyrocketing divorce rate, the American family may well be on the verge of extinction in the next twenty years," Falwell warned, with concern toward what he called "common-law, communal, homosexual, and transsexual 'marriages.'" Falwell hoped that his evangelical audience, and America at large, would return to the "Bible pattern of the family." This return was, to him, the only way to protect the nation from "total collapse."[52]

More subtly than Falwell's techniques, evangelical organizations like Focus on the Family emphasize family values and a return to the "Bible pattern of the family" in a way that conflates "whiteness with existing social norms, values, structures, and institutions."[53] When Focus on the Family promotes male headship and stay-at-home moms in two-parent homes as the "biblical" way to live,[54] it excludes those whose access to such lifestyles is unachievable due to redlining and the race wage gap while also problematizing multigenerational households.[55] Such a "color-blind" approach, at the heart of contemporary evangelical teaching, attempts to hide the ways in which the "taken-for-grantedness" of whiteness leads to stereotyping people of color for their failure to meet white standards. White people's dominant stature in the United States, and in evangelicalism in particular, provides them with the means to conform to those norms and set the agenda for others who might not have the same economic and social resources.[56]

Purity Culture Discourse: Moving Beyond Whiteness-as-Normative

How we understand evangelicalism has shifted since the 2016 U.S. presidential election of Donald J. Trump, who was elected by an overwhelming majority of white evangelicals.[57] With the rise of Trump and his particular iteration of white Christian nationalism came the burgeoning critique of exvangelicals, former evangelicals who have "deconstructed"—reassessed and dismantled previous beliefs—from the subculture/religious tradition. Exvangelicals have reported on, opined about, and started Twitter (now X) wars against Trump's evangelical allies. Much of exvangelicals' critique of evangelicalism has centered on the double standards set forth by purity culture. Reporter and exvangelical McCammon describes her own "feelings of shock and anger that the same leaders who ordered us to remain sexually pure until marriage and who condemned Bill Clinton's moral failings in the 1990s would not only tolerate but embrace and promote Trump."[58] Collaborating mostly online through avenues like Twitter (now X) and Reddit, exvangelicals have found solidarity and connection with others who have likewise deconstructed from evangelicalism.[59] As McCammon argues in her book, these deconstructed exvangelicals often draw on the very tools of their childhood and adolescent faith (e.g., Scripture, the Golden Rule) to challenge and critique it. This can lead to a shift toward social justice, such as reading the story of the eunuchs (i.e., sexual minorities) in Isaiah 56 as welcoming and celebrating queer folks. But because "the master's tools cannot dismantle the master's house,"[60] exvangelicalism—like any movement—also runs the risk of replicating the very structures it tries to upend through its strategies of critique.

Consider how in the fall of 2021, several exvangelical influencers posted a photo of themselves naked in Joshua Tree with the caption "Purity culture parents, be warned: indoctrinating your daughters may cause religious trauma, . . . wild self-acceptance & naked frolicking through the desert."[61] On Instagram, the group was called out for naming their experience as normative, ignoring their privileges as a group made up entirely of conventionally beautiful, light-skinned, able-bodied, cisgender white women. "It's really harmful when folks in deconstruction spaces don't decenter themselves, particularly if they hold multiple privileged identities," commented one person. "This is why you don't find many BIPOC people in these deconstruct[ion] circles . . . it's basically another version of white feminism," wrote another.[62]

The women featured in this photo responded to criticism differently—from humility to defensiveness to outright rage. One photographed influencer, Alice Greczyn, responded by insisting the criticism itself was baseless: "I don't think holding people accountable for moral crimes they didn't commit is valid."[63] Despite being called out by both white folks and people of color for promoting white feminist ideals of sexual liberation in their photo, Greczyn refused to believe she and her peers did anything wrong. Greczyn is one of the subjects of Sara Moslener's 2022 article on the "Dilemma of Purity Culture Recovery." Moslener argues that these women, and Greczyn in particular, "[fail] to acknowledge the diverse experiences with that narrative" of sexual liberation. Their emphasis on embodiment and sexual liberation refuses to take seriously the long history of Black and Brown women's hypersexualization and the experiences of asexual and disabled folks.[64] "Being able to experience sexual pleasure after years of sex-negative indoctrination can be an act of resistance," Moslener writes. "But acts of personal resistance do not address purity culture's collective harms."[65]

Like the Joshua Tree incident, many exvangelical critiques of purity culture have failed to fully address the movement as a white supremacist project or name one's moral responsibility as a former participant in it. Purity culture remains for them either an ill-advised project in sexual ethics or the evangelical church's responsibility, something individuals need to heal or move on from, not an opportunity to recognize one's own complicity within it. Put simply, youth raised in purity culture are *victims* and church leaders, parents, and organizations like True Love Waits are *perpetrators*. Take Emily Joy Allison's book on #ChurchToo[66] in which she calls her readers to "reject, dismantle, and replace purity culture."[67] The narrative she constructs leaves little room for her to recognize her own complicity in purity culture as someone raised and socialized as a straight white woman (though she herself is queer), as well as the complicity of her peers. This is difficult ground to tread, of course, especially as she writes about the sexual violence that she and others experienced in purity culture. To speak of complicity and agency in this context is easily translated as victim-blaming.

But purity culture *is* imbued with white supremacist ideas—that is, the perceived superiority of white beauty, white values, and white beliefs.[68] And though the preceding critiques have been foundational to bringing the harm of purity culture to the public eye, these white exvangelicals miss the ways in which their experiences with purity culture are seen through their white embodiment. Many critics focus primarily on the plight of young white people like them, without a robust articulation of how their race impacts their experiences in purity culture. In fact, race is mostly erased from these critiques (e.g., white women are just *women*) with only some acknowledgment of the particular burden purity culture places on youth of color. The stories, voices, and insights of white women are centered in anti-purity culture discourse while those of people of color are marginalized or wholly excluded.[69]

We could surmise, generously, that this exclusion is because purity culture affects people of color differently because of their unique embodiment. Purity culture, as a white supremacist structure, was always about white women's purity, and so white youth are its primary target and therefore primary victims—even as purity culture sets up Black and Brown women's sexuality as a foil.[70] Books like Tamura Lomax's *Jezebel Unloosed* and Monique Moultrie's *Passionate and Pious* speak to the purity teachings within Black communities, which are not equivalent to the messages of white evangelical purity culture.[71] However, it may be more accurate to say that people of color are not centered in contemporary evangelical purity culture critique because of white supremacy itself. Their stories are not deemed "normal" enough and therefore cannot be thought to represent the experiences of "normal" purity culture victim-survivors.

And yet much of the critique by white exvangelicals and researchers wittingly or unwittingly ignores the contributions of Black and Brown folks[72] who have been sounding alarm bells on purity culture since the beginning.[73] Korean American minister Mihee Kim-Kort has unequivocally named purity culture as a force of not just sexism and heterosexism but white Christian supremacy. "Through the force of religion, the cultures and systems of purity seek to control any bodies that would threaten the concept of purity—especially black and brown bodies of those whose sexual identities are deemed unintelligible or reprehensible according to institutional powers," she writes.[74] For her, purity culture exists within the broader frame of U.S. culture and global cultures as being about power and the normalization of whiteness. That is, purity culture is not just about the specific experiences of young white women at daddy-daughter purity balls but a reflection of systems of power that divide the world into "binaries of black or white, colonizer or colonized, father or daughter, male or female, chaste or defiled."[75] Like Kim-Kort, Black feminist Brittney Cooper describes purity culture as part of a larger white Christian supremacist project that has regulated sexuality for white women and Black folks throughout U.S. history. She writes that such gatekeeping and surveillance "has always been about the propagation of a socially acceptable and pristine nuclear family worthy of having the American dream, a family that was heterosexual, middle class, and white."[76] This is similar to the early American purity campaigns where young white women were expected to uphold this "American dream" for the sake of maintaining the social hierarchy. This will be explored further in chapter 3.

We are at a point in purity culture discourse where even those outside evangelicalism or exvangelicalism know, to some extent, the harm it causes: certainly about the misogyny and antiqueerness. On TikTok, a queer comedian sings the Christian anthem "Awesome God" to her audience. As they sing back, she points to them and yells, "Trauma! Trauma! Trauma! Trauma! Trauma!"[77] The song itself has become shorthand for religious trauma, and yet, as another TikTok user points out in her response, the writer of the song was Rich Mullins, a proto-exvangelical dissenter. While his song has come to stand in for the evangelical church experience, youth group, antiqueerness, and purity, Rich Mullins himself, had he lived beyond his tragic death at forty-one, would have likely been aligned more with the queer comedian than the institutional power of evangelicalism.[78] Why is it so easy to assume that the former youth group kids at a queer comedy show have religious trauma? What of the evangelical teens who found kinship in an outsider like Rich Mullins? Purity culture discourse has become so flooded with such shorthand that we miss the nuances of young people's lived experiences and desires and what they compel us to do in response.

As for those responses: exvangelical solutions to purity culture often look something like white liberal feminism, which prioritizes individual freedom and personal healing over intersectional analysis and community action. We saw this in the story of the influencers at Joshua Tree. Women need to reclaim their (white) bodies as adults. Queer folks need to have as much shameless sex as possible. Individual experience becomes a point of reference for justice. *Purity culture demanded I abandon my desires as a woman; therefore, healing from purity culture means shamelessly embracing my desire.* While this is a necessary step for some people, ultimately it does not take seriously systemic harm. Not only did purity culture shame white women's desires, but it also propped them up as moral exemplars against Black and Brown womanhood. We need a deep understanding of the damaging conditions of purity culture that does not lose young people in a sea of clichés and shorthand descriptions. We also need to ethically engage those conditions in commensurate ways. What would it mean for Greczyn and others to look at their participation in purity culture as teenagers and recognize the harm they caused—for, say, espousing homophobic and racist views—and recognize the context they were in that led them to hold such views? Turning to an understanding of sociohistorical, racial, and gendered development of children is an important first step toward answering that question.

Conclusion

While we have not heard directly from Ariana and Ariah about what their purity rings may or may not symbolize for them, my friends Cassie and Jenny can offer an alternative narrative to those of the twins' mother and her critics.

It was January some years ago when we sat in the back room of The Tipsy Pig, sipping cocktails and hearing all about Cassie's new relationship with Andrew. Cassie was in her early thirties then and in her first adult relationship—her first *sexual* relationship, we knew this meant. All three of us had grown up going to predominately white conservative evangelical summer camps and churches and learned the common teachings of abstinence until marriage, that masturbation is a sin that only boys struggle with, and the importance of modesty, meaning no spaghetti straps even in one-hundred-degree heat lest we cause the boys to stumble. All three of us had since left that world behind.

Somehow we arrived at the topic of purity rings and how, after more than a decade, Cassie and Jenny still wore theirs. Cassie got her ring in college, after an idea came to her in prayer. She does not call hers a purity ring but a *needs and wants* ring, a way to remember that all of her needs and all of her wants are protected and surrounded by God, she said.[79] She wears the ring on the middle finger of her left hand, her own little form of rebellion, reminding herself and her Christian peers that she is more than her marital—or virginal—status. Jenny bought her ring in Ireland as a way to remind her then twenty-something self never to make an important life decision based on a guy. Borrowing from her evangelical upbringing, Jenny held the boundary of no sex until marriage in her dating life, but she found that the men she dated were always trying to change her mind on this, as early as the first or second date. All the debating and manipulating culminated in Jenny's sexual assault by a guy she met on a dating app. Now her ring reminds her that her desire matters, her pleasure matters, and her choices matter.[80]

Jenny and Cassie were not "forced" or "manipulated" into wearing their rings; rather, they actively translated the ring from a symbol of purity into something meaningful for them, as a needs and wants ring or a personal choices ring.[81] These happened within the bounds of a privileged white middle-class status, where they had the resources to enact their subjectivity in such a way. And, of course, Jenny and Cassie were in their twenties and thirties when they had these realizations. But might we see the same kind of agential moves from fifteen-year-olds as well?

I myself was fifteen years old when I bought a purity ring from The Anchor Room, an independent Christian bookstore in my hometown. The ring was sold by the register, one of those enticing spur-of-the-moment purchases, like gum at a grocery store. My ring was the quintessential True Love Waits ring, made of a malleable metal—I remember this because I found myself constantly chewing on it, and it retained its bite marks till I eventually lost the ring, somewhere (likely) in the corner of my bedroom. I called my ring the vaguely Southern-sounding "Susetta Lynn"—a name that was, I claimed in jest, the sexiest

I could think of. The layers of sarcasm and silliness were not lost on me as a teenager; it was probably what convinced me to wear the ring at all. Because ultimately, I was embarrassed by it. I knew I was supposed to wear a purity ring with humorless pride—I had bought it for myself, reflecting my own commitment to purity and abstinence till marriage—and yet I could not get myself to wear it with any regularity. So it became a joke, an anecdote more than a true reflection of my sexual purity.

Might we imagine, too, how fifteen-year-olds Ariana and Ariah might choose to wear their rings differently? Maybe the rings will represent their needs and wants and will never be given away. Maybe one or both of the girls are queer and their first loves are other girls or trans or non-binary folks who will receive the rings intended for cisgender young men. Or maybe they really do believe that abstinence from all sexual behavior before marriage is what is right for them and they will wear their rings into their twenties or thirties. Even as their parents and religious community prescribe a certain meaning to each of those three rings, Ariana and Ariah may interpret them differently, just as Cassie and Jenny refused to call theirs purity rings. Young people, just by nature of being human, have the capacity for moral agency, even as the choices seem limited or imposed or prescribed by an authority as powerful as white American evangelicalism.

2

Defining Childhood and Adolescence

"Somehow, thirteen was the magical age that set you apart," writes Amber Cantorna in her memoir, *Refocusing My Family: Coming Out, Being Cast Out, and Discovering the True Love of God*. "Approaching my teenage years marked the beginning of my journey from girlhood into being a young woman. To celebrate this momentous occasion, grandparents, aunts, and cousins from out of state came to be part of my special day. Family and friends all gathered together for this coming-of-age ceremony and pledge of commitment."[1]

Raised by a father who had worked for decades as an executive at James Dobson's Focus on the Family, Amber grew up in a theological and economic epicenter of purity culture. In addition to the certificate commemorating the pledge she signed in the presence of family and friends and the ring placed on her left ring finger by her father, Amber received a hope chest in this special coming-of-age ceremony. "This gift undoubtedly pointed to my wedding day and future family," she writes. "Already stocked with cookbooks and crocheted doilies, I was to continue collecting my future dreams and storing them inside for when I settled down and got married."[2] Amber writes that she did just that, filling the chest with intentions, desires, and prayers both that her family held for her and that she held for herself. Amber's hope chest contained the purity pledge that was given to her, pre-written and fully formed. It also contained a letter she wrote to her future husband in which she chose her own words of commitment and desire—desire for a blue-eyed, musically talented man who would love playing with their children.

Amber writes of her adolescent self as unaware of and lacking language to describe her identity as a gay woman. She knew that she didn't see why actor Jonathan Taylor Thomas was such a big deal among her friends. And she had strong feelings of love and affection for her girlfriends. Most of all, she knew that she had a reputation to uphold as part of a "Focus family" due to her dad's job and role in the community.[3] Over the next fourteen years—years of confusion, dawning understanding, prayer, and discernment—Amber would eventually come out as gay. She would marry a woman named Clara, understanding that the surprisingly gender-neutral pledge her father presented to her at her coming-of-age ceremony still fit. God did choose a person for her—a person who happened to be a woman—and the two of them displayed her hope chest in their home throughout their marriage, adding items that were personal and meaningful to them.

At age thirteen, Amber was invited to cross an invisible threshold into a new season of becoming. Her community made explicit the expectation that she was becoming a young adult and therefore taking on more responsibility for her own spiritual well-being and, by extension, those around her. And yet, as she writes of her teenage years in *Refocusing My Family*, she clearly felt the weight of the expectations she perceived from parents, community, and God greatly restricting how she moved about in the world and the choices she made. She lived in the push and pull of being a dependent child under a strict religious narrative while also embracing the freedom to drive a car, declare a major, choose a church, and even negotiate with her parents to change piano teachers.

Amber's understanding of thirteen years old as a "magical age" for a girl was not unique to her. For more than a century, the early teen years have been understood as a turning point in a person's life, a threshold between childhood and adulthood. These years are marked by typical developmental changes like puberty and, in the United States, key moments like entering high school (around age fourteen) and getting a driver's license (around age sixteen). But what these years hold in terms of symbolic meaning—a time of rebellion and deviance, a time where one solidifies one's identity, a time of progressive maturation, and so on—has been negotiated throughout time and space. Purity culture advocates, including men like Amber's father, speak of childhood and adolescence as stable categories, holding the same essential meaning from present day back to "biblical times." At the height of purity culture in the 1990s and early 2000s, young white women like Amber were perceived to be innocent yet dangerous if led astray; they were ignorant and moldable yet had a great responsibility to their families and churches. This understanding of adolescence has its origins in early modern notions of childhood and turn-of-the-twentieth-century perspectives on adolescence in the United States.

The Innocent Child and Deviant Adolescent

There is no universal definition of childhood or adolescence. "The category of the child is notoriously unstable, the meaning of which shifts, expands, and contracts according to history, nation, culture, legal statute, context, and discourse," writes gender historian Steven Angelides. In the Anglophone West, our understanding of who is a child is largely the result of laws around age of consent or sex offense, where adolescence is subsumed under the larger category of childhood.[4] In Alabama, for instance, the age of consent is sixteen, meaning sixteen is "the age at which an individual can legally consent to sexual intercourse under any circumstances."[5] In California, the age of consent is eighteen.[6] Moral crises—what I will describe later as moral/sex panics—tend to define for themselves who counts as a child.[7] For example, in a 2009 Lacey, Washington, sexting case, a middle-school boy named Isaiah and two of his friends were charged with Class C felonies for transmitting child pornography when they shared a nude photo of Isaiah's fourteen-year-old ex-girlfriend Marguerite.[8] Despite all of the players being under the age of consent in Washington,[9] these teenagers faced the very adult felony charges for disseminating child pornography.[10]

As in the case of Isaiah and his friends and codefendants, the label "teenager" further complicates the question of who is and is not a child. Teens stretching from age thirteen to nineteen live in a gray area. In some states, sixteen-year-olds are considered adults, whereas eighteen- and nineteen-year-olds are adults virtually everywhere. Biology—in other words, puberty—is also an insufficient milestone with which to categorize young people, as there is not a set time in which physical changes occur. Youth could be grouped together by grade, age, biological milestone, or geography (in the case of state-by-state age-of-consent laws), and one would find tremendous overlap between any two groups. When exercised, the categories of adolescence and childhood are broad enough to prosecute or acquit young people of sexual crimes, serve political or social agendas, and determine a person's moral standing. Understood from their Victorian origins, these unstable, shifting constructs of childhood and adolescence have been deployed in racist, sexist, and classist ways to reinforce links between ideas such as purity and femininity, innocence and whiteness, and respectability and the middle class. These categories contribute to our understanding of youth within contemporary evangelical purity culture as well as other purity cultures of the past.

Childhood

When Augustine of Hippo (352–430) wrote "so tiny a child, so great a sinner" about his boyhood misdeeds, the concept of childhood as a period of life wholly distinct from adulthood had not yet been conceived.[11] Nor had adolescence: the North African priest wrote of his puberty years as tumultuous, long before those in their teens were distinctly characterized as "out of control, deviant, criminal."[12] Augustine had a recognizable influence on views of children and youth through Western ethics and philosophy—from Calvin to Kant and into the New World by the Puritans.[13] We could describe the Augustinian view of childhood as a "top-down" model, where children are viewed as disordered from birth and need instruction from above—adults, God, or educators—to reform them into good future adults, Christians, or citizens. The irony of this model, ethicist John Wall writes, is that children are responsible for their bad behavior yet are believed to lack the agency to do anything about it. Like the screaming infant described by Augustine in Book I of his *Confessions*, a child is to be reprimanded—for Augustine, by God—and steered in the right direction.[14]

Calvinist Puritans in the British colonies of North America (1600s) believed, like Augustine, that children were born with the capacity to be "criminal," but they were also born with the capacity to be "rational," akin to being morally good. Children had a moral duty: "The child, however young, was handed the responsibility for its own salvation."[15] By the Enlightenment (1715–1789), children were seen as neither good nor evil but vulnerable to the influence of malevolent peers and adults.[16] Enlightenment thinkers believed children to be passive and vulnerable, like "camelions," as John Locke wrote.[17] They became good or bad depending on the company they kept.[18] Like the top-down model described previously, these children needed "an *external* guiding force to monitor and direct the balance between passion [i.e., pleasures] and reason."[19]

By the early nineteenth century in Western thought, the prevailing view of children as neither good nor evil yet easily influenced shifted again with the birth of the social purity movement, a moral/sex panic described in more detail in chapter 3. "Innocence . . . was assumed to be an inherent quality of childhood as well as a virtue that must be taught."[20] At least, that was the case with white, bourgeois children. In the nineteenth century, white middle-class children were believed to be sensate—that is, they experienced the world through their senses and were in turn affected by the sensory world. Children were ultimately, then, corruptible, especially when it came to sex. "Pure children were assumed to be de facto asexual," write feminist sociologists R. Danielle Egan and Gail Hawkes. "However, if sexual curiosity or worse still precocious activity was present in a formerly innocent child, its manifestation was the result of a deviant outside influence."[21] Those influences were often other children, particularly older or poorer children. Working-class children and their families were believed to be immoral, "dirty, bawdy, and sexually suspect"—especially for how the sexes intermixed in work and play.[22] Therefore, it was essential that bourgeois children were protected and sequestered in the domestic sphere with their mothers, who were also believed to be sexually disinterested and pure.

Although feminist historians have argued for the porousness of the separate spheres—especially toward the end of the nineteenth century when women participated in reform movements like women's suffrage[23]—the prevailing bourgeois view of the time was that the innocent child and pious mother belonged inside the home while fathers worked and ventured outside the home.[24] This Victorian ideology of the cult of domesticity (also called the cult of true womanhood) taught that white mothers ought to be "pious, pure, domestic, and submissive"—the near opposite of "dirty, bawdy, and sexually suspect"—and that they were the primary moral educators of their children.[25] Here in the hearth, it was the bourgeois mother's responsibility to instill in her children Christian values, including teaching them about sex. This not only benefited the children, who, with their "enlightened innocence" could avoid sexual ills like masturbation and sex with partners of a different class or race,[26] but it held significance to the success of the white, Protestant middle class.[27]

The story of sexual innocence, sensationism, and corruptibility was different for non-white children, especially Black children, in the Victorian era (1830–1900). While white children were presumed to be innocent unless influenced by bad boys and bad girls in the schoolyard,[28] Black children were viewed as sexually precocious, insensate (or unfeeling), and cursed from the start. The presumed racial inferiority of Black persons had been a part of the American story long before the nineteenth century but took a particular shape in the years before and after the Civil War as ideologies of white supremacy were forged as part and parcel to Protestant evangelical identity. "During the nineteenth century," writes Edward J. Blum, "almost every aspect of American Protestantism was permeated by whiteness."[29] This included a little white evangelist, Eva St. Clare, and her creator, Harriet Beecher Stowe.

Stowe's abolitionist novel, *Uncle Tom's Cabin: or, Life Among the Lowly*, offers us a peek into Victorian childhood—or, better put, an imagined Victorian childhood—where childlike innocence functioned in particularly racialized ways. In the Victorian imagination, childhood innocence was "itself raced white, itself characterized by the ability to retain racial meanings but hide them under claims of holy obliviousness," argues historian Robin Bernstein.[30] The perceived innocence of the white child, configured in someone like Eva St. Clare, a Christ figure in Stowe's novel, "secured the unmarked status of whiteness, and the power derived from that status, in the nineteenth and into the twentieth centuries."[31] I rely on Bernstein's *Racial Innocence* to draw a linkage between childhood and racial innocence (as she does), but I draw in a third component, evangelicalism, a growing religious movement of the time.[32] Evangelicalism shapes the moral landscape of *Uncle Tom's Cabin* and illustrates the entanglement between Victorian anti-Black racism, the construction of childhood, and Protestant Christian supremacy that, I argue, has a bearing on us today.

In the preface to *Uncle Tom's Cabin*, Harriet Beecher Stowe—the daughter of Lyman Beecher and sister of Henry Ward Beecher, both evangelical preachers and abolitionists—writes that the purpose of this story (first written as a newspaper serial) was "to awaken sympathy and feelings for the African race, as they exist among us; to show their wrongs and sorrows, under a system so necessarily cruel and unjust as to defeat and do away the good effects of all that can be attempted for them, by their best friends, under it."[33] An ambitious goal, the book set publishing records and, rather apocryphally, became known as the book that initiated the American Civil War. The story follows a number of characters—some slaves, some slaveholders—including little Eva St. Clare, the daughter of a slaveholder, and Topsy, a slave girl.[34]

Topsy is set up as a foil to Eva.[35] If Eva is described as "innocent," "divine," and "always dressed in white," Topsy is "goblin-like," "heathenish," and dressed in "filthy, ragged garment, made of bagging." If Eva has "long golden-brown hair that floated like a cloud around [her head]," Topsy's "woolly hair . . . stuck out in every direction." Her refrain is "I's wicked." Why does she steal? Why does she dress herself in her mistress Ophelia's clothes and parade about? She's "mighty wicked."[36] Topsy asks Ophelia to beat her—often. And Ophelia is not entirely opposed to it. "I's used to whippin'; I spects it's good for me," Topsy tells her.[37] This plays into the common idea of Black children as insensate or unfeeling, that physical beating was a way to steer them in the right direction and mythologized that the beatings were pain-free. Stowe uses this assumption of Black childhood and then challenges Topsy's un-"hurt-ability" by letting Eva penetrate Topsy's outer self (her learned behavior) to get to her essential self (her sensate humanity).[38]

When Eva gets sick and is on the verge of death, she, in her frailty, converts Topsy to Christianity. Topsy has gotten herself into trouble again, this time for cutting up Ophelia's bonnet to make clothes for her dolls. When Eva overhears the family struggling over how to better Topsy, she has Topsy brought to her. On the verge of tears, Eva asks the girl, "What makes you so bad, Topsy? Why won't you try and be good? Don't you love *anybody*, Topsy?" Topsy insists that no, she does not love any person; no one loves her, either, on account of her black skin. In "a sudden burst of feeling"—and, significantly, "laying her little thin, white hand on Topsy's shoulder"—Eva declares, "I love you, and I want you to be good." With this, as a final blow to the assumption of Black un-hurt-ability, Topsy weeps and believes in the Jesus that Eva preaches to her. "Don't you know that Jesus loves all alike? He is just as willing to love you, as me. He loves you just as I do,—only more, because he is better."[39] Bernstein summarizes the significance of this scene: "Only the touch of Eva's 'white hand' combined with declarations of love for Topsy as a 'poor, abused child' transforms 'the black child.' At the moment, a 'ray of real belief, a ray of heavenly love' penetrates Topsy, and for the first time in the novel, she weeps. It is in this scene that Topsy is converted to sensation, into humanized childhood, and even, Eva promises, potential angelhood—'just as much as if you were white.'"[40] Soon after this episode, Eva dies. Eventually, Topsy leaves New Orleans to live with Ophelia in the North and is baptized in the Christian faith.[41] We are told she grows into a proper young woman, not wholly unlike the "true woman" of the white middle class.

While Stowe may have successfully argued against Black insensateness through the figure of Topsy, a Black slave child, she did it through the figure of the innocent white—and, I argue, Protestant—girl-child.[42] The only way Topsy's wicked behavior could end and her insensate nature be penetrated was through a "little Evangelist," a white girl who embodied the innate innocence and goodness of nineteenth-century childhood. Through her evangelism, Eva crossed a cultural line (touching Topsy) in order to "save" Topsy and make a theological and social claim about the fundamental humanity and redeemability of Black people—an ideology that was being challenged in the U.S. South at the time.[43] Although the stories of Eva, Topsy, and others in the novel ultimately evolved to reify the anti-Black stereotypes Stowe sought to dispel, *Uncle Tom's Cabin* shows the entanglement of race, gender, age, and Protestant Christianity in the construct of childhood as it existed in the post-Enlightenment United States. These stereotypes have shifted in the century since, yet its impact on the cultural imagination of white childhood purity persists in both contemporary evangelical purity culture and broader U.S. society.

By the end of the nineteenth century, immigrants from Eastern European countries came to the United States in increasing numbers, complicating the Black/white binary that ordered the country's views on innocence and deviance.[44] At the same time, a new category for age emerged—adolescence—that would bear the racial complexity that childhood innocence could not.

Adolescence

The emergence of adolescence as separate from childhood and adulthood reflected other social recategorizing at the turn of the century, argues queer historian Gabrielle Owen. The passive female and active male, the homosexual invert versus the healthy heterosexual, and the racial othering of non-Anglo-Saxons[45] "functioned primarily as new ways of maintaining existing social hierarchies" and interdependently necessitated the other for definition.[46] That is, if there was a category for health, then there was a category for illness; if there was a category for good, then there was a category for evil. Adolescence emerged as a third category among many binaries and, as such, represented deviance or in-betweenness—sometimes both.

Scholars often name G. Stanley Hall, a turn-of-the-century pedagogue and psychologist, as the originator of adolescence, particularly for his groundbreaking two-volume work *Adolescence*, which links success in this period of a young man's life to the success of a nation. Hall's theory of adolescence was tied to his theory of recapitulation, which states that "the embryos of more 'advanced' species are said to represent the adult stages of more 'primitive' species." Recapitulation, developed first by Ernst Haeckel in the 1860s but expanded by Hall, was weaponized to "rank humans according to racial characteristics, with the white European male ranked above all others."[47] Non-Anglo races, then, were described as child-like or, if sexually mature, "adolescents of adult size."[48] Though Anglo-Saxon children could pass through adolescence into adulthood, those of other races could not; they would forever be adolescents and therefore exist in a deviant state.

Hall's recapitulation theory fits within a broader tradition of developmentalism, consistent in Darwin's writings as well as Hall's. "Developmentalism imagines that change occurs in one direction toward an eventual goal, producing a hierarchy in which earlier stages are inferior stages." This change can happen on an individual level, a species level, or a societal level. "The developmental arrival point"—adulthood, in this case—". . . is defined as inherently normative, evoking characteristics such as whiteness, masculinity, and wealth," writes Owen.[49] Therefore, all who are not white, male, and economically stable adults were considered insufficient in some way. "Through the logic of developmentalism, childhood and adolescence began to function as temporal categories in which any marginalized person or group could be relocated along a developmental timeline as regressive, immature, or undeveloped," she writes.[50] Within Hall's worldview, for young white males, there is hope, with a manly education of wilderness training; for young women, ethnic whites, or the working poor, there is little to no hope for reaching normative white male adulthood.[51]

Hall viewed the period of adolescence as the most important time in a young white man's life, where he could either grow into a healthy "normal" adult or become particularly susceptible to diseases like neurasthenia, a kind of anxiety or melancholia that affected middle- and upper-class Anglo-Saxon men by turning them effeminate and weak (that is, woman-like). Neurasthenia was thought to be caused by the realities of modern society: increased urbanization, too much time indoors, and the exercising of brains instead of muscles.[52] To prevent such a disease from overcoming a young white male, Hall recommended a special education, where boys were encouraged to channel their sexual energies (ever brewing at this time) into physical activity;[53] this was a healthy alternative to repression or chronic masturbation, the latter of which plagued the young Hall.[54] If a young man were able to be properly civilized—that is, outdoorsy but not savage like the "lower" races, educated but not *overly* civilized, like the neurasthenic man—he could develop into a healthy white man, a shining example of his race.[55]

Hall wrote mostly about and to the young adolescent male but gave some advice to young women who were on their way to joining the cult of true womanhood. Education was not good for their "reproductive capabilities," nor did they need to act as rough riders in the great outdoors.[56] Hall saw girls as "more governed by adult emotions." They did not need the same careful education into adulthood, as it was considered dangerous to their reproductive organs. But nor could they, as women, be moral exemplars of their race.[57] Contemporaries of Hall, like sexologist Silas Weir Mitchell, were worried that neurasthenic young women, who were gaining independence through the suffrage movement and economic societal changes, would turn to other women for sexual relationships, becoming sexual deviants or "inverts." Or they would cause the retrogression of society by instituting a matriarchal system.[58] Thus, the "normal" adulthood presented as the opposite of the "deviant" adolescence—or "savage" childhood, in Hall's view—was only achievable by some: most notably white, middle- and upper-class young men.

"As for childhood the nineteenth century aligned childlikeness with animality, the primitive, the savage, and the not-yet-human at the same time figuring the child as innocence, pricelessness, potentiality, and the future," writes Owen, summarizing the conceptualization of childhood and adolescence through the nineteenth and twentieth centuries and hinting at the linkages between age, race, and gender. She continues: "As for adolescence the twentieth century imagined the teen years as out of control, deviant, criminal, and the failed-to-become-human at the same time as it idealized youthfulness, rebellion, and freedom from adult responsibility."[59] Whether positive or negative characteristics, these descriptors come from a dominant white male perspective, often projecting one's own experience of childhood and adolescence onto others. Children and adolescents are treated as deployable symbols—for good, for evil, for everything in between—but not agential humans in their own right.

Pure Girls and Wild-at-Heart Guys

When we think about childhood and adolescence in the United States today, some of the same narratives of innocence and asexuality, deviance and rebellion, that were forged in the nineteenth and twentieth centuries still prevail. Narratives around banning books in Florida and uproar about textbooks teaching critical race theory in Texas are helpful examples here.[60] Children are innocent and influenceable, which is why certain books are to be pulled from the library and textbooks need to teach sanitized histories. Just speaking the word "gay" could queer a child, so the conservative logic goes.[61] A quick survey of articles on adolescence in popular media outlets *The Atlantic* and *The New York Times* are riddled with headlines like, "Why American Teens Are So Sad," "America's Teenage Girls Are Not Okay," "American Teens Are Really Miserable. Why?" "Why Are Teens in Crisis? Here's What the Evidence Says," and "Why Are American Teens So Unhappy?"[62] These headlines alone position teenagers as vulnerable to outside influence, fickle, and in desperate need of adult intervention and protection.

Purity culture follows the same logics as broader U.S. culture in the way it conceives childhood innocence and teenage deviance and potentiality, with an important distinction. Purity culture tends to infantilize white girls, viewing them, like children, as asexual, innocent, and easily influenced by powerful outside forces.[63] At a purity ball—akin to a debutante ball—a young girl pledges her virginity to her father, promising to not have sex before marriage. Her father, in return, promises to safeguard her purity.[64] Researcher Jennifer McGrath describes the bizarre experience of attending the purity ball of a friend when she was thirteen years old. The father and daughter "danced to 'Brown Eyed Girl' while she [the daughter] wore what appeared to be a wedding gown."[65] Christina Reimer calls the message of purity balls "oedipal in nature—that little girls remarried to their fathers until they wed their husbands. Virginity, as guaranteed by the token of the purity ring, is the commodity that is exchanged between men; between fathers and husbands."[66] Like the asexual, innocent child of the post-Enlightenment, teenage girls at the center of the purity ball are thought to be vulnerable to outside influences and therefore in need of male protection.

Teenage boys are not invited to participate in such rituals. They are not pledging their virginities to their mothers the way girls are to their fathers.[67] There is no direct equivalent to purity balls for young men in purity culture, but there are gendered beliefs and stereotypes that link purity culture back to turn-of-the-century adolescent manliness discourse. In his 2001 best-selling book *Wild at Heart: Discovering the Secret of a Man's Soul*, John Eldredge claims that every man yearns for "a battle to fight," a "beauty to rescue," and "an adventure to live."[68] These adventures extend to boys and young men as well. Eldredge recounts the story of rock climbing with his young sons, Sam and Blaine,[69] and calling Sam "a *wild man*" for his maneuvering a tough spot in the climb.[70] He writes, "Sam sort of sidled up to me and in a quiet voice asked, 'Dad . . . did you really think I was a wild man up there?'" Eldredge continues: "Miss that moment and you'll miss a boy's heart forever. It's not a question—it's *the* question, the one every boy and man is longing to ask. Do I have what it takes? Am I powerful? Until a man *knows* he's a man he will forever be trying to prove he is one, while at the same time shrink from anything that might reveal he is not. Most men live their lives haunted by the question, or crippled by the answer they've been given."[71] Eldredge presumes that every young man, including his offspring, desires to be called wild, masculine, and powerful. If men and boys do not attend to their innate wildness, by fighting a battle, living adventurously, and pursuing a good woman, then they will be tempted to seek it out in lesser things, like pornography, masturbation, and addiction.[72] All men were born to be wild, he argues, all the way back to Adam who was formed from the dirt *outside of* the Garden of Eden.[73] Linking this image of manhood to Christian scripture, Eldredge suggests that to believe otherwise is unbiblical or unchristian.[74] This image of so-called "biblical" manhood, however, looks much more like turn-of-the-century manliness than the lives or teachings of the Jewish prophets, Jesus, or the early Christian apostles.

Whether a girl at a purity ball or young man encouraged to pursue "authentic masculinity,"[75] the remnants of Victorian conceptions of childhood and adolescence still linger in purity culture. This is not to suggest an equivalence between early modern and present-day childhood and adolescents. Childhood and adolescence are, after all, social constructs that change in meaning over time. We know, however, that the architects of purity culture nostalgically look to the Victorian era for inspiration, as the primary goal of purity culture is heterosexual marriage with strict gender roles: a father as the "head" who works outside the home and a mother who stays at home to raise the children.[76]

Conclusion

Amber's story gives us a glimpse of adolescence and emerging adulthood shaped by purity culture. Her transition from an asexual childhood to the sexual possibility of adolescence was marked with an abstinence pledge, a purity ring, and a hope chest, all in the presence of extended family and friends. Amber both participated in these rituals and, eventually, queered them as her hope chest transformed from a symbol of heterosexual marriage to same-sex marriage and family. "Old dreams have become new memories," the adult Cantorna reflects, "even when those memories have turned out to look different than my thirteen-year-old self expected."[77]

Tracing the history of the conceptions of childhood and adolescence in U.S. social history can help us make sense of persistent perspectives on the innocence and vulnerability of white girls (of any age) and the fear of sexual deviance in adolescence. These conceptions are entangled in long-held beliefs about race, gender, and age within U.S. Protestant Christianity. Therefore, understanding something about the entanglement and development of childhood and adolescence helps us see that phenomena like purity balls and wild-at-heart young men did not emerge out of thin air. Rather, they are touchpoints along a centuries-long pursuit of characterizing and reifying young people's existence. In the next chapter, we will turn our attention toward how the figure of the white adolescent has been mobilized to quell adult anxieties from the late Victorian era until today.

3

Purity Panics and Young People's "Nation-Saving" Role in U.S. Social History

On a 2019 episode of the popular podcast *You're Wrong About*, hosts Sarah Marshall and Michael Hobbes—two millennial reporters with a love for researching moral panics—discussed what adults have been "wrong about" with regard to teen sexting, the act of sending sexual texts or nude photos of oneself to another person, either consensually or coerced. Amy Hasinoff, author of *Sexting Panic*, joined Hobbes and Marshall as a guest expert, citing how common sexting is among teens and young adults—up to 70 percent participation, depending on how the survey questions are posed and who is being asked.

> HASINOFF: This is not like behavior that is just done by a couple weird people. Like, it's pretty common at this point.
>
> HOBBES: This is not deviant behavior. This is . . . normal behavior. And not sexting is, statistically speaking, the deviant choice.
>
> HASINOFF: Well, I don't know that it's, like, deviant. I mean, it is still risky, so—
>
> HOBBES: *[Laughs]* I just want to be on record as saying people who do not sext are deviant. I just wanted to be crystal clear.
>
> *[Laughter]*[1]

Hasinoff named 2008 as the beginning of the sexting panic with the release of a provocative *CosmoGirl* article on the prevalence of sexting among teen girls, some baseless child pornography charges against adolescents in Pennsylvania, and a young woman named Jessica Logan dying by suicide after her nude photos were spread around her school.[2] These three incidents fueled the public outcry: not only has sexting been construed to be legally and socially dangerous, but, so goes the argument, "the consequences of sexting are [that] you will die."[3] The podcasters laughed at the absurdity of this.

There are many evangelical leaders, legislators, academics, feminists, parents, and media personae in the United States who find teenage sexting to be not a laughing matter but one of dire concern. They see it as a dangerous activity that leads to the oversexualization of girls in U.S. culture, the rise in supply and demand of child pornography, and, as in the case of Logan, death.[4] Borrowing language from gender historian Steven Angelides, "moral/sex panics," like the teen sexting panic, "highlight how the politics of fear and emotion perform a number of social functions" often "beyond" their stated goals of protecting (most often) children from harm.[5] In other words, while cyberbullying and harassment appear to be the real catalysts in Logan's suicide, the adults spreading panic have chosen to broaden the issue to all sexting, including private exchanges between consenting parties.[6] The issue becomes blown out of proportion when any act of sexting is understood "to embody the risks of bullying, harassment, and psychic trauma, and the overarching narrative in the media and educational campaigns becomes one of the *problem* and *danger* of sexting."[7]

Moral/sex panics centered on children (i.e., persons under eighteen)[8] are rarely about the youth themselves—nor their particular actions—but are a reflection of adult anxieties in an unstable society.[9] Moral panics around teenage sexting in the 2010s, or, say, "masturbation phobia" in the 1870s, obscured the larger social instabilities of economic depressions and recessions; increased urbanization; disquiet over growing non-white immigrant populations and Black integration and advancement; apprehension over new technologies; and waves of political unrest that have existed and continue to exist in the U.S. "The need to protect children from sexuality acts as a smokescreen for other social interventions that often go far beyond the bodies and pleasures of children themselves," write R. Danielle Egan and Gail Hawkes.[10] Under the guise of child protection, the subjectivities of children are ignored or erased and replaced by the figure of the Innocent Child. This Child, configured in the United States[11] most consistently as white and economically stable, can do nothing for herself, and therefore her likeness inspires protectionist agendas and incites fear of the other.

White American evangelicals have been at the forefront of recent moral/sex panics such as the pornography panic of the 1980s[12] and the teenage pregnancy panic of the 1990s.[13] But we can trace their involvement even further back to their nineteenth-century itch for reform and into the present day with contemporary evangelical purity culture, a moral/sex panic of its own. Like other stakeholders in moral/sex panics, evangelicals employed the proverbial Innocent Child—and Adolescent—to channel their anxieties about shifts in social power structures, changing cultural mores, and other so-called threats to their normalized white, middle-class life. Young people cease to be agentic persons and are rendered instead into two-dimensional archetypes—innocent victims when they perform their role correctly or corrupt deviants when they do not. They become players on a stage built on societal anxieties.[14]

Three Moral/Sex Panics

From the late nineteenth century to the late twentieth century, the white teenager was situated by sociologists, evangelical leaders, politicians, and her parents at the center of at least three moral/sex panics. The teen herself was not recognized as her own person with legitimate desires but was used as a symbol of purity, in some instances, or a symbol of danger in others. The two earlier moral/sex panics help shape our understanding of contemporary evangelical purity culture as emerging from a longer history of anxiety about the white teen and what she symbolized.

Social Purity Panic: "White Slavery"

Between the late nineteenth and early twentieth centuries, the United States underwent a series of related shifts: the so-called "closing of the frontier" and the sevenfold increase in urbanization, which blurred the boundaries between urban and rural, middle class and working class.[15] The birth of corporate capitalism broadened white bourgeois men's access to leisure time and challenged their perceptions of themselves as hardworking Protestants.[16] The influx of immigrants from Eastern Europe and China complicated the black/white binarism that had dominated the construction of race in the country up until this point. And the Victorian true woman of the domestic sphere was replaced by the new woman, who ventured out into public and fought for her right to vote.[17] These major shifts contributed to a heightened anxiety of the time, giving rise to several moral/sex panics couched within broader reform movements. As with the moral/sex panics of other generations, much of the country's collective anxiety was placed onto the bodies of adolescent girls, to both protect and regulate.[18]

Alongside major cultural shifts of the turn-of-the-century United States came an "ambitious" and widespread reform movement: social purity.[19] The movement maintained that a person's personal purity—whether hygienic, eugenic, racial, or sexual—had an effect on society as a whole. Social purity built on the reform movements of previous generations—for example, abolition—and united leaders who previously had different goals and agendas: feminists, antifeminists, (new) abolitionists, Darwinians, evangelicals, Catholics, doctors, mothers, Black racial uplift reformers, and pedagogues.[20] By the 1890s, the movement had become a national project, encompassing many targets of reform—hygienic practices, alcohol consumption (via anti-saloon, temperance, and prohibition movements), sex work, and obscenity. Social purity reformers worked to eliminate vice to better society. For evangelical reformers, this meant bettering society in order to hasten the Second Coming of Jesus.[21]

One moral/sex panic under the umbrella of social purity was the white slavery scare—the fear of "a widespread traffic in women that sold young girls into virtual slavery"—punctuated by the passing of the Mann Act of 1910.[22] The Mann Act prohibited trafficking young white women across state lines for "immoral purposes."[23] However, the law was broad enough, and the fear of non-Anglos strong enough, that if a white woman were to travel with a man of a different race, he would be suspected of such trafficking. The underlying assumption was that young white women would not willingly travel—in other words, have sex—with a man of a different race. If she did, it was because of her own ignorance or corrupted innocence. According to the logic of social Darwinism, a young white woman's responsibility was to mate with only the "fittest" of men, meaning those of her same (white) race. This was not wholly unlike G. Stanley Hall's conception of race and age a few decades prior. The decisions a young woman made, or was "tricked" into making, had consequences for her and for society as a whole. In this case, it alluded to the possibility of miscegenation and the breeding of "inferior" children. This fear was also associated with Catholic families who raised more children than white middle-class Protestants at the time. It was also heightened due to increased urbanization and the mingling of races and ethnicities in tenement housing.[24]

Focusing on two competing narratives can help us understand the white slavery scare and the social purity movement more broadly: the story of a *pure* middle-class country girl who is deceived by a sly racial other and the story of a *problem* working-class girl who through being "exposed" to sexuality becomes a "sexual delinquent."[25] These two stories show the shifting panic over young women's sexuality within the social purity movement. In the early stages of the movement, young bourgeois women were believed to be—like children—innocent and passive, easily deceivable if put into dangerous situations. By the Progressive Era (1896–1916), however, these young women, like their non-white and working-class counterparts, were seen as having the potential both to be corrupted and for corrupting others. Much of the corruption/corrupting happened in the "cruel, dangerous, and unforgiving" city, a reflection of the growing fear and suspicion of urbanization, particularly for how it provided means for heterosocial and interracial activities.[26] The city was where bourgeois women led anti-saloon and anti-prostitution reform, not where they raised a family or socialized.[27]

Reginald Wright Kauffman's 1910 cautionary tale *The House of Bondage* was one of many white slavery novels that warned young women and their mothers about the dangers of city life.[28] In the novel, a sixteen-year-old country girl, Mary Denbigh, runs away to New York City with a young Hungarian Jew named Max. She expresses love for Max[29] but also for the thrill of freedom for life in the city: "New York, it appeared, was a city of splendid leisure. Its entire four millions of population spent their days in rest and their nights in amusement. . . . As [Max] spoke, though she did not know it, the far-off orchestras were calling her, as if the sound of the city deafened her to all other sounds, as if the lights of New York blinded her to the lights of home."[30] Mary and Max never marry as she was promised they would. Instead, on their first and only night together in New York, Max convinces her to drink wine. Never having drunk before, she has too much and slips into a deep sleep. When she wakes up the next morning, she's naked and now a boarder—an "inmate"—in one Madam Rose Légère's brothel.[31] Girls like Mary in these white slavery novels were often described as wholly vulnerable and innocent, easily taken in by deceptive non-Anglos like Max. The books were written to warn these girls and their mothers of dangerous men whom they could innocently and ignorantly fall into the company of. The true villains were the men; the young women: helpless, passive, and easily fooled.

As a moral/sex panic, the white slavery scare juxtaposed the alleged trafficking of young white women with the reality of Black chattel slavery in the antebellum era. *The House of Bondage* was seen as an abolitionist novel just like *Uncle Tom's Cabin*, but for another race of people.[32] In fact, white slavery tracts "de-emphasized the brutality of chattel slavery in order to punctuate the horrors of white slavery."[33] The subtext is that these innocent young white women were not deserving of the horrors they faced—less so than the Black enslaved folks a generation before. In this is the erasure of these young women's sexual and moral agency, to choose to travel or fall in love with a man of another race. J. Shoshanna Ehrlich writes, "Although unspoken, the complexities of these racial attitudes (regarding the white slavery scare) indicates that the bodies of young white women, who were the ones most likely to be making the perilous journey from the bucolic country to the city, were regarded as more deserving of protection that the marginalized and potentially corrupting bodies of young black women."[34] These girls were instructed to "just say no" to city dance halls, theaters, ice cream parlors, hotels, streets, and parks where they could potentially, in passive construction, *be trafficked*.[35] This moral/sex panic also, of course, erased the experiences of Black people who were a generation or two removed from enslavement yet faced the brutality of white supremacy ramping up in the post-Reconstructionist era. This was a time when young Black men were lynched precisely for allegedly raping white women.[36]

While it is unfair to make a direct comparison, contemporary evangelical purity culture echoes some of these early twentieth-century ideas about racial purity. Scholars like Seth Dowland and Jane Dailey have traced, for example, the influx of Christian schools in response to mid-century integration efforts.[37] The white evangelical homeschooling boom in the 1980s followed the same trajectory: If public schools were a dangerous place because of interracial socialization, anti-Christian teaching, and behavioral permissiveness, why not fully control a young person's education at home?[38] In a *Homeschoolers Anonymous* blog post,

Gary (a pseudonym) writes about his insular, white homeschooling community in the western United States. Gary reflects on how intentionally designed his world was to insulate him and keep him from interacting with children of other races. He writes: "Turns out that when our parents told us they were homeschooling us to 'protect' us, it was to 'protect us' from integration. Often times it seemed it was particularly to 'protect' my sisters (and other girls) from interacting with the males of other races."[39] It was an unspoken rule that he and his sisters marry within their white race. The assumption was of purity—that his people (white Christians) were not to mix with *those people* (Black or Brown Christians or non-Christians). Gary suggests that the courtship model—popularized by purity culture writer Joshua Harris and his book *I Kissed Dating Goodbye*[40]—is inherently racist: "How can your daughter marry someone of another race *if you get to pick her husband?* Simple, she can't."[41]

At the turn of the century, evangelicals played a significant role in propagating the white slavery scare as it erased young white women's agency, portrayed non-Anglo men (including Catholic and Jewish men) as villainous, and reified middle-class Protestant values. In the nineteenth-century United States, evangelicalism emerged from three "streams" of domestic Protestantism: "a Baptist tradition that emphasized an individual's autonomy to claim salvation, a Wesleyan tradition that longed for the perfection of humanity, and a Reformed tradition that focused on God's authority over all creation."[42] Reflecting its aim of social outreach and its Wesleyan perfectionism, nineteenth-century evangelicals were at the forefront of social change, fighting for abolition, the reformation of prisons, and better treatment of the mentally disabled and against societal greed.[43] Much of these reform movements came out of the revivals of the Second Great Awakening, with leaders such as Lyman Beecher in the 1850s and Frances Willard of the Women's Christian Temperance Union (WCTU) in the 1880s.[44]

Due primarily to the labor of the WCTU, the "largest women's organization in [the] nineteenth century," the white slavery scare became part of public discourse by the turn of the century. The WCTU saw evangelical Christian morality as the "solution" to white slavery and societal impurity more generally.[45] Like other female-led purity reform organizations of the time, the WCTU weaponized "Christian piety and fierce support for women's equality" to fight for their vision of a pure society, a society with a single standard of morality for both men and women that "deeply invested in the value of an orderly respectability" and purity.[46] Part of this task was to raise the age of consent from the single digits in some U.S. states to upward of sixteen to eighteen years of age.[47] These laws portrayed young white women as vulnerable and in need of state protection against predators—the non-Anglo men who wanted to take advantage of them and "their youthful innocence." Reformers sought policies that would strengthen laws to essentially make it illegal for young women to freely consent to sex under a certain age.[48] These laws, then, functioned to erase young white women's sexual agency and place them under the protection of the purity reformers and the legal state.[49] "Closely entwined . . . with the belief that young women *could not* give true consent," writes J. Shoshana Ehrlich, "was an equally powerful belief that they *should not* be permitted to consent to sexual relations."[50] At the same time, these purity laws reified the image of the Black, Eastern European, or Jewish man as sexual predator. The WCTU in particular "often depicted African Americans, immigrants, and Catholics as aliens in the country who endangered the safety of the nation."[51] Ehrlich writes, "By denying the possibility of authentic female sexual agency, the reformers sought to encode a narrow vision of respectability into law."[52] This respectability reflected white Protestant bourgeois values that often challenged the perspectives and experiences of non-Anglo, working-class, Catholic, and immigrant women.

Indeed, the lived experience of working-class and immigrant young women posed a "girl problem" for reformers in this time period. These city girls did not fit the script of the young white woman as perpetual victim (the Mary Denbighs of the world) but seemed to actively participate in and pursue sexual behaviors, including sex work. The growing psychology and sexology of the time supported the belief that the "awakening of desire was a natural part of puberty in females and males alike." Therefore, it was expected that a modern girl would desire sexual pleasure. This did not allay the fears of purity reformers, however, who sought to curb the sexual behaviors of young women living in the cities.[53] They were particularly concerned with the environments these girls lived in, blaming the poverty and overcrowding of the tenement districts for the girls' sexual deviance. The reformers believed that working-class and immigrant girls were sexually delinquent because their families "failed to organize their lives in accordance with middle-class standards." Children ought to be "sheltered from the burdens of the adult world," according to these standards, and protected from the "moral dangers of the workplace." Purity reformers believed that once a young woman's sexual desire was "unleashed" through exposure to sexual touch or by witnessing the sexual behaviors of others—commonplace in crowded tenement communities—"her natural reserve would be eroded, thus leaving her vulnerable to the temptations of the flesh." There was hope for reform, however, but primarily for white ethnic immigrant and working-class girls; Black young women, as we have seen, were believed to be inherently sexually promiscuous.[54]

In some ways, this shift in concern from the innocent country girl to the so-called female sexual deviant opened the door to embracing female subjectivity and sexual agency in U.S. law and society. This was perhaps true of white middle-class women in the 1920s—flappers—who participated in the growing heterosocial youth culture. Eventually, concern for the "problem girl" subsided as the social purity movement came to a close. In the postwar years, the anxiety of the Cold War would be transferred onto a new "problem girl," the delinquent teen, but rather than purity reformers, evangelical psychologists and conservative political thinkers would drive the discourse.

"The Way We Never Were": The Family Values Panic of the 1970s

Sex, gender, religion, and youth culture changed tremendously from the eve of the 1920s through the Cold War era in the United States. This period saw sexual norms common among the working class and immigrants—norms such as liberalism and valuing sexual pleasure—spread to the middle class. Companionate marriage was on the rise, rooted in values such as equality, happiness, and pleasure. The sexual desire and fulfillment of not just men mattered, but women too. Easy-to-obtain divorce became a reality for many.[55] The Kinsey Studies of the 1940s and '50s disrupted commonly held assumptions about the ubiquity of same-sex desire, premarital sex, masturbation, and other previously illicit sexual behaviors.[56] In terms of gender, the separate spheres shattered as many middle-class women joined the workforce, American life became more commercialized, and women won the right to vote. In this time, write historians John D'Emilio and Estelle Freedman, "Female purity lost much of its power as an organizing principle for enforcing sexual orthodoxy as young women and men together explored the erotic."[57]

A youth subculture blossomed in the 1920s, in part because of coed spaces like movie theaters and amusement parks and the invention of the car. White middle-class youth now, like urban working-class and immigrant youth previously, had the opportunity to socialize together without parental oversight. The double standard, which was challenged by the previous generation's purity reformers, still existed between the genders. For boys, that meant they would have sex with the girls they would *not* marry in order to get experience but not hurt their future wives. Still, young men would "push," while girls "set the limit."[58] Adolescent behavior, including sexual behavior, was a growing concern for purity reformers and religious leaders, especially for those who viewed youth as the great hope for the nation. They feared that youths' access to pornography corrupted them and led to juvenile delinquency—a threat to the country's future.[59] "The minds of youth, still in formation," writes R. Marie Griffith of the time, "needed protection from corrupt literature intended to arouse sensation and encourage debauchery, lest they be overtaken by lust and cease to be functioning citizens contributing to a well-ordered society."[60] This pivot to focusing on youth and their sex lives would become an important theme in the growing neo-evangelical movement of the postwar era.

The concerns of these decades culminated in what I am calling the family values panic of the mid-century. The movement, bipartisan at first, was grounded in the belief that the strength of the American family correlated directly with the strength of the nation. "As the family goes, so goes the nation."[61] This ideology dates back to Progressive Era concerns for the family, particularly the purity crusades against personal vices that disrupted healthy families and affected the purity and strength of the country. These early purity campaigns and policies especially focused on women and children as vulnerable, as explored in the previous section.[62] In the decades that followed came policies that reflected both liberal and conservative views of the family. In the 1930s, the New Deal rollout reflected the liberal concern for the family, especially with programs like the Fair Labor Standards Act, which reduced child labor. Growing fears of socialism led conservatives to link government intrusion to the destruction of the family.[63] Thus, many conservatives rejected New Deal policies that would have strengthened the family for being too "red."

The misremembering of the 1950s and early '60s as a conflict-free, ideal, *Leave It to Beaver*–type era was critical in the emergence of family values rhetoric. Feminist historians have long argued that the elusive "traditional family" sought by liberals and conservatives alike in the late '60s and '70s was merely an illusion, belonging to a reinterpretation of the unusually stable 1950s.[64] What these memories leave out are "the deep prejudices confronting minority families, the anxieties produced by the Cold War, the financial pressures on the majority of families, and the limited choices afford[ed] to most women."[65] The "traditional family" never existed in the way we think it did—at least not in a single period of time. Stephanie Coontz calls this the "elusive traditional family" or "the way we never were."[66] Against such a "nostalgia trap," in the 1950s and early '60s, juvenile delinquency was on the rise, threats of atomic war made kids cower under desks, race riots overwhelmed the North while segregation thrived in the South, and the Red and Lavender Scares found enemies among all.[67]

By the 1970s, political and social liberals and conservatives agreed that there was a countrywide decline in family values but could not agree on the cause or how to address it. Liberals were primarily concerned with economic problems—for example, the rise in divorce rates, the decline in wages, the weakness of the Black family—and solutions—for example, universal childcare, welfare, and so on.[68] Conservatives were concerned with the moral permissiveness birthed out of women's, gay, and civil rights. Second-wave feminists eschewed traditional marriage, enjoyed greater sexual freedom with the accessibility of the contraceptive pill, and demanded equal treatment in employment.[69] Gay men were perceived as the fault of weak, effeminate fathers.[70] Some neo-evangelicals, especially those with roots in the South, saw the integration of schools as particularly concerning for the American family, as it could lead to miscegenation and the weakening of the white race.[71] It was the partial success of the aforementioned liberation movements that overturned the "consensus" of the postwar era, that is, the perceived stability, especially of the nuclear family.[72] The solution of these conservatives was not to create welfare programs like the liberals but to address what they saw as the underlying moral issues.[73]

Politically conservative evangelicals were particularly keen on weaponizing the language of family values, so much so that by Reagan's election in 1980, "family values" was presumed to have always been a partisan concern and one uniquely tied to conservative evangelicals.[74] With their disappointment in the first evangelical president, Jimmy Carter, white evangelicals became an important voting bloc for the Republican party. "The vision of family values created a bond between evangelicalism and political conservativism," writes historian Seth Dowland. Evangelicals mobilized family values through their homeschooling initiatives and programs like Promise Keepers, which "rall[ied] men to return to the faith," as well as joining already established political agendas like anti-abortion.[75] This was the time of the "culture wars," where conservative evangelicals—eventually the Christian Right and the Moral Majority—believed themselves to be at war against immorality.[76] Influential pastor and expatriate Francis Schaffer[77] encouraged his fellow evangelicals to find "co-belligerents," those with whom they agreed on moral and political issues but not necessarily religious views. For example, this concept of co-belligerency helped transform abortion from being a "Catholic issue" in the early 1970s to being of concern for conservatives of differing religious affiliations (including white Protestants and Mormons) and belonging under the banner of family values.[78] Dowland continues, "The phrase ['family values'] was capacious enough to accommodate a variety of initiatives but specific enough to mark boundaries between conservative evangelicalism and broader society."[79] Through creative political maneuvering and strategic co-belligerencies, conservative evangelicals became a powerhouse for conservative politics.

Both Schaffer and James Dobson, a leading evangelical psychologist, believed youth had an important role in the so-called culture wars, especially when it came to the issue of sexual purity. Dobson and his growing radio and educational empire, Focus on the Family, responded to the family values panic by addressing the role parents played in the raising of godly children—the underlying assumption being that children, and youth especially, have a responsibility in saving the nation. Dobson's first book, *Dare to Discipline*, came in response to what Dobson saw as over-permissiveness in child-rearing, thanks in part to popular experts like Dr. Spock.[80] Dobson called his appeal to white, middle-class family values and structures "traditional" or "biblical," not, more accurately, *Victorian*. "Like purity reformers . . . before him," writes Moslener, "Dobson deployed tropes of sexual morality and national stability in order to make claims about personal morality and citizenship."[81] Drawing on G. Stanley Hall's developmentalism and recapitulation theories and through the language of therapeutic discourse,[82] Dobson reached back to the nineteenth century to reinstate Victorian bourgeois family structures and gender norms, thus using white, middle-class, two-parent families as a "rubric" for all families.[83]

Dobson, whose influence extended into contemporary evangelical purity culture, emphasized the important role of youth in the fate of the civilization. But he did so differently from his nineteenth-century predecessors. A premillennial dispensationalist, Dobson believed that a period of tribulation (war, death, plague, natural disasters) would occur prior to Christ's return. Youth would act as a beacon of hope in a time of impending doom. Because of this, Dobson was particularly concerned with controlling adolescence, making sure teens lived up to their potential. Much like Hall before him, Dobson saw adolescence as a "critical moment" in a person's development.[84] In his 1978 book *Preparing for Adolescence*, he advises parents to focus their energies on the *pre*adolescent child, who was most "pliant and receptive" to their guidance. Once a child reached late adolescence, it may be too late to intervene in a teen's choices—decisions that could affect not just the individual but the family and nation as well. "Beware: if you let this fleeting moment escape unnoticed," writes Dobson, "you may never get another opportunity."[85] Just as bourgeois Victorian parents (especially mothers) had a role in instilling moral values in children, Dobson taught that parents have a responsibility to teach and discipline their children so that they do not conform to the "new morality" of contemporary American society.[86] Only then could they be a beacon of hope.

Preparing for Adolescence was written for both boys and girls, yet this text and the other guides that Dobson wrote for and about teenagers relies on strict gender norms, norms that were being challenged by second-wave feminists at the time. To Dobson, boys were wild and their natural inclinations toward sex needed to be tamed by women. Women needed to remain in the private sphere as moral authorities for their children—though not the "heads" of families, for that was the job of men.[87] Children ought to be disciplined and taught that sex belongs only within the context of a heterosexual marriage. Dobson believed that adolescents' "sexual morals were last line of defense against the rampant moral relativism that threatened family stability."[88] Like the purity reformers of the nineteenth and early twentieth centuries, Dobson placed his anxiety—and parents' anxieties—onto children, especially adolescent girls. Teenage girls, and later adult women, were responsible for keeping men's sexualities in line. As an adolescent, this meant guarding her virginity.[89] "The stability of the family required that sex be confined to marriage, and the continued existence of the nation—and indeed, of civilization itself—depended on maintaining the cohesiveness of the family. . . . [Evangelical leaders] therefore had to do everything possible to deter their young people from losing their virginity before marriage," writes historian Daniel K. Williams.[90] Making a connection between sexual restraint and economic restraint, Dobson and his contemporaries believed that a woman's job was to "civilize" men's "aggressive energy" into capitalistic enterprises. Failing to do so meant the "endangering of civilization itself."[91]

The evangelical view of the integrity of the family, youth's role in it, and the fear of liberal sexuality expressed by Dobson and his contemporaries laid the foundation for evangelical purity culture to thrive in the 1990s and beyond. Much of the same rhetoric was used in this new moral/sex panic to come—and, indeed, many of the leaders and spokespeople remained the same—but this time with flashier, teenage-tailored messaging. Just as the "flower children" of the 1960s and '70s had their own youth subculture, young evangelicals were invited to actively participate in the culture war as a youth subculture unto itself.[92]

Contemporary Evangelical Purity Culture: The Beginnings

In July 1994, tens of thousands of teens gathered in a stadium for Christian rock music and to make a pledge to God, their parents, and their future spouses to not have sex until marriage.[93] In the decades following this first True Love Waits (TLW) rally, thousands of events like this would invite teens from all over the country and throughout the world to promise to remain abstinent until heterosexual marriage.[94] TLW was the brainchild of Southern Baptist youth pastor Richard Ross, who was distraught to learn that "religious devotion was not a deterrent for adolescents engaging in sexual activity."[95] This led Ross to develop the abstinence-based sex education program, which grew out of a fifty-six-member youth group and into a government-funded campaign,[96] hosting interdenominational rallies and producing branded consumer goods, including a TLW Bible, planners, and purity rings.[97] At the same time, because federally funded abstinence campaigns akin to TLW were believed to course correct a nation on moral decline ever since the sexual revolution,[98] evangelical leaders saw that the burden of America's morality rested on the shoulders of these purity-devout teens.[99] The future of the nation, and the future of the teenager's marital, familial, and eternal life, depended on her remaining pure until marriage, no doubt a heavy burden to carry at such a young age.

Like the social purity panic and family values panic before it, contemporary evangelical purity culture defined *purity* to include a wide variety of appropriate behaviors and ideologies. "Instead of being forced to make lists of acceptable and unacceptable sexual activity," writes scholar Christine Gardner, "the [evangelical purity] campaigns [could] focus on purity, thus subsuming sexual activity under the general category of lifestyle choices pleasing to God."[100] That meant regulating a teenager's choice of clothing, friends, and media consumption as well as her sexual activity.[101] Using the language of the "slippery slope," movement leaders taught that any intimate touch between opposite sexes, like kissing, could lead to premarital sex.[102] This movement was not as overtly concerned with racial purity; however, white supremacist ideologies were embedded in how its leaders spoke and wrote about "social norms, values, structures, and institutions."[103]

Contemporary evangelical purity culture was about body control, argues scholar Heather Hendershot, which looked different for adolescent girls and boys. Boys were taught that their bodies are out of control, even violent. They were taught, then, to channel that dangerous desire into physical activity, like weightlifting or football.[104] But if this was not possible, ultimately the girl was responsible for managing the boy's desire because her desire for sex is not predicated on uncontrollable physiology, according to proponents of the movement. Harkening back to Victorian ideas about women's moral authority, purity culture taught that women do not desire sex as boys do; they desire love and will endure sex in order to get it. This does not encourage boys to understand their sexual desires as normal, and therefore manageable, but ultimately excuses sexual violence. If the boy could not control his body with his girlfriend, it was ultimately her responsibility to stop him from advancing. Unlike the purity reformers of the late nineteenth century, addressing the gender double standard was not a high priority for the purity movement of the late twentieth century.

Girls were taught a more complicated set of lessons about their bodies. A girl's purity must be protected at all costs. If she had sex, she was "damaged goods." And she ultimately had to submit to higher male authorities despite being less desirous of sex than her male counterpart. Though it theoretically applied to boys and girls equally, purity was ultimately the responsibility of young women—and, indeed, young *white* women who were "upheld as the ideal embodiment of sexual purity," even as purity culture existed in communities of color.[105] In her study of evangelical colleges, Donna Freitas writes that "evangelical girls are taught to protect their purity on four levels: mentally, emotionally, spiritually, and physically."[106] An evangelical girl was taught by purity literature and teachings to be "asleep" sexually until her "prince comes along (at God's command) to 'wake her.'"[107] The only appropriate time for such awakening is heterosexual marriage. In the meantime, girls were taught not to flirt, not to spend too much time fantasizing about future marriage vows (especially not about the wedding night), and to dress modestly so as to not tempt good Christian boys. Thus, purity culture required a level of "self-surveillance," writes Amy DeRogatis. "Evangelical young women who pledge to live the purity lifestyle are caught in a bind of constantly talking and thinking about the one thing they cannot do."[108] The payoff for all this waiting and self-surveilling was supposed to be amazing marital sex.[109] This reward was permanently lost to girls who did not remain pure before their wedding night.[110]

If such a young woman did not remain pure, the consequences extended beyond her own self and body to God, to her father (to whom she has broken a vow), to her church, to her future husband, and to society itself. The language of nuclear warfare is embedded in a lot of evangelical sex education curricula. A Silver Ring Thing video production compares sexual protection in the form of a condom as akin to letting a child play with an atom bomb. In the video, the bomb inevitably explodes, reinforcing the message that there are national, and global, consequences for sexual impurity.[111] In the 1997 TLW curriculum, *Until You Say I Do*, a teenage girl named Sarah's sexual relationship with an older man is compared to the state of the United States prior to the attack on Pearl Harbor. "Just like America ignored the message of the surprise attack, Sarah ignored all of the warnings in her relationship with Gary. She felt confident and in control of the situation, but she was setting herself up for a surprise attack." Beneath this text are the words: "Be Ready for Battle."[112] The war language equates a young person's purity with the strength or weakness of a nation.

None of this means that girls—and, for that matter, boys—were merely pawns of purity culture and its teachings. We know that many teens chose to be a part of purity culture, and their decisions to wait to have sex were, indeed, decisions *they* made. Hendershot writes that teen participants in purity culture did "not merely internalize the chastity directive without substantial questioning, negotiation, and varying degrees of resistance. . . . Through their own Bible study, teens may end up rethinking, or at least complicating, the very rules that adults say the Bible teaches unequivocally."[113] Girls had opportunities to interpret what *purity* meant to them. (Was it waiting to have penile-vaginal intercourse or waiting to French kiss?) There was room within purity culture for some sexual and moral agency for young women, though officially, the options presented to her were limited.

Conclusion

As we have seen, the categories of age, race, gender, sex, class, and religion are inextricably entwined within moral/sex panics and reform in the United States. Studying these panics through a singular lens does not reveal a full picture as to why young white women were placed in the center of these discourses, why adolescents could save the nation or harken the Second Coming of Jesus, or why purity was the ultimate goal for evangelical teenagers. Taken together, these intersecting categories provide a complex story of how and why young, middle-class white women, in particular, have been and continue to be protected, shunned, stigmatized, or used for particular political and religious agendas. This pattern has only continued into the present day as evangelicals and exvangelicals navigate how to respond to the young women and queer youth who grew up within contemporary evangelical purity culture.

The Child and the Teen have been used for political and religious agendas as a means to expel adult anxiety in uncertain times. In the process, the *real* child and *real* adolescent are erased. What if, instead, we saw girls like Mary Denbigh of *The House of Bondage* as an agential young woman in her own right, who wittingly followed Max to New York as a means to escape her middle-class life in the country? What if we believed that the teen girl at the center of James Dobson's evangelical culture war was one who understood her sexuality as her own, whether she had sex outside heterosexual marriage or not? The coming chapter will provide language and opportunity to explore the child and the adolescent as agents in their own rights and as expert guides in reading purity culture through a new lens.

4

Reimagining Adolescent Sexuality and Agency

In the final scene of Act I of the Broadway musical *Spring Awakening*,[1] the teenage schoolboy Melchior pulls himself on top of Wendla in the hayloft while their families are at church.

> Wendla: Melchi, no—it's just—it's . . .
> Melchior: What? Sinful?
> Wendla: No. I don't know . . .
> Melchior: Then why? Because it's good? Because it makes us "feel" something?

The stage directions read: "Wendla considers, then suddenly reaches and pulls Melchior to her. She kisses him. He holds her, and gently helps her lie back."[2] The writers of the musical adaptation of this nineteenth century play describe the hayloft scene as lovemaking—though its original German author, and any astute feminist, would interpret the number of times Wendla says no and hesitates as an indication of date rape.[3] Still, it is this scene of penile-vaginal intercourse (PVI)—or penetrative date rape—that is positioned as the pinnacle of the story and the height of Melchior's sexual discovery. It is a moment that he arrives to by himself, through his self-taught lessons on sexuality, written down in a series of essays.

As a story written and performed in the perspective of teenagers, a primary theme of *Spring Awakening* is the failure of adults to properly teach their children about sex. The motif is laid out in Act I Scene I as Wendla begs her mom to teach her where babies come from, but her mother refuses to tell her. You could interpret *Spring Awakening* as an indictment against adults for not treating children as sexual and moral subjects. They are treated, instead, as wholly vulnerable and thus in need of control and protection, much like the protectionist agendas and policies we have already explored. In the cast's singing, "O, I'm gonna be wounded / O, I'm gonna be your wound," they evoke the etymology of the word *vulnerable*: to wound.[4] These are vulnerable, wound-able children. Therefore, you could also interpret *Spring Awakening* as a revelation in child sexual agency, albeit a cautionary tale. Tragedy befalls most of the children in this play.[5] Premarital sex (or rape) leads to abortion leads to death.

I imagine, instead, a reading of *Spring Awakening* that resists both of these interpretations through queer theory critique and what childhood studies scholar John Wall calls "childism," or the critical lens that "deconstruct[s] adultism across research and societies and reconstruct[s] more age-inclusive scholarly and social imaginations."[6] This queer and childist lens leads me to ask different questions of the play's characters and its moral messaging. Instead of centering the penetrative sex/rape in the hayloft as the defining moment for Melchior—one that leads to the "success" of procreation—what if we centered another scene? Not long before Wendla meets Melchior in the hayloft, Mortiz comes by Melchior's house to return his handwritten essay on "The Art of Sleeping With. . . ."[7] Mortiz is anxious and overwhelmed by sex and turns to Melchior to help him understand what makes it so alluring. In the stage production, the boys—Moritz and Melchior, now joined by the company of others—sing their inner longings and imagine what girls might erotically desire too. Melchior sings his part "as if in some hypothetical woman's voice":[8]

> Touch me—just like that.
> And that—O, yeah—now, that's heaven.[9]

While this is being sung, Melchior stands behind Moritz, using Moritz's hands to caress Moritz's body.

There is a certain queerness to this scene in the fumbling or failure by the teens onstage and also by and because of their offstage parents in failing to teach their children about sex. This scene "privilege[s] the naïve or nonsensical." Indeed, through Melchior's essay and song, "'the naïve or the ignorant may in fact lead to a different set of knowledge practices,' where 'learning takes place independent of teaching.'"[10] Learning takes place, instead, in the company of other boys and in the touching of their own and each other's bodies. Drawing on the work of queer theorist Jack

Halberstam and Kate Ott's definitional essay, I call this "orgasmic failure," or "a recognition of adolescent sexual subjectivity that values the erotic ethical encounter with self and other."[11] This scene is not one of PVI—it is not even necessarily imagining heterosexual sex, as two boys in the company are revealed to be queer lovers. Rather, it shows the complex desires of young people that may or may not lead to adult forms of sexual play. By centering this scene rather than the hayloft scene, we get a peek into children's sexual lives apart from the strictures of adult thinking, which gives us adults the freedom to understand youth on their own terms.

This analysis of *Spring Awakening* reveals the tensions between agency and vulnerability, autonomy and interdependence in childhood and adolescence. Moving beyond the historical-social constructions of the white Child and Teen as embodiments of helplessness, as easily duped and in need of adult protection and surveillance, I consider the philosophical arguments for understanding the sexual and moral lives of young people, especially young women and queer youth. The prevailing wisdom throughout the Western philosophical tradition has been that children are not moral agents because they are not autonomous subjects. Autonomy is something that can be reached by a certain age or stage of life and if one is a certain gender or race (i.e., male, white). I unpack this prevailing view and rehearse some of the common feminist and childhood studies critiques in order to construct an opposing liberative queer and childist view of adolescent subjectivity and agency that recognizes young people's full agency and vulnerability as sexual and moral beings. It is through this lens that we will read narratives of purity culture in the next chapter.

Adolescent Sex and Sexuality in the Contemporary United States

Our contemporary Western conceptions of sex and sexuality are different from those of the Victorian era when *Spring Awakening* was first written and in which the story is set despite how timeless the play reads. Like childhood and adolescence themselves, child and adolescent sexualities are "profoundly" culturally constructed.[12] Philosophy, the hard sciences, and the social scientific disciplines of anthropology, psychology, and sociology have tempted us into thinking that there is such a thing as a universal, natural, or global childhood and adolescence, especially an asexual childhood and a sexually developing adolescence. Yet, as scholars in the Foucauldian tradition have shown, even these presumably "objective" fields of study are imbued with power structures of whiteness, eurocentrism, adult-centrism, and heteropatriarchal assumptions that prevent us from having a truly objective view of childhood and adolescence.[13] Here I want to specifically turn our attention to contemporary understandings of child and adolescent sexuality in the United States, which are riddled with assumptions about who teenagers are, what their sex lives are like, and what value we are expected to place on their sexual behaviors.

From a feminist theoretical understanding, "Sexuality *is an embodied component of the human capacity to know and a way to communicate and form of expression of one's self-understanding. . . . Sexuality is more than the sum total of our sexual behaviors* and [we] reciprocally gain understanding from others when expressing our sexuality. Our sexuality is *developed in personal (and systematic) relationships affected by social, biological, psychological, cultural and spiritual forces*."[14] Sexuality, then, is a part of who humans fundamentally are (ontologically) but develops both outwardly and inwardly through a person's lifetime in relationship to a wide range of factors. With this comprehensive understanding in mind, sexuality is not something beholden to adulthood, nor is it only or primarily about what is often considered "sex," or genital contact of any sort. Sexuality "can (but doesn't have to!) include . . . sexual orientation, gender identity, ways we express or explore our sexual feelings alone or with other people, sexual interactions or relationships, and our feelings and thoughts about any of those things and about sex in general."[15] Sexuality can also more holistically describe a person's being-in-the-world, as an embodied person's means of self-expression. Sex, then, is one mode of sexual self-expression, whether solo (masturbation) or with others (vaginal, anal, oral, or non-penetrative sex).[16]

In the present-day United States, child and adolescent sexualities are written and spoken of primarily through the language of risk. The Centers for Disease Control and Prevention's ten-year "Youth Risk Behavior Survey" includes statistics on sexual behaviors alongside drug use, violent behavior, and suicidality.[17] Articles on adolescent sex tend to frame the need for education alongside the harrowing statistics of teen pregnancy rates in the United States (highest in the developed world), sexually transmitted disease occurrence ("Young people account for approximately 50% of all new STIs reported each year, and approximately 20% of all new HIV diagnoses"),[18] teenagers' failure to use condoms (fewer than two-thirds of those engaging in sexual intercourse),[19] and how significantly more Black children are initiating sexual intercourse before the age of thirteen than white or Hispanic children.[20] These articles and studies imply *sex* to mean *intercourse*, primarily PVI,[21] and suggest that the goal of medical, religious, governmental, or educational interventions is to reduce the problem of child/teen sexuality (expressed through intercourse) by promoting either comprehensive sex education or abstinence-only-until-marriage education, depending on the institution. The underlying message of many of these articles, through their careful methodologies and data gathering, is that adolescents are engaging in one fundamentally dangerous behavior (PVI), and we adults and institutions need to stop them (by promoting abstinence) or redirect them (by promoting condom use) in order for them to become "sexually healthy adults."[22]

No doubt sex can be risky for teens. Children and youth are uniquely vulnerable due to their physical size, dependence on parents or guardians for food and shelter, and comparably less experience in the world than adults. These factors also put children and teens at risk for domestic and sexual violence.[23] But this story of risk, vulnerability, and violence is not the only story we can tell about adolescents, nor should adults be the only ones *telling* the story. Despite the panicked messages of the preceding articles and studies, American adolescents—here young people between the ages of thirteen and nineteen—engage in PVI at a much lower rate than they did a generation ago; teenage pregnancy rates are much lower too.[24] Teens also have different means of expressing themselves sexually, through sexting and accessing pornography on their phones in the privacy of their bedrooms.[25] They have a broadening definition for what sex is, including oral, anal, and vaginal sex as well as mutual and solo masturbation.[26] Teens have a broader range of categories for describing their sexualities (queer, asexual, demisexual, pansexual, bisexual) and gender identities (agender, gender fluid, gender expansive) than generations previous.[27] They have greater, and safer, avenues for coming out through organizations like the Trevor Project and the Safe Schools Coalition, social media, and other online communities as well as through religious organizations like Beloved Arise, led in part by other young people.

While teenagers have demonstrated their capacity to articulate their sexual subjectivities and exert their sexual agencies, adults and their institutions continue to regard children and teens as unformed adults, incapable of making reasonable or rational choices about their own bodies. They assert that children and teenagers need to be passively protected and educated by well-informed adults in order to one day enact their full rational potential as adults.

The Jigsaw Puzzle of Adolescent Subjectivity and Agency

A young person's sexuality is solely a product of neither one's biological determinism (nature) nor the culture they inhabit (nurture) but is made up of a combination of their biology, family systems, nationality and ethnicity, gender, class, race, (dis)ability, religion, and so on.[28] A young person may find their sexualities to align with the worlds they were shaped in and by, or they might find their sexualities to be in direct opposition to those worlds.[29] Borrowing a metaphor from sociologists Stevi Jackson and Sue Scott, we could compare a child's cultural understanding of sex and sexuality (or "sexual scripts") to a jigsaw puzzle. A child may have two or three pieces—she knows that adults kiss and sometimes get married; she knows that she must sit with her knees together when she is wearing a sundress; and she knows that the adults at church comment on her long, shiny hair but not her drawing skills. But she does not have all the puzzle pieces, nor does she always know how the pieces fit together or even if they "belong to the same puzzle."[30] There are two possible lessons for the girl with the jigsaw puzzle, suggests pastoral theologian Barbara Blodgett.[31] Lesson One comes from those whom Blodgett calls feminist theologians of the erotic. They tell the girl that the puzzle pieces always come together to form a beautiful picture—and if they do not, then she has the wrong puzzle. She just needs to tap into her God-given intuition and creativity to discover the pieces laid out for her and how they fit together. That is, *eros*—or the divine power of the erotic—is always good and therefore any experience of sexuality that is not good is not truly erotic. This lesson does not help the girl understand the sexual script, nor does it take into account the realities of heteropatriarchal oppression that she cannot easily escape.

Lesson Two comes from Blodgett in her reading of feminist psychoanalysts. This lesson is very different—it states that there are two puzzles that got mixed together. One puzzle shows a beautiful picture of romance and love. The other shows a harrowing picture of disavowing the erotic and of unequal power dynamics. With this lesson, the girl needs help discerning how to separate out the puzzle pieces and how to interpret the image each puzzle creates. She needs help locating the often-missing puzzle pieces of "those relating to desire, pleasure and physical sexual acts,"[32] as well as the pieces that make sense of "the dynamics of gender, power, and culture, which are not easily teased apart."[33] And yet, one might ask, as feminist Elizabeth Gish does, whether this second lesson unfairly insists that the girl cannot solve the puzzle on her own. Rather than giving girls the "resources and space to better interpret" the puzzle pieces, Blodgett suggests that "this is the job of adults such as herself."[34]

We can imagine, too, how a queer child of any gender might engage with the puzzle and internalize the lessons they receive. A queer child might find themselves confused why their puzzle is not coming together the way they are told it should. The puzzle may appear to be that beautiful picture promised in the first lesson, but it is only a facade—a stock photo, not a masterpiece. Or maybe the queer child tries to steal a piece from another puzzle—the "straight" puzzle—with the hopes that it will fit into their own jigsaw. The mixing of puzzle pieces, this time, is intentional, done by the queer child to help them make sense of their world. As for Lesson Two, it is the same for the queer child as it is for girls: an adult must step in to help them tease out what is truly part of their puzzle and what is not.[35] We can imagine this as the adult queer man saying, "It gets better!" or the evangelical youth pastor saying, "Your struggle with same-sex attraction is a phase; you will find that perfect woman one day."

These two enduring lessons represent prevailing views of children's and adolescents' sexual subjectivity and agency, which render youth as either completely agential—to the point of transcending their vulnerabilities—or wholly vulnerable, passive, and in need of adult protection and guidance. They also erase the racial, socioeconomic, and ethnic differences with which a child may engage with their puzzle pieces. These lessons assume young people, especially young girls, to be a homogenous group.

We can see how these two lessons are reflected within purity culture discourse as well. In Lesson One, exvangelical feminists challenge a tradition of hating women's bodies and situating sexuality only within the context of heterosexual marriage. Lesson One subverts the patriarchy by insisting that women and girls do have the erotic power to choose what is best for their bodies apart from male dominance.[36] They invite victim-survivors of purity culture to pose naked with them and freely say, *I accept myself just as I am!*[37] In Lesson Two, we see white girls painted as vulnerable victims of their culture, particularly in how they have been socialized to disavow their own desires in relationships with others. This lesson reinforces the victimization narrative, where girls can view themselves as hurt by purity culture in a million different ways but never have to be responsible for any harm they have caused. Lesson Two's solution is not to empower young people to make sense of their worlds but to continue to tell them how they *should* feel: purity culture should have made you feel used, powerless, and objectified. Now that you're free, you should feel empowered, sensual, and uninhibited. Writing from a Christian theoethical perspective in which "sin, sexuality, and the human capacity to create meaning are deeply entwined," Blodgett invites adolescent girls into the typically adult male world of theological participation.[38] Yet Blodgett does not trust adolescents to navigate that world without adult supervision.

Perhaps it is not that children lack the reasoning to solve the puzzle, nor that they are only on their way to understanding or need adult supervision, but given the right "resources and space," they can interpret the puzzle on their own.[39] That is, through social structures that promote a child's self-determination and through reflective relational experiences, a young person can make sense of sexual scripts in a way that does not demand a particular interpretation but invites her participation.[40] This task requires that we have a more complex understanding of child and adolescent ways of being that are not beholden to adult concepts of subjectivity and agency. I argue for understanding youth ways-of-being through a queer, feminist, and child-centric lens that resists the normative assumptions of the child as developing toward normative adulthood and as unidirectionally dependent on adults.

Western Foundations in Subjectivity and Agency

Two major schools of thought—the Kantian tradition and developmental psychology—have shaped our understanding of childhood and adolescent subjectivity and agency in the West. The Kantian tradition and developmental psychology, esteemed as universal and global, and thus acultural, have been rightly challenged first by feminists and then by childist and queer theorists, who attend to the complexity of youth subjectivities and agencies outside a heteronormative, Western, adult-centric lens.

Enlightenment Autonomy: Immanuel Kant

The Age of Enlightenment in the Anglophone West (seventeenth and eighteenth centuries) exalted the individual person with his rights, liberties, and freedom from governmental or ecclesial tyranny. Of course, as generations of scholars from the margins have shown, Enlightenment projects were never intended to be truly universal, just universal among white European men or white landowning men. With global political revolutions and their expanding colonial domination, the fading power of the Catholic and Protestant Church, and the declaration of *I think, therefore I am*, the primary philosophical concerns shifted away from the collective to the individual—the individual adult male. As for children, then, the concern of some Enlightenment thinkers was in socializing boys into the ideal free-thinking man. "Childhood is patterned, in a way, on Enlightenment science itself: the march of progress in understanding nature now being applied to the march of progress in selves," writes John Wall.[41]

Enlightenment philosopher Immanuel Kant (1724–1804) established the adult- and androcentric view of autonomy and agency that feminist and childist scholars have been contending with ever since. In his defining essay, "What Is Enlightenment?," Kant urges his fellow adult European brethren to "dare to know." He celebrates the autonomy and rationality of the adult male mind in its ability to reason apart from its "self-imposed nonage." That is, only laziness or cowardice stand in the way of a man's ability to know freely, apart from the constrictions of the Church or government.[42] Autonomy, or self-legislation, was the key ingredient in Kant's understanding of the morally capable man.[43] Like many in his cohort of Enlightenment-era philosophers, Kant linked moral reasoning with moral behavior.[44] Kant described a "tug-of-war" between a man's inclinations ("desires, needs, and motives") and his duty.[45] Practical reason leads a man to determine what his duty is in a given situation, regardless of how he feels about his choices or any outside forces or influences, a priori.[46]

Women, however, were excluded as agents in Kant's moral universe because of their need for men's protection (lack of autonomy) and because of their inability to choose duty (lack of agency) over their natural inclinations toward beauty (lack of rationality). In his text *Observations on the Beautiful and the Sublime*, Kant writes, "Women will avoid the wicked not because it is unright, but because it is ugly; and virtuous actions mean to them such as are morally beautiful. Nothing of duty, nothing of compulsion, nothing of obligation! Woman is intolerant of all commands and all morose constraint. They do something only because it pleases them, and the art consists in making only that please them which is good. I hardly believe that the fair sex is capable of principles. . . ."[47] Children, too, are excluded from Kant's ethics insofar as they are not fully rational adults. But their exclusion, unlike women, is only temporary. Through "top-down" moral education, boys can overcome their animal-like nature and become rational thinkers.[48] "Everything in education depends upon establishing correct principles, and leading children to understand and accept them," Kant writes in his treatise *On Education*.[49] A product of the Enlightenment, Kantian ethics elevates the autonomous individual without recognizing the ways in which all humans, not just women and children, are interdependent.[50]

Women and children were not the only persons to be excluded from Kant's moral imagination. In his writings on anthropology and race, Kant extended his exclusion to Black, Asian, and Native American men as well, "questioning . . . the natural capacities of non-White races for moral agency and reasoned intellect."[51] In his essays "On the Different Races of Man" and "Natural Characteristics," Kant categorized the races, naming the white race as having superior morals, intellect, and artistic style over other races.[52] While some scholars have deemed Kant's writing on the construction and valuation of race to be "tangential" to his ethical work, others, like James Samuel Logan and Emmanuel Chukwudi Eze, show that Kant's views on race shaped his moral imagination through and through.[53]

Developing Morality: Erik Erikson and Lawrence Kohlberg

Indebted to the Kantian moral imagination came the work of developmental psychologists Erik Erikson (1902–1982), Lawrence Kohlberg (1927–1987) and his predecessor Jean Piaget (1896–1980), and their critic, feminist Carol Gilligan (1936–).[54] Developmentalism in the United States was established by the work of Charles Darwin, Herbert Spencer, and G. Stanley Hall's theories of human progress and recapitulation, that an individual person grows up in a pattern similar to the growth of a species. Childhood and adolescence played an important role within developmentalism, as these ages mark where the most significant changes occur. Through the work of Hall and his contemporaries, developmental psychology—and its study of children in particular—became an established and thriving discipline by the interwar period in the United States.[55] The premier developmental psychologists of the twentieth century viewed an individual's lifespan as a series of stages from infancy through adulthood.

The Danish artist-turned-child-analyst Erik Erikson was one of the twentieth century's most well-known psychologists.[56] Erikson theorized lifespan development as a series of stages marked by identity crises or "turning point[s]," characterized by growing autonomy and an increased, individuated sense of self.[57] Like Hall before him, Erikson believed adolescence to be a critical stage in a person's development. Marked by "genital maturation," uncertainty about one's future career, and their place in the teen subculture,[58] adolescence for Erikson was a period in a young person's life in which they forged their sense of self vis-à-vis their peers. He called this the tension between "identity versus identity confusion," which he linked to Freud's psychosexual stages.[59] For Erikson, adolescents are preoccupied with others' opinions and how they fit into the in-group and distinguish themselves from those in the out-groups. They desire peers with whom they can commiserate over their changing bodies and anxiety about their future choices while also constantly test each other's "loyalties in the midst of inevitable conflicts of values."[60] If adolescents have space for self-expression, apart from their parents and authority figures, they will pass through this stage into the next with "psychosocial strength."[61]

Erikson's eight stages of human development depict only his understanding of Western white male development despite claiming universal application. Erikson tips his hand in two later chapters in *Identity: Youth and Crisis*, in which he describes the development of the female child (chapter 7) and the Black child (chapter 8). Carol Gilligan, a student and critic of Erikson's, summarizes his articulation of female adolescence as different from male adolescence. For the teen girl, "She holds her identity in abeyance as she prepares to attract the man by whose name she will be known, by whose status she will be defined, the man who will rescue her from emptiness by filling 'the inner space.'"[62] That "inner space" is both metaphorical and physiological for a girl, representing her need for relationship (unlike male autonomy) and her vaginal cavity or uterus. Erikson writes that

> Emptiness is the female form of perdition . . . but standard experience for all women. To be left, for her, means to be left empty, to be drained of the blood of the body, the warmth of the heart, the sap of life. How a woman thus can be hurt in depth is a wonder to many a man, and it can arouse both his empathic horror and his refusal to understand. Such hurt can be re-experienced in each menstruation; it is a crying to heaven in the mourning over a child; and it becomes a permanent scar in the menopause.[63]

Erikson draws on Freud here, suggesting that from babyhood, a girl is traumatized from having been born without a penis.[64]

As for his attentiveness to racial difference, to his credit, Erikson recognized the impact of social and historical traumas on Black folks in the United States as he was writing in the late 1960s. He suggested that because of the impact of slavery and colonization on African Americans, "they had constrained . . . identity options."[65] The Black individual (read: boy) had to interpret his identity in the midst of negative images of himself and thus retain not a "positive identity" but a negative one, or "an identity based on opposition to mainstream social forces."[66] Yet Erikson writes of a collective demand for identity apart from dominant white culture. His chapters on female and African American human development show Erikson's commitment to not taking "a life out of history, that life-story and history, psychology and politics, are deeply entwined."[67] Yet by placing girls and Black boys outside of his normative model for child development, Erikson tempts us into placing non-white non-boys into a category of deviance. Difference, here, suggests inferiority.[68]

While Erikson focused on childhood psychosocial development, Lawrence Kohlberg created a model for child moral development, borne out of the work of Jean Piaget. Briefly, in his study of middle-class French boys, Piaget noticed that children had similar patterns of thinking at similar ages.[69] Piaget believed these stages developed biologically "in interaction with the child's practical experiences in the world."[70] Important to Piaget's stages of development was a child's growing autonomy, or sense of freedom from his subjection to another's authority ("heteronomy").[71] Kohlberg expanded Piaget's work to look not just at cognitive development but moral development in children and adults. Kohlberg identified three levels and six total stages of moral development that one must pass through chronologically.[72] Ultimately, Kohlberg concluded that moral reasoning—as a reflection of autonomous thinking—was a key to moral maturity. And the specifics of those reasons mattered tremendously: doing the right thing as a means to avoid punishment (stage one) involves much less moral maturity than doing the right thing because it is lawful to do so (stage four) or because it reflects one's abstract and universal values (stage six). Like Erikson's six psychosocial developmental stages, Kohlberg suggested that his six stages were universal across gender and culture and that this was the only path for young people to develop morally toward "fully autonomous rationality."

Gilligan points out that those who did not belong to Kohlberg's original study of eighty-four white boys curiously did not reach the higher stages of moral development. Indeed, "Women appear deficient in moral development when measured by Kohlberg's scale."[73] Girls' behaviors suggest that they value relationships over rightness, intuition over "the primacy and universality of individual rights," and are thus unable to reach the higher levels of moral development.[74] Gilligan suggests, as a remedy, the careful listening to girls' and women's voices. By placing female voice and experience at the center of her study, she challenges the assumptions of developmental psychologists like Erikson, Piaget, and Kohlberg that "people are by nature separate, independent from one another, and self-governing."[75] While Gilligan offers an important counter to the androcentrism of developmental psychology, ultimately her feminist reinterpretation suffers some of the same pitfalls of those she aims to critique. That is, her ethic of care still tempts us to view childhood as a process of becoming and maturing, where time is "simply passing by."[76] There is a logic to developmentalism that assumes a linear teleology from babyhood to adulthood that does not account for a person's difference or agency, nor does it consider a child's particular stage in life as morally good beyond looking toward the next stage.[77] The field of childhood studies emerged in the mid- to late twentieth century in response to this critique of developmentalist theories.[78]

The Childhood Studies Response

Childhood studies, or the "new sociology of childhood," formed as an academic discipline in the 1980s with the purpose of studying "children and youth beyond the (then and still) dominant paradigm of developmental psychology." Rather than studying the patterns of children over a lifespan, childhood studies places the agential child at the center of its research; children actively participate alongside the adults who study them, even changing the nature of research in the process.[79] In privileging children and their phenomenological experiences, childhood studies scholars recognize how young people are both formed by their cultures and social networks and are also "active participants in and interpreters of these environments in their own right."[80] In this is the recognition of a multiplicity of childhoods and children who are not measured against the same narrow rubric as bourgeois white boys.[81]

One of the primary mottos of childhood studies is "being not becoming."[82] That is, children are not just on their way to becoming mature adults—through moral reasoning (Kohlberg) or self-identity (Erikson)—but are already their own moral person by merely being in the world. By focusing on who youth are to *become*, we miss the unique ways children already *are*: creative, vulnerable, moral, curious, and clever. Childhood studies pushes us to consider the ways in which children are agents in their world, even at a young age, creating and interpreting the world around them. Still, there is need to caution against the extremes of these two key tenets of childhood studies: the *being* of childhood and the agential child. A refusal to recognize becoming over or alongside being might hinder us from recognizing the complexities of childhood subjectivity and agency. While it is important to recognize that children are not "*merely* in the process of undergoing change," it is not helpful to replace this child with "a kind of denaturalized child which exists in a here-and-now."[83] As for agency, childhood studies, in its insistence—rightly—on recognizing the agential child, often does so "to the point of a fetish." That is, for scholars Spyros Spyrou et al., "the thrust of approach and conception [of childhood studies] continues to favor singular—if socially, culturally, and historically embedded—subjects who display, or must be allowed to display, creativity and active engagement of the world in the here and now."[84] An overemphasis on agency eclipses the ways in which children are uniquely vulnerable due to their experience in the world and reliance on adults to meet their needs.[85]

The two prevailing Western views on childhood and adolescent subjectivities and agencies—the Kantian and developmental schools of thought—understand children and youth through narrow lenses. For Kant, children (along with women and men of color) are "unformed" or imperfect humans.[86] Children cannot make rational choices for themselves because of their "nonage" or reliance on others to think and act on their behalf. In Erikson, Piaget, and Kohlberg, too, children are defined by "what they lack" and are moving toward: from a bond of trust with one's primary caregiver to an individuated sense of self (Erikson), from following social conventions to thinking for oneself (Kohlberg). Those who do not follow these trajectories toward adulthood—marked by "separation, autonomy, individuation, and natural rights"—are deemed deviant or, as in the case of Gilligan, in need of alternative developmental models.[87] Within these developmental models, there is little consideration of a child's agency as she is swept from one stage or level to the next. In response, childhood studies rejects developmentalism for not considering the individual agencies and personhoods of the children these previously discussed psychologists have studied. But in this focus on being over becoming, agency over passivity, childhood studies scholars risk fetishizing children and ignoring their complex vulnerabilities and interdependency.

Agential Teens and "The Rebelution"

In contemporary evangelical purity culture, we see the remnants of Kantian and developmental thinking in how youth are understood as subjects and agents. A kind of "stageism" undergirds purity culture as young people are thought of as merely "on their way" to adulthood.[88] Many of the lessons of purity that youth receive are in service to something they will experience in adulthood (i.e., heterosexual marriage), not for the here-and-now. Nancy Leigh DeMoss and Dannah Gresh write in *Lies Young Women Believe*: "One of the main reasons why God designed marriage was so that it would be a picture for us of His passion and His sacrificial love for His people. And that's one reason why He wants marriages to be pure. If your future marriage has the potential to show the world the incredible love and grace of God, doesn't it make sense that Satan would want to try to destroy that picture?"[89] In other ways, the pendulum has swung to an overemphasis on agency as we see in childhood studies. So much emphasis is on what a young person has the capacity to do (e.g., save the nation from sin) that they are no longer recognized as vulnerable.

An intriguing example of this comes from evangelical teens Alex and Brett Harris[90] and "The Rebelution."[91] In the mid-2000s, when Alex and Brett were sixteen years old, they created a website with the purpose of encouraging their fellow teenagers to rebel against "low expectations" placed on them as teenagers. "What if we told you that teenagers can make a difference in transforming the world? What if we told you, teenager, that your community *needed you* to step up and wield your God give[n] talents and gifts?"[92] Arguing that adolescence is a socially constructed stage of life developed in the early twentieth century (see chapter 2), Alex and Brett made a case for teenagers being treated as agents of change, not as children waiting to grow up. "The teen years were meant to be a season of daring, high hopes and real achievements—a one-time-only opportunity for a guy or girl to set a course for a truly remarkable life," they write.[93]

If this were the full story, we could think of The Rebelution as youth exerting their agency in positive ways, even as a rebellion against the kind of developmental stageism described previously. You can almost hear Alex and Brett use the language of "being not becoming." However,

The Rebelution got itself into trouble by recapitulating the kind of sexism and heterosexism that is at the heart of purity culture, thus reinforcing the familiar power dynamics at the heart of conservative evangelicalism. Discussion on The Rebelution's gender-segregated forums led to the creation of the Modesty Survey in early 2007. Young women around the world anonymously submitted hundreds of questions about modesty to The Rebelution. Guys were then invited to respond. More than 1,600 "Christian guys (of all ages)"—most of whom were teenagers[94]—replied with answers ranging from subtle to overt sexism.[95] "One primary purpose of modesty is to prevent men from 'falling' on account of a woman's unguarded body," writes one of these guys, describing modesty as a balcony on a roof. "You don't have to hide the fact that your house has a roof or that you are a woman. . . . But you do have to do what you can to protect the lives of your guests and the purity of your brother."[96] The Modesty Survey determined that "75.6% of guys say that they have less respect for an immodest girl than for a modest one."[97] The Rebelution website reinforced these patriarchal understandings of modesty by featuring guest blog posts by adult thinkers prominent in 2000s evangelicalism: Nancy Leigh DeMoss, John Piper, and C. J. Mahaney.[98]

The Rebelution's Modesty Survey is a helpful example of young people exerting their moral agency. This was a survey created by young people and responded to by young people with only a few adult voices giving credence to what the youth discovered among themselves. But just as the Kantian tradition and developmentalism centered the male experience as normative/active and women as passive, these same dynamics played out within The Rebelution's creation and promotion of the Modesty Survey. Guys were considered "experts" by nature of being young men. They were considered the active ones (lust-filled, sex-pursuant) and future leaders. The predominant message for girls was that they needed to be concerned with men's sexualities; therefore, they themselves were asexual and passive. What would it look like if these teenagers were able to see the power and privilege they exerted through the distribution of this survey and its results? What would it look like to hold young men like Alex and Brett accountable for the survey at large?

What we need is a model for understanding youth as moral agents and sexual subjects that is capacious enough to acknowledge that subjectivity and agency are not age- or gender-dependent. At the same time, such a model must acknowledge, too, that subjectivity and agency are necessarily shaped by one's particular positionality in the world—their race, age, gender, sex, socioeconomic status, and so on. We ought to have the imagination to see youth as vital members of the human race, from whom we can learn and not just teach, who are neither the saviors of humanity nor in need of paternalistic protection. From The Rebelution's Modesty Survey, we learn that teenagers desire to make meaning in the world and live out their values as Christians. They refuse to let their age determine their worth. However, these particular teenagers could not, as a whole, address the sexism and heterosexism playing out before them. Rather, they recapitulated the power dynamics of the larger system of evangelical purity culture.

Orgasmic Failure: Queer Subjectivities, Interdependent Autonomy

Predominant and prevailing Western views of child or adolescent subjectivity—as unformed or becoming—presume an intelligible or normative childhood. A child grows up toward adult maturity, from asexual to sexual, from deviant to normative. Real children resist these pat categories and directions. When it comes to the "shape" of child and youth sexuality, "it cannot be known, defined, or supposed in advance," write Egan and Hawkes. Child and adolescent sexual subjectivities are not intelligible; they require adults to "get more comfortable with ambiguity."[99] This does not mean that children and youth fit into the category of the abstract, deviant other. Children resist all stable knowledge.[100] As queer theorists have argued, childhood (and with it, adolescence) is queer. "For no matter how you slice it," writes Kathryn Bond Stockton, "the child from the standpoint of 'normal' adults is always queer."[101] Childhood and adolescence challenge and "frustrate the adult-centric, neo-liberal, white, heteropatriarchal construction of sexuality."[102] Children do not grow *up* to normative adulthood, as they are thought or expected to, but grow sideways and out, or toward what Wall calls "narrative expansion."[103]

Imagine a seven-year-old girl who cuts and styles her hair after a Backstreet Boy, begs for the "boy toy" in her McDonald's Happy Meal, utters the phrase "I wish I were a boy" in the mirror—yet cries, embarrassed, when she's asked, "Are you a boy?" at recess. The first half of the child's experience presumes a trajectory—though itself queer—toward gender dysphoria. Yet the child's actual behaviors do not so neatly align themselves to this teleology; the child is upset that she is *called* a boy despite wanting to *be* a boy. She resists, though not intentionally, any "normal" gender development. From Hannah Dyer's work on the queer aesthetics of childhood, this child's response is an example of queer affect or what is "excess of the socio-symbolic order and arrive to us 'as surprise or interruption, . . . suspending knowable or teleological time and unhing[ing] proper boundaries and habitual social relationalities.'"[104] We are surprised, as the child is, that she is upset by how her gender is perceived on the playground. Because queer affects "must be discarded in order to 'grow up,'"[105] the surprise the child experiences at recess must be collapsed into a "normal" adult's intelligible articulation of childhood. It was as if the child decided, there at the playground, *I now know I want to continue being a girl.*[106]

Unlike this collapsing of a child's complex experience of herself in her gender, Wall writes of narrative expansion as the "ethical aim" of childhood, that "life's complex narratives may achieve an increasingly diverse wholeness. All the many, various, and conflicting parts of one's life story—its multiple pasts, futures, and presents as a self with others—may be invested with a more rather than less narrative unity."[107] This unity allows for the child's queerness to remain intact, intensify even, as she develops in other ways—in relationships with others, in her self-expression, and in her understanding of the world and her place in it. Thus, I offer here a view of youth subjectivity as *becoming* (growing sideways) but without a normative teleology, a *being* but not a static or stable kind of being.

As complex subjects, children participate in their moral universes not as parrots of adult behavior nor with the same moral responsibility or culpability as adults. Not rational, autonomous agents, children are *interdependently autonomous*.[108] Children need adults to survive and to grow toward greater moral understanding, but adults also need children to disrupt them and help them decenter themselves toward greater moral responsibility.[109] Children "disrupt in the moral sense of demanding changes in the world." When a child is born, parents shift their schedules, change their spending habits, reallocate rooms in their home. Communities make space for another child in day care. A child's name is added to a household census form. And with every new child comes new moral questions. Should the child (and her community) have access to lead-free water? Should the child (and his guardians) have choice in what school he attends?[110]

Children, too, are disrupted by others and thus have a role in moral world-building. "Even the youngest child is obliged to exceed herself in response to others, to create new relations beyond her present horizons, to expand her own moral worlds," writes Wall.[111] Those moral worlds expand through a child's lifetime. For example, Baby Ellie relates to the global poor "through the cheap labor that went into making her toys," but her relation to them is limited. Ellie cannot make sense of her relation to the poor due to her lack of narrative experience (i.e., her lack of cognitive abilities in understanding where toys come from, beyond her toy bin). But as she grows in narrative complexity, she will have a growing sense for how her world intersects with others' and a growing response-ability to the poor.[112]

Similarly, we can consider the difference between a child's having and giving reasons.[113] Three-year-old Teddy asks his playmate if he needs help putting his toy together. Teddy does a kind thing and likely knows it is a kind thing, but when pressed, he is unable to articulate *why* it is a kind thing. He is participating in his moral universe, even as a young child, whether he can articulate his moral reasoning or not. This is directly counter to Kantian and Kohlbergian notions of autonomy, which narrowly define moral reasoning as "increasingly independent and sophisticated reason-giving" that exists only in adulthood (Kant) or develops over a person's lifetime (Kohlberg).[114] "The inability of a child to explain [his] actions fully," such as Teddy offering help to his classmate, "does not necessarily make [his] behavior less morally weighty, less intentional, or less rational."[115] Even if Teddy understands that offering a helping hand is a kind thing to do, that does not guarantee that he will do that kind deed again.

In emphasizing the importance of children's moral agency, feminist social ethicist Cristina L. H. Traina draws on the work of Black feminist and womanist scholars who emphasize the significance for Black women in recognizing their agency and dignity in the midst of oppression.[116] This does not erase Black women's vulnerability but reminds them "that they have not borne their mistreatment passively."[117] These scholars resist the easy narrative that a victim is, and must always be, passive against perpetration to risk being deemed complicit.[118] Rather, we ought to see how even young children are complicit—as in active participants in—their abuse, though they are not responsible or culpable for the acts of violence done to them. For an example, a child may acquiesce to her father's abuse in order to ensure she and her siblings are fed that night. This does not make the beatings she receives her fault; rather, it shows her creative participation in her broken family system toward what she understands to be a greater moral good (provisions for herself and her siblings). Feminist philosopher Lisa Tessman calls this idea "burdened virtues"—sometimes the morally right thing to do (acquiesce) would not be viewed as morally good under perfect circumstances. It is not the child's fault that "someone 'set up the world up like this.'" Traina continues. "For children, who manifestly 'do not set the world up,' Tessman's burdened virtues provides a realistic way to think about moral action and about how systemic evil bears down to shape children's moral formation."[119] Children retain their moral agency but ought not be held responsible (especially legally so) for their actions to the same degree as adults.

As children like Ellie and Teddy reach adolescence, their moral worlds expand toward greater participation and greater response-ability. Ellie may learn that not just her toys but her clothes come from cheap labor overseas. Out of this, she may choose to wear only vintage, secondhand clothing (much to her peer group's dismay) as an expression of her moral agency. Her articulation of *why* she is wearing these thrift-store clothes could be viewed as simplistic to adult sensibilities ("Child labor is wrong!"), but her reasoning reflects her self as a moral subject. For Teddy, his kindness in day care might extend to his relationships in adolescence. He may find that his kindness functions in a particular way because of his brown skin. That is, the children, now teens, may have a greater recognition that how the world is "set up" is even more constraining due to their race (Teddy as South Asian) and gender (Ellie as female). Teddy may feel extra pressure to be viewed as the "kind one" among his white peers and teachers to fulfill his predetermined role as the model minority. Ellie may feel pressure to look and dress a certain way as a girl that collides with her convictions about child labor.

With these complex and dynamic understandings of adolescent subjectivities and agency, we have a broader conceptual framework for adolescent sex and sexuality that moves beyond the risks of STIs, pregnancy, and moral/sex panic. As queer subjects, adolescents participate in their moral and social worlds in ways that do not always make rational "adult" sense. For instance, adolescents today prefer maintaining relationships through texting and sexting more so than hanging out at the mall or going on dates as did previous generations of teens.[120] As interdependently autonomous agents, adolescents disrupt adult assumptions that sex must lead to the "success" of procreation or orgasm. Returning to the language of "orgasmic failure" introduced at the beginning of this chapter, adolescent sexuality, with its inclusion in the larger narrative of human sexuality, "resist[s] a goal of self-mastery of sexual behaviors . . . embrace[s] a praxis-based approach that values experiential knowledge and unhinges 'teaching' from particular centers of power . . . [and] release[s] ourselves and our relationships from a linear developmental logic that views change or ending as a loss."[121] That is, (1) adolescent sexuality is not caught up with the outcome of a particular sexual behavior, as other motivations such as pleasure and curiosity are centered in a teen's experience. (2) Learning is done by doing and through peer-to-peer interaction, especially as adults fail to offer holistic sexuality education. And (3) relationships themselves do not need to be lifelong to be significant (meaning childhood loves are as "serious" as adult relationships). Therefore, orgasmic failure is descriptive rather than prescriptive, except in how it directs adults to have a more expansive view of sexuality. We will explore this concept further in chapter 6.

Conclusion

In 2009, the traveling production of *Spring Awakening* made its way to Midwest stages. I was nineteen years old when I sat in the back of a Cleveland theater, watching the story of adolescent sexual desire and confusion alongside my friend and her high-school-age brother. I remember blushing when the actors mimicked masturbating on stage. I felt sick to my stomach (and, admittedly, intrigued) when Melchior exposed Wendla's breast to the audience. I drove back to my evangelical college on the Sunday of spring break, feeling things in my body that I had not been invited to feel in my Christian context: desire, curiosity, *thirst*. I became obsessed with *Spring Awakening*, a story I had known nothing about until I saw it on stage; I wrote about it in the Arts & Culture section of my school newspaper: "A musical exploring the themes of teen pregnancy, suicide and abortion doesn't seem [appropriate for students at an evangelical college]. But the Tony Award-winning musical 'Spring Awakening' allows [college] students to grapple with these themes from a Christian perspective."[122] This was my story—not that of "teen pregnancy, suicide and abortion" but of trying "to grapple with these themes from a Christian perspective." Adult failures, I knew well. I was not yet aware of how little I knew about sex, but I had a queer felt sense that I was being duped. *Maybe sex isn't* always *bad outside marriage. Maybe it's normal for girls to want to have sex, too.* I did not have the resources within my evangelical Christian context to make sense of my questions or my awakening sexual feelings either. So I set out to understand it on my own, by writing about *Spring Awakening* in the school newspaper and listening to the soundtrack on a loop.

I think of my late adolescent obsession with *Spring Awakening* as a subtle, but nonetheless real, form of resistance to the messages I had grown up with in purity culture in my church and now my evangelical college. I had not ever accepted wholesale everything those evangelical cultures had taught me about sex; just a peek at my stacks of journals from the time shows the constant frustration, wrestling, disagreement I had with what I had been told. But there was something about the story of the German Victorian schoolchildren that gave me permission to have those feelings of frustration, to wrestle, and to disagree—in fact, *Spring Awakening* helped me realize that that was what I *had* to do, in order that my fate did not end the same as the victimized Wendla or Moritz. Not unique to me, this is the reality of many teenagers who grew up in purity culture: they disagreed, they negotiated rules, they sought out answers not just from Bible study leaders but from their friends or media. Listening to the narratives of adolescents themselves, apart from a normative adultist lens, helps us recognize the ways in which white adolescents not only suffered under the oppressive structure of purity culture but were also simultaneously agential, creative, and resistant to its teachings.

5

Reading Adolescent Narratives Against the Norms of Purity Culture

Growing up a preacher's kid, Danny subscribed to Focus on the Family's evangelical alternative to *CosmoGirl*: *Brio*. Every issue featured a "Brio girl," a reader who fit qualities of the magazine's ideal girl, or what Danny describes in a 2021 *Chatner* piece as "homeworkfulness, tidyment, toothbrushery, boyfriend control, projects, social studies, haircut-mindedness, eyes on the prize, gel pens for devotional journals, Bible For Teen Girls, limited field hockey, one hour on the family computer, being on time, dishwasher awareness, college prep. . . ." "My bitterest regret," Danny writes, "is that I was never selected as a Brio girl." Danny imagines how great a Brio girl he would make—he, a trans man, now in his thirties. "I'd make a killing on devotional companions to [hormone replacement therapy] with folksy little asides about dealing with acne and avoiding pornography if T changes your libido."[1] He cites relevant Bible verses corresponding to each week on testosterone.

Danny writes extensively about growing up evangelical and transitioning later in life in his collection of essays, *Something That May Shock and Discredit You*. He uses the narratives, scripture, and themes of his childhood and adolescent faith to "ground and locate [himself] in the stories of transformation that were already familiar to [him]."[2] Jacob wrestling the angel and being given a new name. The Rapture and Second Coming of Jesus. The flood in Genesis 6–9. The narratives of evangelicalism help him interpret the contours of his childhood—the feelings, the questions, the confusion—as well as his gender transition in his early thirties. But they do not him provide any clear cohesion to his life's story. He writes,

> My childhood was not especially useful to my adulthood, which I found bitterly disappointing. One thing that came as a relief to me was the realization that absent any sort of narrative about biological destiny or the

> magic of chromosomes, everyone's description of their internal sense of gender, their own sense of themselves as male or female or anything else, always sounded a little ridiculous, always depended on shorthand and substitution. Any attempts to justify or ground said feelings in externalities inevitably resulted in a sort of half-hearted list of hobbies, interests, toy preferences, instinctive reactions to certain forms of dress or speech or address.[3]

Danny is frustrated, but ultimately delighted, that there is not a clear trajectory from girlhood hobbies (climbing trees and so on) to his transition. Rather, what he retains are "all the many, various, and conflicting parts of [his] life story—its multiple pasts, futures, and presents as a self with others," as John Wall writes.[4]

In his essays, Danny does not describe his life story as one shaped by a trajectory from Christian to agnostic or evangelical to exvangelical. Nor is his life story shaped by a trajectory from girl to man or as unhappy closeted childhood to happy uncloseted adulthood.[5] His collection lacks the narrative cohesion that is typical of so many stories of both coming out and leaving a faith. Danny instead provides this image of complicated, complex narrative wholeness—a growing sense of how his faith and queerness connect and expand his sense of self. Inspired in part by Danny's essay collection, I am attempting something of this complex narrative integration by centering, reading, and analyzing the experiences of adolescents in purity culture—by way of personal narrative—while resisting an adultist lens that views adolescents as unformed subjects or merely "on their way" to adulthood.[6]

Agency, Intelligibility, and Narrative: Analyzing Youth Choices

Giving adolescent girls and queer youth epistemological privilege, I center their experiences within purity culture.[7] It is a characteristically feminist value to center personal experience, especially women's experiences, as it challenges the Western, male-centric assumption of objectivity.[8] Feminist scholars have long argued that there is no "view from nowhere," as "all knowing is embodied knowing."[9] Therefore, I consider the experiences of adolescent girls and queer youth as valid sources of knowledge, no less than adults' experiences or classic sources of knowledge like texts and tradition. Young people's experiences are studied "*in the plural*," for no single experience ought to be deemed universal.[10] Their experiences—unique, complex, conflicting—can provide "moral insight."[11] That is, by focusing on firsthand accounts of lived experience, I uncover the moral choices teenagers make in light of conservative sexual norms of purity culture.

Narrative is one way to crystalize lived experience into observable data.[12] Narrative is both interpreted by its readers and self-interpreted by the author herself through the act of writing.[13] In this way, personal narratives are not the same as ethnography or unmediated "objective" truth because autobiography has embedded meaning within it. Autobiography "is always an apologetic of the individual. Autobiography is one of the ways to answer the question of what my life *means*."[14] Personal narrative, memoir, and autobiography[15] are written toward narrative cohesion. One way to provide cohesion is through plotting one's life experiences toward a telos of "moral significance."[16] The author chooses which stories to tell and in what order to arrange them for the purpose of making a moral claim about their life. *I once was lost, but now I'm found / was blind, but now I see*. We find a good example of this with the genre of evangelical conversion narratives. This narrative genre was especially prolific in the mid-eighteenth century but has its origins in Paul of Tarsus's Damascus Road experience or Augustine's turn to Catholicism from the heretical Manicheanism.[17] This genre of story is still being written and published today. In fact, all of the memoirs and personal narratives read for this chapter could be called evangelical conversion narratives, though the conversion is not necessarily from sinner to saint but saved to sinner, straight to queer, believer to skeptic.

But not all real, lived adolescent experience can fit neatly into a linear or intelligible logic as autobiography and memoir suggest it can. I resist any author's attempt at constructing an adult-centric, intelligible narrative by my looking at the specific choices the adolescent makes apart from their adult self's backward moralizing. For example, Linda Kay Klein writes about breaking up with her high school boyfriend, Dean, because she believed at the time it was what God wanted her to do. "*But how dare I call myself a Christian? I spent my morning primping. I spent my afternoon making out with my boyfriend. Then I spent my evening leading a Bible study!*" she wrote in her diary as an adolescent.[18] The adult narrator Klein interprets breaking up with Dean as morally wrong, believing it was a choice made out of the sexual shame imposed on her by her evangelical Christian context.[19] She characterizes her younger self as foolish, eager to do the right thing. While all that may be true, my concern lies with how Linda, the adolescent girl, acted, especially vis-à-vis the norms of sexual purity. Linda acquiesced to the norms set by her spiritual community—purity in body, mind, and spirit[20]—even as she felt uneasy about her decision.[21] The adult Klein sets herself up for a "bifurcated life story."[22] Her narrative is structured to suggest that everything of her time in purity culture was bad and everything after or beyond purity culture was good. This binary logic merely recapitulates developmental models of adolescence—that adolescence is unformed adulthood or a special time of progress and growth—especially the lack of childhood/adolescent agency. I resist the adult-centric impulse by centering the adolescent's "present as accomplished fact," not their "processes of becoming"—becoming adults, exvangelicals, out queer folks, and so on.[23]

The Norms of Purity Culture

Based on my reading of purity culture texts and exvangelical memoirs[24] and through conversations with folks with a broad range of experiences,[25] I have identified four sexual norms that are nearly universal within purity culture:

Norm 1: Sex is only appropriate in the context of heterosexual marriage, which is the ultimate goal of all romantic relationships.
Norm 2: Purity extends beyond abstinence, but penile-vaginal intercourse (PVI) is still the normative sexual experience.
Norm 3: Young men will do anything for sex; young women will do anything for love/romance.
Norm 4: Young women have responsibility to stop boys from "going too far," yet they do not have the agency to make decisions about their own bodies.

I consider how young people *queer* these norms—by attempting to align or disavow, conform to or deviate from these norms—just by their nature of being adolescents. Here I am drawing on queer theorists

Kathryn Bond Stockton's and Hannah Dyer's conceptions of queer childhood and Gabrielle Owen's queer adolescence. While the normative Child is white, middle-class, and asexual, the real, actual child never quite lives up to this standard. Real children are simultaneously innocent and precocious, well behaved and fussy, passive and active, and represented by all socioeconomic classes, races, sexualities, nationalities, and genders. Children do not follow the scripted paths of or to adulthood—toward "full stature, marriage, work, reproduction, and the loss of childishness"—described by developmental psychologists as linear and teleological.[26] Children do not "grow up" as much as they "grow sideways," in "serpentine" fashion.[27] With Owen's work, I further imagine a queer adolescence, situated in the in-betweenness of innocent childhood and mature adulthood. The Teen is conceived as "out of control, deviant, criminal, and the failed-to-become-human at the same time as it idealized youthfulness, rebellion, and freedom from adult responsibility."[28] I argue that this erases the ways in which the teen is—*is*, not just becoming.

Purity culture reflects these conceptions of Child and Teen with its future focus toward marriage and reproduction; its presumption of child and feminine passivity and innocence; its view of adolescents as out of control and deviant, in need of adult control and surveillance; and its construction of whiteness (white values, white beauty, etc.), middle-class socioeconomic status, and cisgendered heteronormativity. But as queer theorists suggest, real, living, breathing teens do not neatly fall into these normative categories. Not all teens desire marriage, and when they do, their relational path is not as linear as *first comes love, then comes marriage, then comes the baby in the baby carriage*. Not all young women are white, cisgender, and straight, nor are they passive non-agents as the above norms would suggest.

I draw attention to the ways teens deviate from or fail to conform to these norms—thus, how they *queer* them. For example, some teens choose to interpret purity culture's centering of heterosexual intercourse as the pinnacle sexual experience to mean they can engage in anything *but* PVI before marriage and still remain pure virgins. Some teens do the opposite: because the rubric for "pure" is so broad, they treat any level of intimacy as equivalent to intercourse and respond with varying forms of penitence. My focus here is primarily on teenagers' actions (their agency) more so than how they deviate from ideal Child or Adolescent subjectivity through their racial identity and class location, as I am narrowing in on middle-class, white narratives only. I am also not beholden to how their adult selves understand their behavior as good, bad, fully formed, or in the process of becoming. With all this, I attend to the silences related to race in order to expose the moral effects of whiteness within purity culture.

Norm 1: Sex is only appropriate in the context of heterosexual marriage, which is the ultimate goal of all romantic relationships.

Brenda grew up "casually Catholic" but began attending an evangelical nondenominational church when she was twelve. There, her "sexual fascination skyrocketed, and with it [her] anxiety about 'saving [herself] for marriage.'" Brenda was told the importance of waiting to have sex till marriage and that if she waited, marital sex would be "amazing."[29] The lessons she learned reflect what purity culture writer Dannah Gresh promises: "*If* you will wait [to have sex], *then* it will be exciting!"[30] Brenda took pride in her virginity as a young person: "One Friday night, while my peers were somewhere indulging in hard lemonade and indiscriminate hand jobs, we Christian teens were dressed in white, promising our purity to the Lord. I signed a virginity contract in the presence of my parents."[31] A little older, Brenda married the first man she had intercourse with as a way to assuage the guilt she felt for having premarital sex. She was promised "the greatest possible sexual fulfillment" in marriage because she had no memory of sex with another person.[32] But Brenda discovered she did not enjoy being married, it did not alleviate her feelings of guilt, nor did it stop her young husband from cheating on her.[33]

Orienting adolescents toward happy, healthy heterosexual marriage is not a goal unique to purity culture. Christians have been concerned about *who* has sex and *in what context* for millennia, at least since Paul's first epistle to the Corinthians.[34] In the twentieth century, American Christians looked to the Bible for clarity on sexual norms. With the help of the Revised Standard Version (RSV) translation committee, they were given an interpretation of Greek and Hebrew that was inclusive of their modern sexual concerns. One primary ethical concern was homosexuality, the neologism that made certain sex acts symptomatic of a disease (nineteenth century) and an identity (mid-twentieth century). The word *homosexual* first appeared in English in the Bible in the 1946 RSV. Ironically, "it was Protestants' faith in the Bible's timelessness and enduring relevance that served as a key mechanism for these textual changes," writes historian of sexuality and religion Heather R. White. "Protestant biblicism thus does in practice what it opposes in theory: it generates new meanings for biblical texts."[35] In part because of these translation maneuvers, purity culture proponents use verses like Leviticus 18:22—one of the so-called "clobber texts" used to defend a homophobic stance—to make a quick, strawman argument that shuts down debates before they happen.[36] Purity texts written to girls include statements like "if you're a normal, red-blooded girl, then I bet you want to be attractive to the opposite sex."[37] To respond with *What if I am gay?* would be countered with *It's a sin to be gay* or, more commonly now, *Same-sex attraction*[38] *is not a sin per se, but to act upon it is.*[39] At the same time, purity culture chooses which aspects of broader culture it wants to use in its arguments, generally critiquing the secular world for "mak[ing] sex seem common, casual, and cheap."[40] For example, this same author, Gresh, warns of the dangers of sexually transmitted infections (citing the CDC) while also arguing for abstinence pledges, which have been proven to not be effective means of delaying sex.[41]

Within purity culture, arguing for heterosexual marriage as the proper "container"[42] for sex both *reflects* broader Christian and U.S. cultural ideals of marriage and sexual risk and *raises the stakes*. Purity culture teaches that (1) sex belongs only in marriage between one man and one woman;[43] (2) Christians should not date anyone they do not intend to marry;[44] (3) sex in marriage is enjoyable, even more so when the husband and the wife are virgins;[45] and, therefore, (4) sex outside marriage is painful and/or regrettable. From girlhood, young white women are especially taught that they are "called to save the deepest treasures of [their] beauty for just one man" in a "covenant marriage relationship."[46] God has already chosen who this man is, and rather than initiating a relationship with a guy—even a godly one—she must wait for him to pursue her, in either a dating or courting relationship.[47] Queer folks are, of course, excluded from this equation as purity culture does not advocate for queer relationships or marriage (see norm 3 for more on this). Despite the pedagogical nature of this norm in so many realms of their Christian lives, not every young person participated in purity culture in the same way. Some actively partook in it. Others resisted its harmful ideologies in subtle, even unwitting ways. That is, as Stevi Jackson and Sue Scott write, we need to be careful not to understand youth as "brainwashed" or "in rebellion against dominant discourses." This binary makes us "lose sight of the actualities of their everyday experience and practices."[48] So how did young people navigate this normative lesson?

Addie writes about a phone call with her high school boyfriend, Chris, who tells her, "I don't think we should be together unless we're serious about marriage." In the second person, Addie writes either about or to her younger self: "The word *marriage* doesn't scare you the way it maybe should. In the language of evangelical relationships, marriage is the pinnacle, the goal, a summit that you've been climbing toward. You are only a sophomore in high school when this conversation occurs, but you are certain that Chris is the man you will marry."[49] Addie does not marry Chris. As she describes in her memoir, *When We Were on Fire*, Addie later begins to understand how Chris used these evangelical norms of marriage to control her. He sought her out as "submissive, compliant, unformed."[50] But as a fourteen- and fifteen-year-old girl, she believed marriage to be the "summit" and that she would marry her first love, Chris. She *wanted* this. "You *want* mania," Addie writes of her young self. "When you are fourteen, truth matters less than the sound of your own heart pumping in your ears, the excitement of being swept into something greater than yourself."[51]

It is important to see that Addie *wanted* to date with the intention of marriage. She was not a brainwashed, unthinking marionette. She was heavily influenced by purity culture and vulnerable to manipulation—as the older Addie recognizes—but she also expressed her agency in her short-lived romance with Chris. Toward the end of their relationship, Addie planned a birthday date for him, which he tried to back out of:

> "No," I said.
>
> "What?"
>
> "I said *no*, Chris." I tried to steady my voice. "I planned all this stuff for your birthday. You have to come over. We had *plans*."[52]

After she and Chris broke up, Addie dated other young men: "I wanted to see what it was like—to kiss someone just for the fun of it, without a three-page contract, without any thoughts of marriage."[53] Addie understood her kissing many different guys as rebellious, even as this behavior is considered typical in contexts other than purity culture.

Addie writes of this season of dating as the year she "found [her] voice."[54] Addie, like other memoirists, writes that she had no identity (or an unformed identity) while in purity culture.[55] While girls like Addie may have been reliant on evangelical purity culture for their values, beliefs, and tastes in music, clothing, and Saturday night activities, they were still full sexual subjects, even as children. She may have "found her voice" in the sense that she was finally confident to name what she wanted, even as it went against the desires of the men in her life—but Addie had a voice the whole time.

Brenda, who we met earlier, was not "bother[ed]" by the rules surrounding marriage. But ultimately, she engaged in premarital PVI before marriage, albeit to the man she eventually married. In some respects, Brenda's narrative is consistent with the warnings of the purity culture. Gresh writes, "Making poor sexual choices will bring consequences. I am not talking about pregnancy or AIDS or STDs. I am talking about the cancer that eats away at the heart."[56] Brenda refers to her relationship with her first husband as a "pursuit of folly." "After having sex with Brandon, I'd sit on the toilet, trying not to cry. . . . I was shut off from my intuition and my Creator, running off the fumes of teenage hormones, ignited by sparks of shame."[57] According to the logic of purity culture, marrying her husband should have erased the guilt and shame that Brenda felt. But Brenda's feelings of shame only increased in her marriage. "Sex remained sinful, and I blamed the guilt-ridden sensation on my wretched self," she writes. "Purity culture has the power to convince us that even married sex is a sin if done the 'wrong' way."[58]

In Klein's book, Jo uses tiger/lamb language to describe the expectation that a young woman is supposed to be "a lamb—chaste and pure as the driven snow until you are married. And then you have to be a tigress in bed."[59] In this way, purity culture reinforces the binary between childhood innocence and informed, mature adulthood; it presumes a linear progression from one to the other where childhood and its queer affects are "discarded."[60] Brenda does not fit this progression at all. She had conflicted emotions that do not make sense within purity culture: she cried on the toilet after having sex with her husband. She should have been happy and sexually satisfied within her young marriage, assuming she upheld her responsibility to please her husband—but she was not happy at all.[61]

Norm 2: Purity extends beyond abstinence, but penile-vaginal intercourse (PVI) is still the normative sexual experience.

Jo tells Klein:

> I had one half-kiss[62] at the age of sixteen that made me brush my teeth for ten minutes afterward. He kissed me but I did not kiss him back. I think I mostly just stood there, kind of horrified and fascinated at the same time. But I felt guilty, ashamed, dirty for years. . . . I thought I was dirty and ruined, a soiled package.[63]

Jo's description of her half-kiss exemplifies how *purity* is not merely synonymous with *abstinence* but is much more far-reaching, involving a young person's whole "body, mind, heart, and spirit."[64] In defense of its long and often quite specific list of impure behaviors, thoughts, and desires, purity culture texts often cite the first clause of Ephesians 5:3 (NIV): "But among you there must not be even a hint of sexual immorality [*porneía*]. . . ."[65] The following are some of the behaviors thought to be impure:[66]

Oral sex
Sexting
Wearing certain clothes, especially "Belly rings. Miniskirts. Short shorts. Low-cut shirts."[67]
Watching certain shows on TV
Being alone with a date in an apartment or house[68]
Wearing a lot of makeup[69]
Associating with "a wild, partying, sexual nonbeliever"[70]
Mutual masturbation
Anything that involves genitals
Anal sex
Petting parties[71]

Rainbow circles[72]
Hooking up
Feeling each other up
Making out in public
Dry sex or dry humping
Watching romantic comedies as they are considered "female porn"[73]
Showing cleavage
Looking at Abercrombie & Fitch posters
Listening to music or watching movies that use "sexual humor and language"[74]
Hand jobs and blow jobs
Masturbation
"Talking on the phone with a guy after bedtime hours"[75]

Moving away from the language of *abstinence* to the language of *purity* was an intentional strategy within purity culture.[76] While abstinence implied abstaining only from PVI, purity includes all of the behaviors and desires listed and more. Gresh explains it this way: "Well, you can abstain from sex and not be pure, I think. Purity is more all encompassing. It's about your thought life. It's about your emotional life. It's about everything, whereas abstinence is obviously a lot more about the technicality of sex."[77] Having a broader understanding of purity "has the practical result of eliminating the need for evangelical abstinence campaigns to explicitly define what constitutes sex," writes researcher Christine Gardner.[78] As the preceding list indicates, penetration is not the only behavior that "counts" as sex, therefore extending the sexual norms of purity culture beyond the context of the bedroom. No wonder Jo felt dirty with her half-kiss.

Purity culture emphasizes avoiding a broad number of behaviors because they might lead to PVI. In an extreme example, DiMarco suggests that back rubs and tickle fights are foreplay.[79] "All this stuff we've been talking about is all made to lead to one ultimate thing—sex."[80] This emphasis, even obsession, with avoiding behaviors that can lead to PVI (as well as avoiding PVI itself) gestures to purity culture's connections to white supremacy. In white supremacist logics, whom one has sex with and reproduces with matters tremendously. White people must reproduce with other "fit" companions, those who are 100 percent[81] racially white in order to produce white offspring. While DiMarco and her contemporaries are likely not thinking about this specific goal in their guidance for youth, this connection cannot stay fully hidden below the surface.

Jo, Linda, and Val describe feelings of shame that were birthed out of a broad definition of purity. Rather than being an alternative to the *just say no* of abstinence rhetoric, the standard of purity made even seemingly innocent acts feel dirty, as if the teen were just one step from having PVI. DiMarco and others call this the "slippery slope."[82] Scholar Elizabeth Gish refers to this as "harm and damage rhetoric."[83] This rhetoric unambiguously suggests that if a young person engages in so-called impure behaviors, she is "damaged goods." In the logic of purity culture, this could involve merely thinking or desiring impurely. Linda shares:

> I had left the evangelical church but its messages about sex and gender still whirred within my body. Even after I calmed myself down and apologetically kissed my boyfriend goodbye, I couldn't let go of the lingering fear that we had gotten too close to having sex this time, that I had gotten pregnant, and that my sexual sins would soon be exposed to the religious community I'd left but still desperately wanted to approve of me. Eventually, I'd walk to the local drugstore and buy a pregnancy test. I was still a virgin, but taking the test was the only way I could steady my breathing.[84]

Linda was not alone in her midnight drugstore runs. Val says: "Surely you've heard of 'the phantom baby'? How nobody has had sex but they all think they're pregnant? I've never met an evangelical woman who doesn't irrationally believe she's pregnant at some point."[85] Like Val, Linda believed she was sliding down the slope so fast that she would somehow get pregnant from behaviors that could not, in reality, cause conception.

These personal testimonies emphasize purity culture's harm to young women's sense of agency over their bodies. Their stories also show the ways in which these young women made sense of the puzzle pieces before them, to borrow a metaphor from chapter 4. Jo was given enough information to believe that kissing—even a "half-kiss"—was dangerous and dirty, so she brushed her teeth. (Not to mention that Jo turned away from the kiss, even if she could not stop the boy's initiation.) Linda was afraid that getting "too close to having sex" was the same as having pregnancy-possible PVI sex, so she chose to get a pregnancy test.

We could think of these choices—brushing one's teeth, getting a pregnancy test—as trauma responses or pitiful or just plain strange.[86] Or we can imagine these actions as the girls' failed attempts to conform to the dominant sexual norms of purity culture—that is, a failure in the sense that it complicates the adult-centric valuing of success, mastery, and narrative closure.[87] Linda and Jo fail to live up to the norm of purity culture—in other words, they behave in ways that are considered impure by some—by kissing and getting "close to having sex." They also fail by not reaching the final telos of their actions. That is, a successful kiss would be one that is returned or fully received—not a "half-kiss." Successful sex would be intercourse that leads to reproduction. Jo and Linda achieve neither, exemplifying instead a queer act of failure.

Scarlet and Alma found different means of interpreting the puzzle pieces of purity culture—not by conforming but more actively resisting or negotiating the norms that shaped their evangelical worlds. Scarlet says: "We're rolling around naked; he would be rubbing his penis on my vagina but not in it; I would have orgasms from it. But I still, in my brain, I could be like, 'We're not having sex.' I would still be a virgin."[88] Scarlet interpreted the purity culture script in such a way that allowed her and her boyfriend to lie naked together and mutually masturbate one another. She negotiated the boundary set to her by purity culture and pushed against it. This did not free her from the totalizing effects of the norm, however. Like most of the stories explored in this chapter, shame accompanies Scarlet's behavior. She says how the further in her boyfriend's penis would penetrate, the more she "would recoil and freak out."[89]

Alma describes masturbation as a means of surviving "so many years of chastity":

> I had to find ways to do it without totally breaking the rules so I didn't hate myself for it. I would fantasize that I was with my future husband and we were on our honeymoon. Or I would think about that verse that they always referred to in order to say, "don't masturbate": "If you sin with your right hand, cut it off." I figured, "Well, I won't use my hand then." . . . "Oh, I have this marker that just happens to be here, or this pencil or whatever. Oops! I don't know how that got there!" . . . And I also used to arrange these little pointy tissues in my panties so that they would rub against me while I walked.[90]

Alma found ways to live into her sexual agency "so that [she] didn't hate [herself] for it." She masturbated, a behavior condemned by most, though not all, evangelical writers.[91] Borrowing from the playbook of evangelical biblicism, Alma used a literal interpretation of the Bible—"if you sin with your right hand, cut it off"—to creatively justify her sexual choices. Even in her fantasy, Alma conformed to norm 1 as she imagined herself having sex with her future husband on their honeymoon.[92]

Scarlet and Alma both resisted the norms of purity culture in important, though limited, ways. Scarlet insisted that sex meant PVI, which gave her the rationale to participate in non-penetrative acts with her boyfriend. The closer to penetration she got, though, the more shame and guilt she felt. Alma found creative means of pleasuring herself that still took into consideration scriptural mandates about abstaining. We could describe both Alma's and Scarlet's choices as *queer*, as neither act—mutual masturbation nor solo masturbation—leads to the "success" of heterosexual intercourse. Their behaviors are queer *and* still means to conform to the norms of purity culture. As Scott and Jackson write, these young people were not necessarily intentionally rebelling against the system. Rather, they were interpreting the sexual scripts—the jigsaw puzzles—before them in ways that made sense to them in their contexts and in their unique subjectivities. Their stories invite us to reflect on the actuality of adolescent behaviors, to not make moral judgments about whether masturbation (solo or otherwise) is a moral or immoral behavior. These young women's stories help us understand *their* moral reasoning, how they make sense of their choices within the broader frame of conservative sexual ethics.

Norm 3: Young men will do anything for sex; young women will do anything for love/romance.

Brandon Wallace's memoir *Straight-Face* traces his experience growing up Baptist in the South, discovering he was gay as a child, and then hiding from his desires for years and experiencing inner turmoil as a result. From this internal chaos, Brandon developed a split identity. He had his true self he kept quiet and deep inside himself, and he had his "Straight-Face," his externally facing self that presented as the perfect Christian man. Brandon writes,

> On one hand, I had these teachings: I had to be pure, undefiled by the world, and without sin for God to really love me, and that meant being totally clean in thought and action. It also definitely meant not being "a gay." But on the other hand, I had these feelings—these thoughts—that I couldn't help. I had these attractions which I was told were an abomination, but I simply had no control over them. I looked at some of the boys my age and just wanted to be close to them, but then I heard over my shoulder from preachers—my own preacher—that God hated the way I felt, and that I was probably doomed for an eternity of damnation because of it.[93]

Brandon felt the tug between wanting to be straight and wanting to present his real self to the world. One strategy he tried was looking at heterosexual pornography to try to turn himself straight. Even though looking at porn was a clear violation of norm 2, teenage Brandon understood that being gay was somehow a worse sin than looking at explicit videos.

In his best-selling men's book *Wild at Heart*, John Eldredge summarizes the prevailing view of gender within purity culture: "Gender is a more fundamental reality than sex."[94] Eldredge's comment emphasizes how purity culture values not only *sexual* difference between "biological men and women" (i.e., the primary and secondary sex organs, hormones, and chromosomes that lead to licit heterosexual, married, monogamous intercourse that produces offspring) but also *gender* difference. Sexual difference and gender difference are inextricably linked within purity culture: a person's gender ought to reflect their biological sex.[95] Even more so, as Eldredge insists, gender is thought to be more essential than the body's sexual makeup. That is, the soul or spirit of a person—apart from the body—is gendered, and those genders are either feminine or masculine.[96]

To understand how this norm is negotiated by adolescents in purity culture, I narrow in on one aspect: how desire itself is gendered. This norm is rooted in early Christian doctrine, most easily traced to the teachings of Augustine of Hippo in the fifth century. Drawing on common Neoplatonic thought of his day, Augustine taught that there are two parts of the inner self: the intellect/mind (the part made in the image of God and most associated with masculinity) and the body (the un-Godlike quality in humans most associated with femininity). In a

Prelapsarian world, the intellect/mind successfully ruled over the body, just as the man ruled over the woman. Augustine imagined that in this Prelapsarian world where the genders were properly ordered, humans could have sex without lust or pleasure.[97] Procreation, the primary purpose of sex, would be a rational act, "like shaking hands."[98] After the Fall, the genders became disordered.[99] Augustine taught that Eve was the one enticed by the serpent; Adam knew better but did not want Eve to live outside Paradise without him. Adam's sin, therefore, was his "losing male rank by obeying his wife (his lower self), rather than making his wife obey him as her 'head.'"[100] As a result, man's base, bodily nature continually refuses to submit to man's intellectual nature, as exemplified by involuntary arousal (i.e., an erection).[101] Augustine's theology leaves little room for women's agency or desire; instead, women are blamed for "stimulating" lust in men.[102] This theological anthropology contributes to a culture of victim-blaming and gender double standards, which we will explore more in depth in norm 4. It also contributes to reifying sex and gender normativity, which erases queer possibilities.

"God created us all to be sexual beings, either male or female," write Ethridge and Arterburn in *Every Young Woman's Battle*. "Our femininity or masculinity is an expression of who we are. We are sexual beings from the time we are conceived until we die and leave our earthly bodies for our heavenly home. . . . You are a sexual being all the time, and that's something you cannot change."[103] We could credit Etheridge and Arterburn for having a holistic vision for sexuality, which broadens it to include behaviors outside the bedroom. However, they unapologetically reinforce the binary in this statement: there are two ways to be gendered, either/or. Those two genders are inseparably linked to two biological sexes. That is, to be feminine is to be female and have a vagina; to be masculine is to be male and have a penis.

The authors continue on to assert that because of our biological sex and gendered difference, we desire differently—and we desire in only two ways:

> So while young men are primarily aroused by what they see with their eyes, as a young woman you are more aroused by what you hear and feel. . . . In addition, a male can enjoy the act of sex without committing his heart or bonding spiritually with the object of his physical desire. This

> is the ultimate act of compartmentalization, and guys are masters of it. Never assume a guy feels what you feel.[104]

These gendered differences in desire are often communicated something like "Most of the time guys give *love* to get *sex*, but girls give *sex* to get *love*."[105] Both guys who want love and girls who want sex are deemed deviant, even if they are heterosexual. This frame is so reified that it is used to warn young women of young men's true desires. DiMarco warns girls that even a man's desire to talk to her is suspect: "They spend hours listening to you because maybe, just maybe, it might lead to something more, shall we say, something physical." She reassures her reader that this is not because this guy is a "scumbag"; this is just how men are. They "have different wants and needs."[106] Per this worldview, guys' masculine desire for sex and young women's feminine desire for love inevitably lead to the act of PVI (see norms 1 and 2), which again is exclusively binary: "God designed the male and female bodies so the penis fits perfectly inside the vagina during the act of sexual intercourse. . . . God wants you to enjoy sex, and that is why He gave you a body part, the clitoris, that has no other purpose but to give you sexual pleasure. Yay, God!"[107] We can resonate with Ethridge and Arterburn's joy in the clitoris's one role, especially as disinformation about the clitoris, and gynecology in general, is pervasive in conservative Christianity and beyond. However, Ethridge and Arterburn limit the joy of clitoral stimulation to marital PVI only—an unfortunate limitation as only a small percentage of cisgender women experience orgasm through vaginal stimulation alone.[108]

Purity culture writers articulate these gender and sex norms as descriptive—*this is how it is*—and prescriptive—*how it ought to be*. In writing about queer clothing choices, DiMarco says that "femininity is how you were made. You were made a girl." Citing Deuteronomy 22:5,[109] she asks, "Why would he [God] care enough to let his people know that it's not appropriate for girls to dress like guys and guys to dress like girls?"[110] Ethridge and Arterburn devote the afterword of their book to speaking directly to women who "desire other women."[111] They write that "unlike your sex or ethnicity,"—and gender as it is tied to sex—"homosexuality isn't some predetermined condition that was passed onto you genetically when you were conceived in your mother's womb. A person develops these desires through a variety of different experiences, but you are not powerless to develop different, more healthy desires."[112] They write that "hundreds" of "former" queer folks have converted from homosexuality to heterosexuality and recommend the now-defunct conversion therapy group, Exodus International, as one possible solution.[113]

Young queer folks of all genders have had to navigate these gender and sex norms and locate their desire within this frame. As much as Brandon "watched, and watched, and watched" straight pornography, he could not escape his queer desire. He writes, "The entire time though, my eyes always went back to watching the guys. Sometimes, I would even get frustrated when a woman would get in the way, and then I would get mad at myself for getting frustrated about that."[114] By early adolescence, Brandon began dating girls, though desperately wishing he was holding hands with the boys he liked instead. Recognizing his desire as deviant, Brandon "would get angry with [himself] and feel defeated." The straight relationships he formed were not all distasteful. He enjoyed the "companionship" he experienced with girls, even though he did not desire to be sexual with them.[115] This too is a queer desire, a deviation from the masculine expectation to only desire sex from girls, not friendship.

Brandon had a felt experience of his deviance and made painful moves to conform to the norms of purity culture because of it. Ultimately, though, he could not fully live into the norms without losing a sense of himself as a full subject in the process. Brandon bifurcated his adolescent self. He had his public "Straight-Face" and his inner, private gay self. His contemporary, Garrard Conley, describes something similar, imagining the two parts of himself splitting. "I am both [my father's] son and not his son. I am both native and tourist. A speaker of tongues he does not yet know. Believer and nonbeliever."[116] Brandon and Garrard used their agency for the sake of survival, not to rebel or revolt against a harmful system. Choosing to hide their sexuality did protect them from the harm they would have experienced from their families of origin and their churches.

Brandon and Garrard negotiated their desire within purity culture through hiding and splitting as a means of protection from the harm that they feared in their churches and families. The harm they experienced came from this rigid construction of gender, believed to be inextricably linked to sex. We can imagine how their stories would have been even more complicated had they not been white, middle-class boys. Being, say, Latino immigrants with little command of the English language would have put the boys in more economically and socially precarious positions in intersection with their sexual identities. Coming out could mean more than severing a relationship with a parent—a difficult enough loss—but it could mean not having the same access to resources like extended family in the United States or the language acumen to find shelter if their families kicked them out. Garrard and Brandon's white identity—along with language and citizenship status—offered them a certain level of privilege, even as they navigated really troubling realities internally and in their homes and churches.

Norm 4: Young women have responsibility to stop boys from "going too far," yet they do not have the agency to make decisions about their own bodies.

Jane remembers being in youth group and writing down her "'biggest sin' on a small piece of paper," which was then nailed to a "large, wooden cross." Jane had written down the words "struggling with sexual sin" on her little piece of paper. "I just believed I was *thinking* about sex too much," she reflects.[117] Both Jane and her husband arrived at marriage with very little to no sexual experience and were excited for the kind of sex life they were promised growing up. Their expectations were not met: "There were so many nerves. And for me, the nerves went to guilt, because even though we were married . . . I started just feeling terrible. I was really scared of my husband's body; I was afraid to touch him. I felt sick, just awful, dirty, like what I was trying to do was wrong. We couldn't get through it, we had to stop."[118] After many painful attempts at having sex with her husband, Jane was eventually diagnosed with vaginismus, "a condition in which involuntary muscle spasm prevents vaginal penetration."[119] The trauma Jane experienced aligned with not only this norm of purity culture, that she was responsible for men's behaviors, but the heteronormativity of norm 3 as well. "I realized that I wasn't straight, I was attracted to girls too, and I had been in the past," she says. Jane realized that she was bisexual, something she says she had been repressing until adulthood.

This fourth and final norm builds on norm 3's insistence on two distinct genders with opposing desires. Norm 4 highlights further tension within that binary. Purity culture teaches that it is a young woman's responsibility to guard men's sexuality, to make sure he does not let his sexual desire "rule over him," to borrow language from the Augustinian tradition, and to make sure that she herself does not "cause her brother to stumble."[120] Purity culture discourages young women from exploring their desires and naming what pleasures or experiences they really want. Purity culture, rather, encourages self-surveillance to the point of hypervigilance. DiMarco tells young women to imagine "a cameraman with you, shooting all your moves. Then at the end of the night your entire family is getting together to look at your slide show."[121] DiMarco elsewhere writes that "Having read this book, you know what God wants from you," equating purity culture—and DiMarco's own writing—with the voice of God.[122] Young people are told that they know what is right but that they are ultimately powerless to remain pure "without Jesus."[123] This, again, sets young women up to be expected to bear the burden of harms done to them, and it does not encourage them toward truly understanding their desires apart from the desires of a boyfriend or a patriarchal God. Put simply: young women are thought to have responsibility without agency and young men agency without responsibility.[124] Many young women describe their experiences within purity culture as traumatic, a form of religious trauma syndrome,[125] or "body theodicy," as theologian Katie Cross calls it, even if they were not sexually assaulted.[126] As with Jane's experience of vaginismus, many women exhibit physiological symptoms similar to those of rape victim-survivors, a phenomenon documented by psychologist Tina Schermer Sellers and others.[127] It is no wonder with the kind of psychological pressure authors like DiMarco put on women that they grow up to experience somatic resistance to sexual pleasure.

While purity culture teaches young women that they have no agency or desire, it teaches young men that they do not have control over their bodies. Their sexual desires are described as wild, uncontrollable beasts.[128] "Every time you make it too easy on him by showing him how willing and ready you are, you lose out," writes DiMarco. "He starts to think of you less and less as a potential girlfriend and more and more as a great hookup or onetime make-out session."[129] In purity culture, both boys and girls are at risk of losing control, but losing control looks different for each gender. Heather Hendershot puts this plainly: "Boys and girls who are repeatedly told that at a certain point they are no longer in control may as a result feel less in control, and it may actually be more difficult to stop sexual activity if one conceives of one's body as a runaway train. Crudely put, when all bodily control is lost, boys give in to their urge to rape and girls give in to their urge to submit to rape."[130]

Meaningful consent does not have a place within purity culture. To teach consent would necessitate female agency and control over one's body, both of which are counter to the logics of purity culture. There are troubling implications for this, to say the least. Without language of meaningful consent, sexual assault is defined only narrowly, as a man violently forcing himself on a woman. This excludes all the ways in which people of all genders are limited in their ability to truly consent within certain contexts, such as when a person is not of sound mind or is being groomed by a person with more social power than them. For example, at the beginning of the #MeToo and #ChurchToo movements, Jules Woodson's story circulated online. As a seventeen-year-old evangelical girl, Jules's youth pastor isolated her in his car and asked her to perform oral sex on him. Because she did so and because the youth pastor did not use violent force, he and the church referred to this as a "sexual incident," not as sexual assault.[131] Feminists have fought hard to articulate that no child or a congregant in the care of a pastor can meaningfully consent to sexual behaviors with them. But within purity culture, unless a woman proves herself to be completely pure, or the *perfect survivor*, she may be blamed for causing a man to rape her.[132]

Feminist theologians and scholars of religion have spent decades contending with conservative Christianity's contribution to "rape culture," or a culture in which sexual violence is normalized.[133] This has become one of the most widespread critiques of purity culture, including within evangelicalism itself,[134] and rightfully so. But in waging this critique, we must take the lead from certain feminist and womanist scholars who urge us not to erase a person's agency, and therefore dignity, in attending to her vulnerabilities. This too sets up the binary of a "good" victim and a "bad" victim. If we only emphasize a woman's vulnerability to being raped, we are tempted to call an act of protection and resistance—like asking her rapist to wear a condom—consent.[135]

To their credit, Ethridge and Arterburn distinguish between sexual assault from sexual sin (i.e., promiscuity, homosexuality, and other so-called impure behaviors). They write: "*No one deserves to be abused, regardless of how she dresses, where she goes, or what she does*. Read that sentence again and believe it. Even if you initiate physical involvement, you have the right to change your mind and choose not to engage in further sexual activity at any point. . . . *Rape and promiscuity are entirely different things*" (emphasis in original).[136] They write that purity has nothing to do with the actions done to them but with the specific choices they make. Just one page later, however, the authors provide a list of "practical ways to avoid being sexually abused or raped," undermining their previous statement.[137] The latter message was internalized by young people like Sofia to mean that she was to blame for her own rape. "All I could think of was the shame aspect of it—*They'll know I had sex*. When, in reality, I was being raped. They'd think I was sinful, like now I was a chewed up piece of gum and no one would want me."[138] If having sex makes a young woman disposable like a Styrofoam cup[139] or used like a junky car,[140] then no wonder young people interpret a violation of their bodies as causing these same outcomes.[141]

Sofia understands that her experience of harm may have been exacerbated because, unlike other young people in this chapter, Sofia is Mexican American, although she attended a white evangelical church growing up. Sofia says that "her 'curvy, Mexican body' was policed as she went through puberty, and that she was made to cover her silhouette more than the other white girls in her youth group."[142] More than just the added burden of covering her body that did not fit the standard of thin, white beauty, Sofia may have felt she would never live up to the "good Christian" standard just by nature of her culture, skin tone, and body type.[143] Latina women often bear the cultural expectation of *marianismo*, that they ought to conform to the "submissive, docile, passive, sacrificial, patient and pure" image of the Virgin Mary. This construction of *marianismo* demands that Latina women either acquiesce to these expectations or maintain the appearance of doing so; otherwise they risk being seen as "the traitorous, evil, and sinful temptress."[144] This is an extra burden Sofia's white peers may not have felt.

Trauma, whether sexual assault or rape, complicates our understanding of agency. We know from decades of research that traumatized bodies exhibit similar physiological behaviors—fight, flight, freeze, or fawn—that certainly do not feel like choices to the victim-survivor.[145] In a *HuffPost* article, Hannah writes about her anxiety disorder that was birthed out of her upbringing in purity culture:

> Dating and sex had felt so dangerous and sinful for so long—not to mention the biblical implications of dating a *woman*. I had trained myself to shut down all bodily desires and now that my desire had awakened, a fight or flight response had been activated. I couldn't seem to convince my body that dating was safe. I realized that while I'd been convinced during my youth that *I* was making the choice to not date or have sex, I had actually been stripped of bodily agency. The fundamentalism of my upbringing had terrified me into submission.[146]

Is it really fair to argue that Hannah had agency over her body's responses? We must listen to young people's stories of harm and take them at their word. Still, our expansive understanding of adolescent agency, described in chapter 4, provides a helpful interpretive tool. What if Hannah's fight-or-flight responses were considered agential, a way that her body *chose* to respond to the situation? This is not the same as calling Hannah *responsible* for choices in the sense that she is morally culpable for the harm done to her. As feminist pastoral care clinician Pamela Cooper-White writes, "Whatever a woman chooses within such violently constrained choices—even if her choices may not look like the 'empowered' woman who fights back—must be understood as resistance, and a strategy of survival."[147] This could include fight, flight, freeze, and fawn.

Sofia, Jane, and Hannah bore unfair responsibility for the behaviors (Sofia) and pleasures of men (Jane) and expressed their agency in very limited ways (Hannah) because of purity culture. Their stories are a testament to the ways in which the norms of purity culture expand far beyond the scope of adolescence and have lasting impact on the adult victim-survivor's life. These traumas are perhaps the reason so many memoirs and personal narratives of purity culture exist: as a way of making meaning of the long-term effects of these normative teachings. These three young women found creative, and at times physiologically automatic, means of resisting or participating in the norms set before them.

Conclusion

Rebekah Matthews concludes her story of leaving evangelicalism, and Christianity as a whole, with a love note to her younger self: "I remember with affection the teenager I was, who secretly recorded Christian radio broadcasts because she wanted to do the right thing, who also knew she wanted more for her life than what was in front of her. I'm proud that I wrestled with my faith; if it had come easily to me, I think I would have been a different kind of person altogether, less able to take life's more confusing aspects in stride."[148] Rebekah, like other young people in this chapter, experienced purity culture in harmful ways, finding herself not quite conforming to the norms set before her, though trying. She felt weird about cussing and avoided TV shows and movies with too much sex, per her mother's and pastor's instructions. She felt sick with shame over her queerness. "I wondered if maybe God could forgive a sin like being gay," her younger self wondered. "Or maybe being gay wasn't even a sin. But there was another, darker part of me, too, that thought maybe it was a sin, maybe God wouldn't forgive me, and maybe I didn't care." Rebekah imagines that had she followed the norms of purity culture she "would have felt less alone."[149] Yet here she is as a thirty-something, "proud that [she] wrestled with [her] faith," proud of the person she had become because of the choices she made.[150]

There are multiple, complicated, overlapping, and conflicting ways that young people, both queer youth and straight girls, navigated the norms of purity culture. Rebekah's story is not Addie's, Brandon's, Jane's, or Linda's. Young people's stories resist any cohesive narrative that states that all kids who grew up in purity culture feel a certain way or behave a certain way. These stories taken together and apart from their adult selves' interpretation do not provide a teleological structure from lost to found, closeted to out, believer to unbeliever. Young people make choices. Those choices sometimes align with the norms of purity culture—though often failed attempts, as with Linda's virgin pregnancy scare—and sometimes they don't. They sometimes make choices that make sense to adults, and sometimes they don't. All these are examples of queer adolescence—not just in homosexual and bisexual desire but through the non-normativity of adolescence.

6

Toward a Post-Purity Sexual Ethic

Lyz knew the girl she was *supposed* to be: the testimony-sharing, committed-to-purity, my-father-will-choose-my-husband girl on the cassette tape Lyz's mother played for their family during homeschooling sessions. "As I listened to this girl," Lyz Lenz reflects in a 2013 essay on the now-defunct blog *The Toast*, "I pictured her, standing at the podium. . . . I imagined her white face framed by thick hair that is brushed into a ponytail, her long skirt falling to her calves."[1] Lyz also knew all the ways she was failing to be that girl despite how similar they were as straight white girls, devoutly Christian and committed to purity.

Lyz describes the spring she and her older sister Jessie attended a youth conference at a megachurch in Dallas. The main speaker at the event was Joshua Harris of *I Kissed Dating Goodbye* fame, a few years before he made it big. Lyz and her peers thought of him as their "holy heartthrob," "as close to a homeschooled celebrity as they came."[2] Harris, just nineteen at the time, spoke to the teen boys and girls about the dangers of lust. "For the next hour, we listened rapt to this man, not much older than us describe to us in clear language precisely what we were feeling and how it was a sin," Lyz writes. Girls needed to dress in ways that did not stir lust in their brothers in Christ. Boys were "encouraged to be respectful of women," to not give into their lustful tendencies, and to ask their parents to hold them accountable.[3]

Lyz found herself between two poles: the girls like Jessie, who "flirt[ed] with that gray area between mainstream femininity and what they had been taught as modesty" by wearing lip gloss and refusing to wear skirts, and the "meek" girls who wore long skirts and clustered closely with their same gender. "I merely sat between the groups, trying to look prayerful instead of bored."[4]

Lyz had been told, both indirectly and directly by the girl on the cassette, that if she dressed modestly and performed the part of a pure Christian girl, then she would be noticed by boys like Joshua Harris. But she wasn't getting noticed. She reflected at the end of the conference, "I wondered if the girl on the cassette was like me. Trying so hard to be good and holy and going unnoticed. Perhaps, we were going about this wrong. Perhaps we too needed knotted shirts and lip gloss." And, just as quickly as this inkling of resistance came to her mind, she denounced it as sinful: "After I thought that, I immediately asked God to forgive me."[5]

All three characters in this story—Lyz, Jessie, and Harris—were marked by privilege, though they navigated that privilege differently within purity culture. White girls like Lyz and Jessie—girls whose culture said they wanted to be noticed by boys—had access to events like the conference at a megachurch, a product of the suburbanization of evangelicalism in the mid-century.[6] While they themselves may or may not have been middle class (Lyz does not specify in her blog post), they were certainly able to access the conspicuous consumption of the middle class through participating in such events. Lyz mentions favorite scrunchies, a church with a gymnasium, pizza, soda, physical abstinence pledge cards to take home with them, and big passenger vans to bring them to and from the event. Out of their privilege, they policed each other. Because of Lyz's proximity to the ideal girl of the cassette tape, she could look down on the girls who seemed further away from it—in this case, the girls like Jessie who "wore shorts and were the ones who snuck in lip gloss and knotted their t-shirts to emphasize their adolescent waists." Lyz was proud to be seen as a "serious girl" for what it might grant her—in this case, the attention of a specific boy.[7]

As a white-passing, heterosexual young man,[8] Harris was given a platform, first through his magazine, *New Attitude*, and then through his books, *I Kissed Dating Goodbye, Boy Meets Girl*, and *Sex Is Not the Problem (Lust Is)*, among his most popular. By the time Lyz Lenz wrote her piece for *The Toast*, Joshua Harris had been a best-selling author for fifteen years, having published millions of copies of *I Kissed Dating Goodbye*. His book's influence on purity culture is "hard to overestimate."[9] However, beginning in 2018, Harris began to publicly share some changes. First he apologized for the negative impact his books had had on young people, and then he asked his publisher (Multnomah) to stop printing copies of his books on sexuality.[10] In 2019, he announced he was divorcing his wife Shannon, whom he had "courted" per his own rules of non-dating, and that he was no longer a Christian.[11] Alongside these public confessions came two publicity moves—or *stunts*, depending on one's perspective. First was his documentary *I Survived I Kissed Dating Goodbye*, which featured testimonies of people who grew up reading his books, describing the specific impact on their lives. Then in 2021, he launched a five-week, $275 course on deconstruction promising to give "a step-by-step process and online community to reframe and reimagine your human journey."[12] After receiving a wave of backlash, particularly from the exvangelical community,[13] he pulled the course, just days after it was announced.

The discourse surrounding Harris's documentary, divorce, deconversion, and deconstruction course is split between those wanting to punish Harris for the harm he caused and those who view him as merely a cog in the machine of purity culture.[14] And indeed, it is fair to ask whether Harris was sincere about his apology, especially as he charged money for his deconstruction course. We might ask, as others have, is Harris just a grifter, always looking for a way to platform himself and make a buck? It is also fair to wonder whether a twenty-two-year-old single man's take on dating and marriage should have been published to begin with. Shouldn't the onus of responsibility fall to the editor and the publisher who read and promoted his work? But just as all young people are agential within their intersecting identities, Harris can be accountable for the harm he caused to young people for the twenty years his books were in print as well as for trying to monetize deconstructing from ideas that he helped perpetuate.

But can we also see how Lyz was an active member of this purity culture ecosystem in which Harris thrived, that she was complicit in her own way, even as she found ways to nudge the boundaries? She attended the conference Harris spoke at. She admired him. She internalized the messaging she received. Cristina L. H. Traina reminds us that agency is not a "zero-sum game." "Even when others are gravely responsible for the conditions of her behavior, a dependent's action is still her action."[15] To say that Lyz has agency does not mean that she is not also incredibly vulnerable, nor does it suggest that she is as complicit as someone like Harris or his editor and publishers. Rather, each person "bears a different responsibility in moral proportion to [their] privilege."[16] If we fail to see average girls as active members of purity culture—as complicit—then we miss seeing all the subtle ways they resisted, too. They wore lip gloss.

They snuck peeks of Nickelodeon at their neighbor's house. They questioned what it meant to be the "ideal girl" on the cassette tape. And if we fail to see average girls as complicit, then we might be tempted to think that liberation looks only like undoing sexism, not also dismantling the deeper entanglements of white supremacy and antiqueerness at the heart of purity culture.

In all the ways we have come to see young people as complex and queer subjects, full and interdependent agents, we might be left wondering what a post-purity culture sexual ethic looks like that acknowledges both the vulnerability and complicity of white youth. Here we return to the language of burdened virtues and orgasmic failure as interventions for those in or coming out of normative white purity culture.

Privileged Vulnerability: White Youth in Purity Culture

As we have come to see, purity culture is a structure aimed at disciplining young people toward "normality" and against perceived deviance defined by racial difference and sexual precocity (adolescent girls) or perversity (queer youth). Young people are given an ideal image to which they must conform, while also questioning whether this image is part of a "sexual prosperity gospel"[17] that "no real person can ever quite conform, though the members of some social categories gain real social privileges by their perceived proximity to [that ideal]."[18] We saw this with Harris and Lyz. None of this, of course, is made explicit, as normality discourse thrives on occlusion.[19] Julian B. Carter writes, "Whiteness and heterosexuality share an unwillingness to acknowledge their own power and the many forms of coercion and violence that uphold their unearned advantages; both prefer to perceive themselves as natural traits, simultaneously noble and innocent of political meanings."[20] We might wonder what kind of resistance and healing an ethic of "mak[ing] whiteness speak its own name" could lead to.[21]

What would it mean if white adults and youth were to become more conscious of their complicity in purity culture? Understanding the ways in which a child develops racially can help answer that question. Children, by age three, can distinguish racial difference and categorize people by race—though they are not particularly good at it. By age five or maybe even earlier,[22] children can internalize the stereotypes espoused by their community and reason and act within resulting belief systems.[23] This is true of white kids as it is with kids of color. While much research has been done on how children of color have navigated their racial identities and racialized structures within the United States, much less research has been done on how white children and adolescents understand themselves as raced and how they talk about and interpret race.[24] This is in part because of the "culture of entitlement," where white people, including youth, do not "question [their] position within the dominant, normative group and instead [accept] all the privileges of race and class that naturally come [their] way."[25] In this perspective, race and culture are what other people (Blacks, Latinos, Asians, etc.) have, not what white evangelical church kids have.

Whiteness "derives its potency precisely from its muteness and invisibility."[26] It thrives on not naming what it is while operating as the "standard" human body in the United States.[27] Borrowing language from Marilyn Strathern, we can think of this as a "social greenhouse," that is, "a closed system, one that feeds off itself, an insular community that doesn't see too far beyond its present conditions and boundaries."[28] A predominantly white evangelical megachurch or a white family in a Midwest suburb insulates the white teen where she and her peers come to understand their own experiences, in their social location and embodiment, as normative. Her taste in music is normative. Her clothing choices and her quiet, feminine sensibilities are normative. Normativity is further reinforced when a member of the community deviates from the norm.[29] When a girl like Cheryl Pierson[30] fights back against her abusive father by killing him, she disrupts not only the sexist violence wielded against her but the white supremacist norm of the patriarchal family, where man is the head of the woman who is in charge of the children. When a girl like Emily Heinrichs[31] joins a neo-Nazi commune, she espouses a version of white supremacy that is too outspoken, too overt, especially for a young woman who is thought to be nice and agreeable. Compared to these extremes, the everyday racism of white youth seems acceptable to others in the social greenhouse.[32] After a mission trip to Uganda, a white girl changes her profile picture to one of African children clinging to her neck with the caption "Called to Serve the Least of These."[33] A white boy casts himself as Jesus in the youth group skit and his sister as the "innocent girl led astray"; he casts his Brown and Black peers as "bad influences" or demons.

Race structures the lives of all children and youth—no matter their racial identity—from their experiences in school to their interactions with law enforcement, how they learn about sex and sexuality, where they live, and with whom they play.[34] These are not systems children choose for themselves, of course, but children interact with them both alongside and apart from their parents or guardians. When we think about how children are socialized racially, we must also "adequately take into account children's active participation, or agency, in social learning processes."[35] Children will not necessarily take on their parents', peers', or teachers' perspectives on race but form their own opinions on race, participate in antiracist projects, or perpetuate racial stereotypes across a wide age range and in spite of any parental or peer socialization.[36]

How does this play out within the slice of white America known as contemporary evangelical purity culture? Much of the published critique of purity culture recapitulates the moral/sex panic language, framing teens—especially white girls and white queer youth—as vulnerable to such socialization (called here indoctrination) and without agency. As exvangelicals Chrissy Stroop and Lauren O'Neal write in the introduction to their book *Empty the Pews*, the 2016 election of Donald Trump by overwhelmingly white conservative evangelicals[37] "demands that voices of those of us who have experienced the religious right from the inside, often being indoctrinated and mobilized for the culture wars in ways that caused us long-term damage, be given a hearing." The alarmist language may be called for here, as the white supremacist structures of evangelicalism are "politically pernicious, reality-averse, and often abusive," as Stroop and O'Neal write and as I have argued in this book.[38] However, their language is such that exvangelicals like Stroop and O'Neal are let off the hook for their own complicity, while evangelicals "out there" are fully to blame. One implication is that all white evangelical women who voted for Trump are brainwashed and have no responsibility for their actions because they are victims of how they were raised or of being women in a patriarchal culture. We need to further nuance this conversation and recognize our own complicity as white people in purity culture.

This victimization of white youth in purity culture is so ubiquitous that even Mihee Kim-Kort, a queer Asian American scholar, forwards the idea. "The only benefits [white girls] glean from their enculturation in this system are institutional approval and protection from the consequences, as long as they don't break the rules of the system," she writes. "They are passive participants with little voice or agency."[39] However, institutional approval and protection from the consequences of impurity are two very significant privileges that white youth may have some sense that they benefit from, even as they are simultaneously harmed by it. A young white woman in purity culture has privileges because of her race and proximity to white men, as daughter and future wife. Because of her conventional beauty and presumed innocence, she gets to stand front and center on the worship team. She gets her pick of the young men in her church because she represents the pure young womanhood that has been advertised to them. A queer white boy's testimony of "overcoming same-sex attraction" is the highlight of the church retreat. He is invited to be the pastoral intern after high school graduation. As bona fide members in the social greenhouse, these young people not only benefit from the privileges of their race and gender performance but are the ones who will keep the greenhouse thriving unless they are willing to take accountability for the choices they have made along the way.

The normative structures of purity culture invited active participation in one's own oppression as well as in the oppression of others. But at the same time, purity culture met the very real needs of the teenagers it embraced (i.e., friendship and chosen family, meaning-making, spirituality, etc.). While it is tempting to imagine this as an all-or-nothing game, where one is either wholly vulnerable or wholly complicit in a system of harm, the reality is that all of us, including the smallest child, has complex and overlapping roles in a death-dealing system like normative white purity culture.

Burdened Virtues

In response to purity culture, there is a temptation to shift blame. Parents and churches are blamed for teenagers' participation in youth group, purity balls, and signing abstinence pledges. Not only that, but adults are also blamed for how those teenagers internalize the messages of normalcy, in believing that a good Christian girl looks a certain way (fair-skinned, thin, feminine, and modestly dressed) or that heterosexual marriage is the ultimate goal or that queerness ought to be blotted out or covered in the pure blood of Jesus. But treating young people as puppets or parrots of adults does not afford them the dignity they deserve as humans, nor does it take seriously the harm they may have caused by participating in a normative system. This does not mean that we ought to hold white evangelical youth morally accountable to the same degree as Jerry Falwell Jr.[40] or as legally accountable as a white supremacist storming the U.S. Capitol.[41] Here it is helpful to return to feminist philosopher Lisa Tessman's concept of burdened virtues.

Tessman's revision of Aristotelian virtue ethics recognizes "systemic and unrelenting" bad moral luck, like racism, sexism, and heterosexism, which, though called "luck," are not to be thought of as coincidental or happenstance. Because of bad moral luck, even when a person makes the most virtuous choice possible, that choice is not "really good at all."[42] Take, for example, Brandon, the queer youth introduced in chapter 5. Brandon's means of surviving in his Southern evangelical world was to split: he had his outwardly facing "Straight-Face" and his internal queer self. This was a tactic that is not morally good—internalizing homophobia, attempting suicide, and watching straight pornography to "turn" oneself straight do not contribute to Brandon's, or anyone else's, flourishing.[43] And yet splitting was likely the best choice Brandon could have made given his circumstances. To give up his straight face and live into his queer identity would not have been a viable or even thinkable solution to Brandon in his situation. Too much was at risk, and his limited narrative experience[44] could have kept him from imagining a world beyond his adolescence, beyond his parents' house, beyond his hometown. What looks like virtuous behavior for Brandon in his situation could be deemed morally bad in other people or in other contexts. And indeed, Brandon's behavior is only partially liberating—and potentially oppressive—to himself. While eventually he was able to come out fully as queer, it was not until adulthood and only after years of harm under purity culture.

At the same time, the concept of burdened virtues is capacious enough to account for how all humans are multiply situated in positions of power and vulnerability. There are ways in which the one person both benefits from and is harmed by the same oppressive structure. Brandon, as a white male, had certain privileges because of his gender and race unavailable to someone like Sofia (chapter 5), the Mexican American young woman who was raped by her boyfriend.[45] Brandon bought into the white hope of the middle-class family with a picket fence. He did not bear some of the same lessons in modesty or in "stop[ping] men from lusting over" him, like Sofia had to because of her gender and ethnicity. While Sofia was told, "If I kept things covered, I wasn't causing guys to lust after me,"[46] Brandon was able to stay up all night looking at pornography. The question is not whether a certain action (hiding one's identity or acquiescing to rape) is morally good in all times and contexts, but whether it is proportionally good—or good *enough*—given the reality of the world we live in. That is, as Tessman urges, what does it mean "to engage ethically under damaging conditions"?[47]

Orgasmic Failure, Redux

With Tessman's burdened virtues, we can begin to see how a moral framework that seriously considers the situatedness of a young person in purity culture as both vulnerable and agential can lead to a sexual ethic that considers the same. That is, what does it mean to ethically engage *as sexual beings* under damaging conditions? Rather than trying to prescribe a post-purity culture sexual ethic that is expansive enough to account for its harms and does not further replicate them, I return to orgasmic failure as descriptive groundwork for future projects. *Orgasmic failure* is a term developed by Kate Ott in light of queer theorist Jack Halberstam's queer failure.[48] As queer failure is a means "to escape the punishing norms that discipline behavior and manage human development with the goal of delivering us from unruly childhoods to orderly and predictable adulthoods,"[49] orgasmic failure helps us recognize that adolescents—and, truly, all humans—do not behave sexually toward a certain telos but are led by their own curiosity, desire, and pleasure. They fail to orgasm, fail to ejaculate, fail to perform in adult (i.e., white, male, heteronormative, middle-class sensible) ways.

We can think of the moral/sex panic around the Mormon practice of "soaking" as a useful example.[50] Described by young Mormons on TikTok, soaking is when a young person's penis is placed inside another person's vagina but there is no thrusting or movement to create friction. Without friction, it does not "count" as having sex; thus, young Mormons can participate in soaking without feeling guilty for having premarital sex. Further, according to the lore, while two young people are soaking, a friend could jump up and down on the couple's bed to create the friction that will cause pleasure to the penis and clitoris. This is called "jump humping." Because the action is done not by the couple in bed but by a third person, the jumper, this makes the practice morally acceptable to the teens. By imagining themselves as without agency, the soaking teens do not have the moral responsibility, or moral guilt, for their behaviors. This is similar to the ways in which young evangelicals would engage in oral sex or anal sex to preserve their virginity, understanding losing one's virginity as a matter of active/frictional PVI.[51]

Although soaking may be rarely practiced and even if it thrives in popular culture only to panic Mormon parents and get a laugh out of the "sexually liberated," it represents queer orgasmic failure and an image of adolescent creativity. We can think of soaking as just what teenagers *do*. Teenagers are creative, and they will use their agency to work with the conditions they exist within. Without robust sexual education, teens may not realize what behaviors can cause pregnancy or sexually transmitted infections. They may not know where to locate the vaginal cavity to have penetrative PVI. Without this knowledge accessible to them, they will participate in behaviors that meet their curiosity, desires, and pleasure. This act of soaking, as a form of orgasmic failure, frustrates adult sensibilities. It does not *look* like adult heterosexual behavior in that it does not include thrusting. It does not *look* like adult monogamous sexual behavior because it involves a third person (the jumper). Adolescents, by nature of who they are in relation to normative adulthood, will continue to queer sexuality. Our understanding of sexual ethics, then, needs to account for this.

Like the Mormons on TikTok or Alma, who only masturbated with markers and tissues in her panties (chapter 5),[52] or Danny, who found Christian scripture to house helpful metaphors for his gender transition (chapter 5),[53] young people find means of expressing their sexualities and genders in systems that were not set up for them to thrive. As a system with rigid norms for what it means to be a white woman and white man, what context sexual pleasure ought to be confined to, and what structure a family ought to take both socially and economically, purity culture demands that its youth conform to its norms or be punished for it. But teenagers fail to conform, both by choice and by the mere impossibility, for most, of reaching white, male, middle-class, heterosexual adulthood. And this act of failure—not true rebellion nor a moral good in any clear, universal sense—taps on the glass of the social greenhouse. It imperfectly, messily draws attention to the ways that the system does not work, not for them as white girls or white queer youth and certainly not for their peers of color.

In this way, I offer orgasmic failure as a post-purity sexual ethic. We tend to think of sexual ethics as sets of prescriptive or proscriptive rules describing what one can or cannot do with their body, especially on an individual level. As we have already seen, orgasmic failure resists this notion of rule-giving and rule-following by describing creative forms of resistance or reinterpretations of sexuality that challenge imposed cultural norms (e.g., not having sex means not having PVI means soaking instead). Orgasmic failure is a sexual ethic in that it is an *orientation toward* a way of being and behaving. It imagines another way to be a sexual being that does not require rigid gender or sex roles, goals toward orgasm or reproduction, or definitions of age-appropriateness. It offers a disruption of and an alternative to normative white sexual ethics.

As I have argued throughout this book, many responses to purity culture emphasize individual sexual freedom over communal responsibility and systemic change. Orgasmic failure, instead, is both an individual/personal intervention and a communal/systemic intervention. It makes space for youth to create sexual ethics out of their own sense of agency, with the tools and experiences already available to them and in interdependent relationship with others. This does not require anyone to reject their sexual subjectivity (like purity culture), nor does it require that they perform sexual liberation in a particular way (like some exvangelical responses). There is space for young people to gender identify in ways that feel integrous to them and to engage in sexual behaviors—or not—as they understand themselves to be emotionally and developmentally ready for.

Orgasmic failure encourages us to see young people as complexly vulnerable and complicit within systems due to age and/or gender and sexuality. With that, it encourages us to name the inescapable power imbalances in all relationships, across age, gender, class, race, and socioeconomic status, among others. As we know from Tessman's burdened virtues, young people will invariably do things that are not life-giving, but the stakes are not as high as heaven versus hell. Where more wisdom and experience are needed, adults act not as all-knowing protectors but conversation partners with young people. Adults and youth both have wisdom and insights to share with each other.

We can imagine how adopting a sexual ethic like orgasmic failure could lead to changes in public conversations around sex and sexuality. Orgasmic failure could alter educators' emphasis on teaching "safe sex" and sexual reproduction. Instead of only teaching proper condom usage toward the prevention of teenage pregnancy and sexually transmitted infections, educators could guide youth toward understanding consent and power dynamics at the intersections of race, gender, sexuality, disability, and socioeconomic status.[54] Beyond mere "yes" or "no," educators could help youth understand how their desires are shaped by the worlds they inhabit and how to listen to the needs and wants of their bodies and their partners' bodies. White, heterosexual, and/or male students could be taught to recognize the social greenhouse and how they might listen differently to the needs and wants of partners who are people of color, queer, or women or do not have the same social privileges and protections they do. This would be grounded in a holistic understanding of sex (including behaviors beyond PVI) that has a multiplicity of purposes (pleasure, connection, stress relief, and so on).

Orgasmic failure could also lead adults toward taking youth seriously in their self-expression. While public discourse today suggests that children cannot possibly know themselves to be queer or trans and must be influenced by media, peers, or adults around them—not unlike the view of the "sensate" child of the nineteenth century—attuning to orgasmic failure helps us recognize that *all* humans are sexual beings, even the youngest child. This allows children to wear the clothes they most want to wear and to be called by the name and pronouns they identify with, and it avoids pushing a child toward white heteronormativity in their relationships across genders. In return, adults are invited to learn from youth as well. Not merely viewing youth as pupils to adult educators, orgasmic failure offers an orientation toward understanding youth as co-learners and even teachers themselves. Sex education, then, is considered "a life-long process."[55] Orgasmic failure, as a queer and child-centric ethic, imagines a liberatory way of being a sexual person under damaging conditions.

Conclusion

In teaching a graduate-level course on God, gender, and sexuality, I invited my students to spend the latter part of a class period imagining their own sexual ethic in light of our reading from queer feminist ethicist Marvin Ellison and the numerous womanist and liberationist theologians we had read throughout the term. Many of my students, like me, grew up in purity culture and were in the process of relearning what it means to be a sexual and spiritual person. Many no longer identified as Christian (despite attending an interdenominational graduate school and enrolling in a theology course) and struggled with talking about God, even in queer, feminist ways. Others hungered for new language to talk about a faith that really mattered to them as a kid but made less and less sense to them as they came to understand themselves as gay, bisexual, or transgender or when they became parents themselves.

I wanted to invite them into the values-based sexual ethics at the center of progressive sexual education, such as the Our Whole Lives curriculum cocreated by the United Church of Christ and the Unitarian Universalists and in the work of feminist sexual ethicists like Ellison, Kate Ott, Karen Peterson-Iyer, and Margaret Farley.[56] But this was all new to my students. For many of them, sexual ethics meant a list of rules. Or they found that the only viable option was a kind of prescribed sense of sexual free-for-all that did not acknowledge, let alone dismantle, the social greenhouse of white supremacy and heteronormativity. So to help them get started, I invited them fill in the blanks: *What ought I do with my body in light of (blank)? Who ought I be in my gender and sexuality in light of (blank)? What beliefs about God and humanity could ground how I engage sexually with myself and others? Are my ethics grounded in certain values like mutuality, justice, pleasure, or (blank)?*

After giving my students time to list their values, I asked them to take the next step and answer the questions: *What ought I do with my body in light of my values? Who ought I be in my gender and sexuality in light of my values?* I trust that my forty students had forty different answers, each speaking to their unique values, their beliefs about God and their bodies, their sexual experiences, their families and cultures. During our debriefing time, one student reported back that they had never been asked to do this before. They had never been invited to construct a sexual ethic in light of their own values. They had never asked to construct a sexual ethic to begin with. Ethics were handed down to them, most likely by their youth group or parents, not something they were invited to cocreate.

Purity culture is a normative project, promoting white supremacist and antiqueer values as it disciplines teenagers toward heterosexual marriage. There is a temptation to respond to purity culture by isolating single issues (say, its sexism) or single players (say, male leaders like Joshua Harris) rather than seeing the interconnectedness of sexism, heterosexism, and white supremacy and the many active participants. A more holistic understanding of purity culture recognizes the systematic and institutional harm it has caused as well as how average people kept it alive. That is, in placing all the blame outside young people or ourselves as young people, we miss all the ways we keep the social greenhouse thriving by uncritically participating in an insidiously racist and antiqueer system.

Can we ask with Tessman, what does it mean "to engage ethically under damaging conditions"?[57] Let's think back to my story in the introduction to this book. I harmed my best friend Blake by responding to the confession "I'm gay" in a homophobic way, as I had been taught to do in purity culture. I had internalized the lesson that one cannot be both gay and Christian. Calling young people complicit or participatory does not mean that they are culpable for the harm done to them by the system or players involved, but it does afford them the agency and dignity to respond differently now as adults. I, too, was vulnerable to harm in purity culture because of my gender, made to feel deeply shameful for my body and sexual desires. And I have a responsibility now to respond differently and to see purity culture for what it really is—a white supremacist, antiqueer, normative project—and to divest from it. What does a moral and sexual ethic look like in light of the damaging conditions of purity culture? While a universal post-purity culture sexual ethic is hard to prescribe, a descriptive ethic of orgasmic failure is a helpful starting place in naming the ways in which young people negotiate their sexual worlds under such conditions. This is a helpful starting place, too, for those of us who see ourselves as adult victim-survivors of purity culture.

Conclusion

We began this book with a story about myself as an eighteen-year-old who, in a defining moment of my youth, chose to deny my best friend's sexuality and align myself with normative purity culture. I had come to wholeheartedly believe that Christian girls ought to behave a certain way, dress a certain way, and sublimate our desire until we marry a good (white) Christian man. My moral imagination had no room for queer teens, certainly not queer *Christian* teens.

Then I went off to college. I attended a conservative evangelical school in the heart of Indiana, where I was suddenly not the only devout Christian girl on the scene. Against the girls who led Bible studies in the residence hall or did a "no makeup month" with their roommates, I felt like I was failing to live up to the ideal of the pure Christian girl. I felt duped, much like Lyz Lenz,[1] for believing that if I performed white womanhood well enough, a good Christian man would want to date me. But just like in my public high school, the guys at Indiana Wesleyan chased after the more conventionally attractive girls who also happened to perform purity just a little bit better than I ever could. So I stopped trying so hard. I spent more energy calling out the hypocrisy in evangelical culture than trying to live up to its standards. With this, purity culture began to lose its power over me, and I started to see through the greenhouse walls.[2]

Beginning second semester my freshman year, classmate after classmate came out to me as gay. At first, I did not quite understand why J. on my floor and N. in my student organization both told me, in subtle, even *funny* ways, that they were gay. Eventually I began to see how I had become a safe-enough space for my peers to come out to. Even back then I knew this alone could not undo the harm I did to Blake in the Starbucks parking lot. But this shift in me—evidenced by my classmates' coming out—was a small act of recompense. I began to find other ways to live into my faith that did not necessitate the homophobia engrained in purity culture. This movement was, of course, slow and progressed in "serpentine" fashion.[3]

My story is just one of many examples of how young people participated in the normative, white structure of contemporary evangelical purity culture. Young white people like myself were actively involved in this system that sought to offer protection over young white women's bodies as a front for power and control and to punish Black, Brown, and queer bodies for their supposed deviance. At the center of purity culture, like other moral/sex panics before it, were adolescents who were thought to be the paragons of innocence and whose purity could save the nation from impending doom. But real teens, like Blake, myself, and all of the teenagers introduced in this book, were not marionettes of adult desires. At times, we chose to align with certain purity culture teachings, and at other times, we rejected them. It is not quite fair to call our resistance wholly liberative, however, as we were burdened by the normative structures within which we lived. White girls and white queer youth could not or would not name their white privileges, thus contributing to the thriving of the insular social greenhouse of white supremacy.

This book has sought to reject the easy binaries presented by purity culture advocates and critics: that a young person is either wholly agential, complicit, and therefore invulnerable *or* wholly victimized, vulnerable, and therefore non-agential. Rather, all humans—youth included—are much more complex subjects. In purity culture, white girls are vulnerable by their age and gender, but they are privileged by their race and by how well they conform to the ideal image of purity and innocence. White male-presenting queer youth are vulnerable by their sexuality but privileged by their race and gender. And yet even their so-called "struggle with same-sex attraction" could be channeled into a powerful testimony that reinforces the normalizing message of purity culture. This book has broken open binary categories and offered new ways to see youth, sexuality, whiteness, and purity culture with an eye toward diverse approaches to human flourishing. To that end, I have used the language of accountability throughout this book as an important step toward that flourishing.

Often accountability is described in contrast to a kind of easy forgiveness or "cheap grace."[4] Victim-survivors of sexual abuse and their advocates have long critiqued the Christian imperative to forgive, as it centers the perpetrator's feelings or reputation over the lives of those whom they have harmed.[5] Accountability, rather, centers the victim-survivor's needs and seeks appropriate recompense for the harm done. There is a true cost. As Michael Jaycox writes, "[Moral accountability] necessarily involves a disturbing transformation of the responsible agent's self-perception, having recognized they are capable of incurring guilt not only for past harms but also for likely future harms in the context of ongoing, unchosen, conflictual relationships."[6] We must face the full truth of the harm we have caused and make amends. That the transformation be "disturbing" means that if we do not find that process to be disruptive to our sense of self and our relationships with those we have harmed, we likely have not yet probed deep enough.

For many of us, accountability is terrifying. We have been primed to think that being held accountable is the same thing as getting "canceled,"[7] so we strive for an unattainable perfection and crumple at any scent of critique. Tema Okun calls this pursuit of perfectionism and fear of conflict the characteristics—or the poisons—of a white supremacist culture.[8] But what if we imagined a different way? I wonder with writer and educator Mia Mingus: "What if accountability wasn't scary? It will never be easy or comfortable, but what if it wasn't scary? What if our own accountability wasn't something we ran from, but something we ran towards and desired, appreciated, held as sacred?"[9] Mingus "dreams" a world in which accountability is something of a daily, weekly, monthly, yearly practice as a flawed and "tender" human, toward the kind of world we want to build collectively. "What if we understood our accountability, not as some small insignificant act, but as an intentional drop in an ever-growing river of healing, care, and repair that had the potential to nourish, comfort and build back trust on a large scale, carving new paths of hope and faith through mountains of fear and unacknowledged pain for generations?" she asks.

I watch my sister-in-law coach her two-year-old toward the practice of accountability. Lydia hit her baby cousin in a fit of excitement. Her mom pulls her away and holds her daughter's hands in hers as Lydia practices saying the word "sorry." *Do you know what you're saying sorry for? You hurt baby Davy.* Sometimes we need a kind parent or guide to remind us of the impact of our harm. I take Mingus's lead and ask, "What if we took more time to dream accountability? . . . What if accountability was so normalized, so everyday, so run-of-the-mill, that it was second nature? . . . That it was something that everyone knew about and you could easily pass a group of children and youth of any age casually talking about it?"[10]

I view this book as a move toward "dreaming accountability," for myself and for my white peers who grew up in purity culture, were harmed by it, and survived it. I have come to see that if I do not hold myself accountable, then I have ignored the harm I have caused. I have disregarded how those with less privilege have been harmed in deeper ways. If I only focus on the sexism I experienced as a white girl in purity culture, then I am tempted to miss all the ways I participated in the perpetuation of heterosexism and racism as well. It is as if I am saying that my trauma is the only one worth healing from. If I am only and always a victim, then I am forgoing the agency I have over my experience and existence. In saying that I have a role other than as someone who is *only ever acted upon*, I reclaim dignity as a human. Accountability and healing do not and should not end with truth-telling, but it is a "vital ingredient."[11] My hope is that through this book, victim-survivors of purity culture, no matter their gender or race, can begin to tell a truer story of their participation in and harm by purity culture as a normative, white supremacist structure. Through that truth-telling, may not only victim-survivors be healed, but may the whole system begin to crumble beneath our feet.

ACKNOWLEDGMENTS

I want to thank my family for all the ways they saw me as a writer (thanks, Natalie Eggeman) and educator (thanks, Sam Baker), well before I could see it in myself.

Thank you to my beloved, Joel Scaria, who has never treated my ambition as a dangerous thing but something to be cherished, even at a cost. Davy bubba has made the stakes of my work so much higher. *You, my sweet being-from-birth, constantly surprise me by being your complex and queer Davy-self.* In so many ways, all six of the niblings have helped me think through this book and its implications for real, living, breathing children: Raphaël, Chloé, Teddy, Alice, Ellie, and Lydia.

Sarah Bailey, my *anam cara*, has been my interlocuter for over a decade now. We have talked about the ideas in this book—we have both *lived* the ideas in this book!—and so much more. I am grateful for all the invisible ways she has supported me and this project.

When I was six weeks postpartum with a list of revisions to attend to, Annie Mesaros brought structure, care, and the wisdom of lived experience into a process that felt even more overwhelming than raising a tiny human. She was my book doula, helping me deliver this project from its still-basically-a-dissertation form into a book that I am so proud of. I could not have done this without her.

I want to thank my friends and colleagues at Drew University who have supported me from when this project was barely an idea, expressed in some nascent utterance in the infamous Circle of Doom. Thank you, Kelsey Wallace, for being my confidant and cheerleader, from our Thai food sob sessions to the hours we spent workshopping sentences across the table at Macrina. Michael Anderson, Hunter Bragg, Desmond Coleman (#TeamDesmond), Gabe Crooks (and Brooke Baker by extension), Sarah Galo, Simeiqi He, Meredith Hoxie Schol, Angie Kirby-Calder, Brinna Kolitz, Jennifer Maidrand, Jesse Mann (Puddleglum!), Hilary McKane (indexer extraordinaire), abby mohaupt, Hamza Radid,

O'neil Van Horn, and Amiel Wayne have all deepened and challenged my scholarship.

I want to specifically thank my Drew dissertation committee, Kate Ott, Traci C. West, and J. Terry Todd. This whole project could be dedicated to the three of them for how they pushed this idea (and me) toward greater depth and clarity. I knew from our first phone conversation that Kate "got" me. She saw the potential of this project before I could and talked about it *as a book* before I did. Kate was the most brilliant, attentive, and generous chair—and now colleague—I could ask for. Traci has been the voice in the back of my head asking, *What about race?* She helped me see beyond white feminism and toward an intersectional critique of purity culture. So much of this book has been shaped by her scholarship on gender-based violence, power, and race. And more than just completely ruining my view of Christian marriage (!), Terry has given me so many categories for understanding American evangelicalism, let alone introducing me to some of my most important conversation partners.

The Purity Culture Research Collective has been an invaluable resource and community for me as I completed my dissertation and underwent the revision process. These colleagues have complicated my understanding of purity culture and purity culture research. Liv Schultz helped me revise my final chapter during one of the early rounds. They reignited my excitement for that chapter and this book as a whole. Jennifer McGrath, Tessi Muskrat, and Rebekah Vickery have been fiercely fun collaborators. Victoria Houser has been a dream to cowrite with and has forwarded my thinking on queer theory and rhetorics (of course). *Forever Sawyer and Houser; Houser and Sawyer?*

I want to thank my colleagues at The Seattle School of Theology & Psychology and the Allender Center. Misty Anne Winzenried has shaped me as a teacher and has helped me grow into my scholarly voice. Dan B. Allender, Rachael Clinton Chen, Sam Lee, Wendell Moss, and Linda Royster have helped develop my understanding of complicity and the ubiquity of sexual harm. And my students: I held so many of their faces in my heart as I wrote, edited, and revised these chapters.

Thank you to Jennifer Hammer for her continued support and guidance through this now many-years process. New York University Press was and still is my dream publisher, and I am so glad she believed in the book, and me, from the very beginning. As a first-time author, I am so lucky to have been under her care as well as the rest of the NYU Press team.

And finally, I want to show my gratitude and awe for my many friends who survived purity culture and whose conversations have influenced my work in important ways: Bethany Berens, Olivia Campbell, Cassie Carroll, Grace Christensen, Asher Greyson, Phil Herbruck, Kate McCollister, Molly Meyer, Nic Mueller, Steven Porter, Rachel Pyle, Nick Rassi, Matthias Roberts, Anna Shaver, Heather Shaver, and Jenny Wharram.

NOTES

INTRODUCTION

1 Sara Moslener credits Donna Freitas for popularizing the term *evangelical purity culture* in her 2008 book *Sex and the Soul: Juggling Sexuality, Spirituality, Romance, and Religion on America's College Campuses* (Oxford University Press, 2008); Sara Moslener, *Virgin Nation: Sexual Purity and American Adolescence* (Oxford University Press, 2015), 186 n7.

2 Thelathia "Nikki" Young, *Black Queer Ethics, Family, & Philosophical Imagination* (Palgrave Macmillan, 2016), 5. This is Young's shorthand for describing the normative white, middle-class family.

3 Sophie Bjork-James, *The Divine Institution: White Evangelicalism's Politics of the Family* (Rutgers University Press, 2021), 5.

4 Bjork-James, *The Divine Institution*, 7.

5 For how purity culture serves rape culture, see Emily Joy Allison, *#ChurchToo: How Purity Culture Upholds Abuse and How to Find Healing* (Broadleaf Books, 2021).

6 "Harm and damage rhetoric" like this is analyzed in Elizabeth Gish, "'Are You a "Trashable" Styrofoam Cup?' Harm and Damage Rhetoric in the Contemporary American Sexual Purity Movement," *Journal of Feminist Studies in Religion* 34, no. 2 (2018): 5–22, https://doi.org/10.2979/jfemistudreli.34.2.03.

7 The *NIV True Love Waits Youth Bible* explicitly embedded purity teachings. The *Revolve* New Testament is designed to look like a teen fashion magazine with the quiz question "Are You Dating a Godly Guy?" plastered on the front. Mark DeVries et al., eds., *NIV True Love Waits Youth Bible* (Broadman & Holman Publishers, 1996); *Revolve: The Complete New Testament* (Thomas Nelson, 2003). See Caroline Blyth, *Rape Culture, Purity Culture, and Coercive Control in Teen Girl Bibles* (Routledge, 2021).

8 Sex Ed for Social Change (formerly SIECUS) overviews the standards for sex education in my home state of Indiana. "Indiana State Profile," State Profiles, SIECUS, October 24, 2023, https://siecus.org.

9 Justin Lookadoo and Hayley DiMarco, *Dateable: Are You? Are They?* (Hungry Planet, 2003); Blaine Bartel, *Every Teenager's Little Black Book on Sex and Dating* (Harrison House, 2002).

10 BarlowGirl, "Average Girl," recorded February 2004, track 10 on *BarlowGirl*, Fervent Records, compact disc.

11 Joshua Harris, *I Kissed Dating Goodbye: A New Attitude Toward Dating and Relationships* (Multnomah, 1997).

12 R. Danielle Egan cited in Stevi Jackson and Sue Scott, "A Sociological History of Researching Childhood and Sexuality: Continuities and Discontinuities," in *Children, Sexuality, and Sexualization*, eds. Emma Renold et al. (Palgrave Macmillan, 2015), 50.

13 Terry Gross, "How the Southern Baptist Convention Covered Up Its Widespread Sexual Abuse Scandal," *Fresh Air*, NPR, June 2, 2022, www.npr.org; Audrey Clare Farley, "The Racist Roots of the Southern Baptist Convention's Sex Scandal 'Apocalypse,'" The Soapbox, *New Republic*, May 30, 2022, https://newrepublic.com; Jina Moore, "How the Atlanta Shooting Shows the Dangers of American Evangelicalism's Trademark 'Purity Culture,'" March 20, 2021, www.businessinsider.com.

14 See Ruth Frankenberg, *White Women, Race Matters: The Social Construction of Whiteness* (University of Minnesota Press, 1993) and Michael Omi and Howard Winant, *Racial Formation in the United States* (Routledge, 2014).

15 I credit Sara Moslener with this insight. See Moslener, *Virgin Nation*.

16 Other scholars have likewise argued that purity culture is a white supremacist project. See, for instance, Madison Natarajan et al., "Decolonizing Purity Culture: Gendered Racism and White Idealization in Evangelical Christianity," *Psychology of Women Quarterly* 46, no. 3 (2022): 316, https://doi.org/10.1177/03616843221091; and Olivia Jayne Schultz, "Purity Culture's Racist Fruit: Centering the Voices of Black Womanists and Feminists in the Deconstruction of Purity Culture," *Arc: Journal of the School of Religious Studies (McGill University)*, 49 (2021): 1–47.

17 Julian B. Carter, *The Heart of Whiteness: Normal Sexuality and Race in America, 1880–1940* (Duke University Press, 2007), 2.

18 See, for example, Shannon Ethridge and Stephen Arterburn, *Every Young Woman's Battle: Guarding Your Mind, Heart, and Body in a Sex-Saturated World* (Waterbrook Press, 2009).

19 See Gish, "'Are You a "Trashable" Styrofoam Cup?,'" 15; and Karen Peterson-Iyer, "Mobile Porn? Teenage Sexting and Justice for Women," *Journal of the Society of Christian Ethics* 33, no. 2 (Fall/Winter 2013): 100, http://dx.doi.org/10.1353/sce.2013.0036.

20 Arguing that the female body is constructed as a "solution to moral and cultural crises" within purity culture, Ligia Crut describes the simultaneous sexualizing and asexualizing of the female body by its teachings as "paradoxical, contradictory, and disturbing" (Ligia Crut, "I'm Taking Back My Body [The Female Body in the 'Purity' Culture]," *Linguaculture* 12, no. 1 [2021]: 118, 121, https://doi.org/10.47743/lincu-2021-1-0191).

21 Heather Corinna and Isabella Rotman, *Wait, What? A Comic Book Guide to Relationships, Bodies, and Growing Up* (Limerence Press, 2019), 72.

22 Seth Dowland, *Family Values and the Rise of the Christian Right* (University of Pennsylvania, 2015), 157–180. See also Heather Hendershot, *Shaking the World for*

Jesus: Media and Conservative Evangelical Culture (University of Chicago Press, 2004), 114–115.

23 See, for example, Stephen Arterburn and Fred Stoeker, *Every Young Man's Battle: Strategies for Victory in the Real World of Sexual Temptation* (WaterBrook Press, 2002).

24 See, for instance, Matt Barber and Brittany Machado, *Give Me Sex Jesus*, 2015, Vimeo, https://vimeo.com; Nadia Bolz-Weber, *Shameless: A Sexual Reformation* (Convergent, 2019); Jamie Lee Finch, *You Are Your Own: A Reckoning with the Religious Trauma of Evangelical Christianity* (Published by the author, 2019); Linda Kay Klein, *Pure: Inside the Evangelical Movement That Shamed a Generation of Young Women and How I Broke Free* (Touchstone, 2018); Kristine Stolakis, *Pray Away* (Blumhouse Productions, 2021), Netflix; Jessica Valenti, *The Purity Myth: How America's Obsession with Virginity Is Hurting Young Women* (Seal Press, 2009); Addie Zierman, *When We Were on Fire: A Memoir of Consuming Faith, Tangled Love and Starting Over* (Convergent Books, 2013).

25 Peterson-Iyer, "Mobile Porn?," 100.

26 Sara Naps (@AlsoNamedSara), Twitter (now X), May 2, 2020, https://twitter.com/AlsoNamedSara/status/1256710062975922180. More on this story in chapter 1.

27 Carol Kuruvilla, "Youth Ministry Accused of Deceiving Queer Teens with 'Bait and Switch,'" HuffPost, August 13, 2020, www.huffpost.com.

28 "What Do We Have to Learn from, as Well as Teach, Young People About Sex?" in Marvin Ellison, *Making Love Just: Sexual Ethics for Perplexing Times* (Fortress Press, 2012), 143–170.

29 Christian Scharen and Aana Marie Vigen, eds., *Ethnography as Christian Theology and Ethics* (Continuum Books, 2011), 64.

30 Scharen and Vigen, *Ethnography as Christian Theology and Ethics,* 64.

31 Heewon Chang, *Autoethnography as Method* (Left Coast Books, 2008), 48–49 as cited in Brent Smith, *Religious Studies and the Goal of Interdisciplinarity* (Routledge, 2019), 14.

32 Smith, *Religious Studies and the Goal of Interdisciplinarity*, 13, 14.

33 John Wall, "From Childhood Studies to Childism: Reconstructing the Scholarly and Social Imaginations," *Children's Geographies* (2019): 1, https://doi.org/10.1080/14733285.2019.1668912.

34 Jackson and Scott, "A Sociological History," 50.

35 I appreciate David Halperin's definition of queer in *Saint Foucault*: queer is "*whatever* is at odds with the normal, the legitimate, the dominant." It is "a positionality vis-à-vis the normative" (David M. Halperin, *Saint Foucault: Toward a Gay Hagiography* [Oxford University Press, 1997], 62).

36 Lauren D. Sawyer and Victoria Houser, "Purity Culture and the Limits of Queer Evangelicalism," *Theology & Sexuality* 29, no. 2–3 (2024): 200–218. https://doi.org/10.1080/13558358.2024.2332982.

37 Kathryn Bond Stockton, *The Queer Child, or Growing Sideways in the Twentieth Century* (Duke University Press, 2009), 2.

38 Hannah Dyer, *The Queer Aesthetics of Childhood: Asymmetries of Innocence and the Cultural Politics of Child Development* (Rutgers University Press, 2020). See also Kate Ott and Lauren D. Sawyer, "Sexual Practices and Relationships Among Young People," in *The Routledge Handbook of Philosophy of Sex and Sexuality*, eds. Brian D. Earp et al. (Routledge, 2022).

39 Ott and Sawyer, "Sexual Practices and Relationships," 264–265.

40 Jaber F. Gubrium and James A. Holstein, "Chapter 12: Narrative Ethnography," in *Handbook of Emerging Methods*, eds. Sharlene Nagy Hesse-Biber and Patricia Leavy (Guilford Press, 2008), 247.

41 Lorraine Delia Kenny, *Daughters of Suburbia: Growing Up White, Middle Class, and Female* (Rutgers University Press, 2000), 137–139.

42 Kenny, *Daughters of Suburbia*, 33.

43 From Anne Lamott, an important thinker in my turn away from evangelicalism: "This is how we make important changes—poorly, barely, slowly. But still, [Jesus] raises his fist in triumph" (Anne Lamott, *Plan B: Further Thoughts on Faith* [Riverhead, 2004], 46).

CHAPTER 1. WHAT WE TALK ABOUT WHEN WE TALK ABOUT PURITY CULTURE

1 Stephanie Drury—SCCL (@StuffCCLikes), Twitter (now X), May 2, 2020, https://twitter.com/StuffCCLikes/status/1256619533017604096.

2 Prominent exvangelical writer and host of the podcast *#Exvangelical* Blake Chastain briefly defines *exvangelical* on his blog: "Similar to the way we use terms like 'ex-husband' or 'ex-girlfriend' to acknowledge a prior relationship that has ended, 'exvangelical' acknowledges an individual's prior place within the evangelical movement and culture that they have since left behind. 'Exvangelical' is an easily accessible shorthand to acknowledge our past experience. It nods to our heritage and how it has shaped us, but does not make any assumptions about what we—individually or collectively—believe now" (Blake Chastain, "'Exvangelical'—A Working Definition," *#Exvangelical*, March 2, 2019, https://exvangelicalpodcast.com).

3 For example, Christopher Stephano (@cjstephanoAITC), Twitter (now X), May 2, 2020, https://twitter.com/cjstephanoAITC/status/1256626216980930566; sheologian (@sheologian), Twitter (now X), May 2, 2020, https://twitter.com/sheologian/status/1256620335304249345.

4 For example, Janey the Small (@JaneyTheSmall), Twitter (now X), May 2, 2020, https://twitter.com/JaneyTheSmall/status/1256623141129818114.

5 Sara Naps (@AlsoNamedSara), Twitter (now X), May 2, 2020, https://twitter.com/AlsoNamedSara/status/1256710062975922180.

6 Sarah McCammon, *The Exvangelicals: Loving, Living, and Leaving the White Evangelical Church* (St. Martin's Press, 2024), 9–10.

7 Ann Swidler, "Culture in Action: Symbols and Strategies," *American Sociological Review* 51, no. 2 (1986): 273.

8 Swidler, "Culture in Action," 273.

9 Amy DeRogatis, *Saving Sex: Sexuality and Salvation in American Evangelicalism* (Oxford University Press, 2014), 6.

10 And any other non-married persons.

11 A purity ball is a ceremony in which a young girl pledges to her father to remain a virgin until her wedding night. For more on the ritual of purity balls, see Elizabeth Gish, "Producing High Priests and Princesses: The Father-Daughter Relationship in the Christian Sexual Purity Movement," *Religions* 7, no. 3 (2016): 1–22, https://doi.org/10.3390/rel7030033.

12 "Bouncing the eyes" describes the action of averting one's eyes from an object of lust (women). This is a practice taught to evangelical men regarding women in chapter 11 of Stephen Arterburn and Fred Stoeker, *Every Man's Battle: Winning the War on Sexual Temptation One Victory at a Time* (WaterBrook Press, 2000), 125–132.

13 Katelyn Beaty, "Commentary: When the Sexual Prosperity Gospel Doesn't Pan Out," *Salt Lake Tribune*, July 29, 2019, www.sltrib.com.

14 Elizabeth Gish, "'Are You a "Trashable" Styrofoam Cup?' Harm and Damage Rhetoric in the Contemporary American Sexual Purity Movement," *Journal of Feminist Studies in Religion* 34, no. 2 (2018): 7, https://doi.org/10.2979/jfemistudreli.34.2.03.

15 DeRogatis, *Saving Sex,* 116.

16 For more on the Quiverfull movement, see Emily Hunter McGowin, *Quivering Families: The Quiverfull Movement and Evangelical Theology of the Family* (Fortress Press, 2018).

17 DeRogatis, *Saving Sex,* 115.

18 DeRogatis, *Saving Sex,* 49.

19 Heather Hendershot, *Shaking the World for Jesus: Media and Conservative Evangelical Culture* (University of Chicago Press, 2004), 91. See also Sara Moslener, *Virgin Nation: Sexual Purity and American Adolescence* (Oxford University Press, 2015), 109; and Linda Kay Klein, *Pure: Inside the Evangelical Movement That Shamed a Generation of Young Women and How I Broke Free* (Touchstone, 2018), 25.

20 Though out of scope for this project, purity culture was exported outside the North American context as well. See Jennifer McGrath, "Pure to Purpose Pipeline: Socializing Purity in White Women's International Aid Work," *Theology and Sexuality* 29, nos. 2–3 (2023): 130–147. https://doi.org/10.1080/13558358.2024.2332979.

21 Moslener, *Virgin Nation*, 119.

22 Moslener, *Virgin Nation*, 113–118. According to reporting by *Jezebel* and ProPublica, in 2003, the year Silver Ring Thing began to receive government funding, more than half of its $1.2 million in revenue came from the U.S. government. See Hazel Cills, "The Rise and Fall of the Pop Star Purity Ring," *Jezebel*, January 25, 2018, https://jezebel.com; and "Unaltered Ministries," Nonprofit Explorer, ProPublica, January 8, 2024, https://projects.propublica.org.

23 Since Reagan's 1981 Adolescent Family Life Act, millions of dollars have been allocated to abstinence-only-until-marriage education in public schools in the United States, through Clinton's welfare reform bill in 1996, Bush's Community-Based Abstinence Education, and Obama's Affordable Care Act (although much less so). See Cynthia Daillard, "Sex Education: Politicians, Parents, Teachers and Teens," *The Guttmacher Report on Public Policy*, The Guttmacher Institute, February 2001, www.guttmacher.org; Melissa Healy, "Clinton Frees $250 Million for Sex Abstinence Teaching," *Los Angeles Times*, March 1, 1997, www.latimes.com; Elana Gordon, "How Sex Education Changed Under the Obama Administration," Side Effects Public Media, January 23, 2017, www.sideeffectspublicmedia.org; John S. Santelli et al., "Abstinence-Only-Until-Marriage: An Updated Review of U.S. Policies and Programs and Their Impact," *Journal of Adolescent Health* 61 (2017): 275.

24 Klein notes the decline, without giving a specific year, in the introduction to her book (*Pure*, 25–26). Renée Roden names the turning point at 2007 when a government-mandated study showed that abstinence-only-until-marriage sex education did not curb sexual behavior in young people at all (Renée Roden, "Britney Spears: An Icon for Purity Culture's Wounded Woman," *National Catholic Reporter*, August 31, 2021, www.ncronline.org). Klein and others have also named a turning point for the contemporary purity movement as 2017 when Joshua Harris apologized for the impact of his best-selling purity culture book *I Kissed Dating Goodbye* and the #MeToo and #ChurchToo movements were born (Klein, *Pure*, 268; Becca Andrews, "Sins of Submission," *Mother Jones*, July 26, 2018, www.motherjones.com).

25 Klein, *Pure*, 26.

26 Devi Abraham, "It's Back: Purity Culture 2.0, Gen Z Style," *Religious News Service*, December 2, 2021, https://religionnews.com.

27 This includes government-funded abstinence-only-until-marriage education, as cited previously.

In late 2023, purity culture once again entered the public conscience when Republican Speaker of the House Mike Johnson admitted to having a pornography blocker called Covenant Eyes on his computer, which alerts his accountability partner when he ventures to risky websites. Perhaps the most absurd thing about this was that Johnson's accountability partner was his teenage son. See Heather Digby Parton, "The Twisted Fantasy Behind Mike Johnson's 'Purity' Pledge," *Salon*, December 27, 2023, www.salon.com.

28 Famously, 'oos popstar Jessica Simpson vowed to remain abstinent until marriage, a topic she was frequently asked about in interviews. See Jessica Simpson, "Eyeshadow Abs," *Open Book* (New York: HarperCollins, 2020). Kindle.

See Cills and Roden.

29 See Victoria Houser, "Crisis Pregnancy Centers: How the Evangelical Purity Movement Funded Thousands of Anti-Abortion Clinics," *Canopy Forum*, July 8, 2022, https://canopyforum.org.

30 Margaret Lamberts Bendroth, *Fundamentalism & Gender, 1875 to the Present* (Yale University Press, 1993), 5.

31 The fundamentals are belief in the virgin birth, substitutionary atonement, Jesus's bodily resurrection, the inerrancy of Scripture, and premillennial dispensationalism (Bendroth, *Fundamentalism & Gender*, 3–4).

32 Bendroth, *Fundamentalism & Gender*, 5; Angela M. Lahr, *Millennial Dreams and Apocalyptic Nightmares* (Oxford University Press, 2007), 14. See also Matthew Avery Sutton, *Aimee Semple McPherson and the Resurrection of Christian America* (Harvard University Press, 2009).

33 See Randall Balmer, *Mine Eyes Have Seen the Glory: A Journey into the Evangelical Subculture in America*, 4th ed. (Oxford University Press, 2006).

34 Barbara G. Wheeler, "You Who Were Far Off: Religious Divisions and the Role of Religious Research," *Review of Religious Research* 37, no. 4 (June 1996): 292, https://doi.org/10.2307/3512010.

35 Wheeler, "You Who Were Far Off," 292.

36 See, for example, Lahr, *Millennial Dreams and Apocalyptic Nightmares*, 5; R. Marie Griffith, *God's Daughters: Evangelical Women and the Power of Submission* (University of California Press, 2000), 2, 21.

37 See Daniel Vaca, *Evangelicals Incorporated: Books and the Business of Religion in America* (Harvard University Press, 2019).

38 Hendershot, *Shaking the World for Jesus*, 1–14.

39 Sophie Bjork-James, *The Divine Institution: White Evangelicalism's Politics of the Family* (Rutgers University Press, 2021), 27.

40 Vaca, *Evangelicals Incorporated*, 8.

41 Isaac B. Sharp, *The Other Evangelicals: A Story of Liberal, Black, Progressive, Feminist, and Gay Christians—and the Movement That Pushed Them Out* (William B. Eerdmans Publishing Company, 2023), 15–16.

42 See John Otis, "Evangelical Christian Churches Gain Ground in Majority Catholic Brazil," *Morning Edition*, NPR, August 22, 2022, www.npr.org; Raphael Tsavkko Garcia, "Evangelicals in Brazil Are Stronger Today Than Ever Before," *Aljazeera*, January 7, 2022, www.aljazeera.com; Daniel Silliman, "Evangelicals Outgrow Catholics in Central America," *Christianity Today*, February 13, 2023, www.christianitytoday.com.

43 Meaghan Winter, "The Fastest-Growing Group of American Evangelicals," *The Atlantic*, July 26, 2021, www.theatlantic.com.

44 See Lauren D. Sawyer and Victoria Houser, "Purity Culture and the Limits of Queer Evangelicalism," *Theology & Sexuality* 29, no. 2–3 (2024): 200–218. https://doi.org/10.1080/13558358.2024.2332982.

45 Sharp, *The Other Evangelicals*, 49.

46 Peggy Pascoe, *What Comes Naturally: Miscegenation and the Making of Race in America* (Oxford University Press, 2009), 77–108.

47 See Brian Donovan, *White Slave Crusades: Race, Gender, and Anti-Vice Activism, 1887–1917* (University of Illinois Press, 2005), 17–36.

48 Jane Dailey, "Sex, Segregation, and the Sacred After *Brown*," *The Journal of American History* 91, no. 1 (June 2004): 119–144.

49 See "Nobody Knows de Trouble I See," in James H. Cone, *The Cross and the Lynching Tree in the Black Experience* (Orbis Books, 2017), 1–29; and Lillian Smith, *Killers of the Dream* (W.W. Norton & Company, 1949).
50 For example, preacher Dwight Moody encouraged segregated seating at his revivals. See Edward J. Blum, *Reforging the White Republic: Race, Religion, and American Nationalism 1865–1898* (Louisiana State University, 2005).
51 See Seth Dowland, *Family Values and the Rise of the Christian Right* (University of Pennsylvania, 2015).
52 Falwell cited in Matthew Avery Sutton, *Jerry Falwell and the Rise of the Religious Right: A Brief History with Documents*, The Bedford Series in History and Culture (Bedford/St. Martin's, 2013), 123–125.
53 Eric Tranby and Douglas Hartmann, "Critical Whiteness Theories and the Evangelical 'Race Problems': Extending Emerson and Smith's *Divided by Faith*," *Journal for the Scientific Study of Religion* 47, no. 3 (2008): 347, https://doi.org/10.1111/j.1468-5906.2008.00414.x.
54 There is, of course, nothing biblical about the nuclear family. See Julia M. O'Brien, "The Economics of Family: Changing Biblical Norms," *Biblical Archaeology Review* 36, no. 5 (2010).
55 See Peter Goodwin Heltzel, *Jesus and Justice: Evangelicals, Race, and American Politics* (Yale University Press, 2009), 91–126; and Anneke Stasson, "The Politicization of Family Life: How Headship Became Essential to Evangelical Identity in the Late Twentieth Century," *Religion and American Culture: A Journal of Interpretation* 24, no. 1 (2014): 1052–1151.
56 Tranby and Hartmann, "Critical Whiteness Theories," 347.
57 Jessica Martínez and Gregory A. Smith, "How the Faithful Voted: A Preliminary 2016 Analysis," November 9, 2016, Pew Research Institute, www.pewresearch.org.
58 McCammon, *The Exvangelicals*, 45.
59 McCammon, *The Exvangelicals*, 9. McCammon defines deconstruction as "the often painful process of rethinking an entire worldview and identity that was carefully constructed for them" (*The Exvangelicals*, 9–10).
60 Audre Lorde, *Sister Outsider: Essays and Speeches* (Crossing Press, 1984), 120.
61 The Instagram post is no longer online. The caption was quoted in an article expounding on the white womanhood on display in Joshua Tree by Sara Moslener: "White Women's Bodies and the Dilemma of Purity Culture Recovery," *The Revealer*, February 7, 2023, https://therevealer.org.
62 These comments are pulled from Alice Greczyn's blog post. See Alice Greczyn, "The Photo: How a Girls' Getaway in Joshua Tree Became a Symbol of White Supremacy and Why I'm Not Here to Do Better," *Alice Greczyn*, November 15, 2021, www.alicegreczyn.com.
63 Greczyn, "The Photo."
64 Moslener, "White Women's Bodies."
65 Moslener, "White Women's Bodies."

66 Emily Joy Allison, *#ChurchToo: How Purity Culture Upholds Abuse and How to Find Healing* (Broadleaf Books, 2021). #ChurchToo is the hashtag for addressing sexual abuse within churches. It came in response to the widespread #MeToo hashtag in 2017. See "#MeToo #ChurchToo," FaithTrust Institute, accessed January 21, 2024, www.faithtrustinstitute.org.

67 Allison, *#ChurchToo*, 114.

68 "Whiteness," *Talking About Race*. National Museum of African American History and Culture, Smithsonian, Accessed January 24, 2024, https://nmaahc.si.edu.

69 Madison Natarajan et al., "Decolonizing Purity Culture: Gendered Racism and White Idealization in Evangelical Christianity," *Psychology of Women Quarterly* 46, no. 3 (2022): 316, https://doi.org/10.1177/03616843221091l. See also Olivia Jayne Schultz, "Purity Culture's Racist Fruit: Centering the Voices of Black Womanists and Feminists in the Deconstruction of Purity Culture," *Arc: Journal of the School of Religious Studies (McGill University)* 49 (2021):1–47.

70 Natarajan et al., "Decolonizing Purity Culture," 316.

71 Tamura Lomax, *Jezebel Unhinged: Loosing the Black Female Body in Religion and Culture* (Duke University Press, 2018); Monique Moultrie, *Passionate and Pious, Religious Media and Black Women's Sexuality* (Duke University Press, 2017).

72 I credit this insight to Sara Moslener. See her article "White Women's Bodies."

73 For example, the Black woman–led Crunk Feminist Collective blog published critiques on purity culture as far back as 2011. CrunkAsHell, "Single, Saved, and Sexin': The Gospel of Gettin' Your Freak On," Crunk Feminist Collective, February 3, 2011, www.crunkfeministcollective.com. Although published anonymously on the blog, the author of this post was later identified as Black feminist Brittney Cooper. The piece is published under her name in Brittney C. Cooper et al., *The Crunk Feminist Collection* (The Feminist Press, 2017).

74 Mihee Kim-Kort, *Outside the Lines: How Embracing Queerness Will Transform Your Faith* (Fortress, 2018), 147–148.

75 Kim-Kort, *Outside the Lines*, 149.

76 Brittney Cooper, *Eloquent Rage: A Black Feminist Discovers Her Superpower* (St. Martin's Press, 2018), 97.

77 Rachel Scanlon (@rachelscanloncomedy), "If you sang along, you've also been traumatized Watch my special 'Gay Fantasy', out now! Link in bio!" TikTok, July 1, 2024. www.tiktok.com.

78 Jenna Ballinger (@jennaforeverawkward), "Miss you man #richmullins #religioustrauma." TikTok, July 1, 2024, www.tiktok.com.

79 Cassie Carroll, Zoom call with author, July 30, 2020.

80 Jenny Wharram, Zoom call with author, July 30, 2020.

81 From Sara Naps's (@AlsoNamedSara) Twitter (now X) post.

CHAPTER 2. DEFINING CHILDHOOD AND ADOLESCENCE

1 Amber Cantorna, *Refocusing My Family: Coming Out, Being Cast Out, and Discovering the True Love of God* (Fortress Press, 2017), 57.

2 Cantorna, *Refocusing My Family*, 57.
3 Cantorna, *Refocusing My Family*, 85.
4 Steven Angelides, "Sexting," *The Fear of Child Sexuality: Young People, Sex, and Agency* (University of Chicago Press, 2019), xxvi–ii.
5 Asaph Glosser et al., "Statutory Rape: A Guide to State Laws and Reporting Requirements," Office of the Assistant Secretary for Planning and Evaluation, December 15, 2004, 5, https://aspe.hhs.gov.
6 State age-of-consent laws also include a minimum age of consent if the perpetrator and victim are close in age. For example, in Alabama, the age differential is two years, so if a seventeen-year-old has sexual intercourse with someone fifteen (below the age of consent but above the minimum age of victim, which is twelve in Alabama), the seventeen-year-old cannot be prosecuted for sex with a minor (Glosser et al., "Statutory Rape," 18).
7 Angelides, "Sexting," xxvi–ii.
8 Jan Hoffman, "A Girl's Nude Photo, and Altered Lives," *New York Times*, March 26, 2011, www.nytimes.com.
9 Glosser et al., "Statutory Rape," 119.
10 The *New York Times* piece that covered this story notes that "if the Lacey students were convicted of dissemination of child pornography, they could be sentenced to up to 36 weeks in a juvenile detention center. They would be registered as sex offenders. Because they were under 15, however, after two years they could petition a court to remove their names from the registry, if they could prove they no longer posed a threat to the public" (Hoffman, "A Girl's Nude Photo").
11 Augustine, *St. Augustine Confessions*, Oxford World's Classics (Oxford University Press, 1998), 38.
12 Gabrielle Owen, *A Queer History of Adolescence: Developmental Pasts, Relational Futures* (University of Georgia Press, 2020), 147.
13 John Wall, *Ethics in Light of Childhood* (Georgetown University Press, 2010), 15–18; Robin Bernstein, *Racial Innocence: Performing American Childhood from Slavery to Civil Rights* (New York University Press, 2011), 36.

John Calvin (1509–1564) believed, like Augustine, that even babies were capable of sin, though they were not as "blameworthy" as older children and adults. He held that unbaptized babies were hell-bound, but that did not make them "*more sinful* and depraved than anyone else." In fact, children were "a little less sinful" than adults "since they had not yet had opportunity to commit actual sin" (Barbara Pitkin, "'The Heritage of the Lord': Children in the Theology of John Calvin," in *The Child in Christian Thought*, ed. Marcia J. Bunge [William B. Eerdmans, 2001], 165–169).

See also Catherine A. Brekus, "Children of Wrath, Children of Grace: Jonathan Edwards and the Puritan Culture of Child Rearing," in *The Child in Christian Thought*, ed. Marcia J. Bunge (William B. Eerdmans, 2001).

14 Augustine, *St. Augustine Confessions*, 29–46.

15 R. Danielle Egan and Gail Hawkes, *Theorizing the Sexual Child in Modernity* (Palgrave MacMillan, 2010), 17.
16 See also Bernstein, *Racial Innocence*, 37.
17 Egan and Hawkes, *Theorizing the Sexual Child*, 18
18 Egan and Hawkes, *Theorizing the Sexual Child*, 34, 46.
19 Egan and Hawkes, *Theorizing the Sexual Child*, 21.
20 Egan and Hawkes, *Theorizing the Sexual Child*, 34.
21 Egan and Hawkes, *Theorizing the Sexual Child*, 46.
22 Egan and Hawkes, *Theorizing the Sexual Child*, 34, 46, 49.
23 See, for example, Samuel Watson, "Flexible Gender Roles During the Market Revolution: Family, Friendship, Marriage and Masculinity Among U.S. Army Officers, 1815–1846," *Journal of Social History* 29, no. 1 (Autumn 1995): 81–106.
24 See John D'Emilio and Estelle B. Freedman, *Intimate Matters: A History of Sexuality in America* (Harper & Row, 1988 [2012]), 176.

During the Victorian Era, white middle-class women were viewed not as "Eve, the temptress" of previous generations but were thought to have fewer base inclinations than men had. Existing on a "higher moral plane than men," these women were the protectors of the private sphere against the temptations of the outside world, including excessive drink, untamed capitalism, and sexual deviance (D'Emilio and Freedman, *Intimate Matters*, 90–91).

See Egan and Hawkes's section on masturbation phobia in *Theorizing the Sexual Child*, 24–31.
25 Bernstein, *Racial Innocence*, 39. For a connection between the Victorian home and James Dobson's Focus on the Family, see Peter Goodwin Heltzel, *Jesus and Justice: Evangelicals, Race, and American Politics* (Yale University Press, 2009).
26 Egan and Hawkes, *Theorizing the Sexual Child*, 41–42. D'Emilio and Freedman, *Intimate Matters*, 102.
27 See also Sara Moslener, *Virgin Nation: Sexual Purity and American Adolescence* (Oxford University Press, 2015), 16. For more on the extension of the cult of true womanhood in middle-class African American communities, see Vicki Howard, "The Courtship Letters of an African-American Couple: Race, Gender, Class and the Cult of True Womanhood," *The Southwestern Historical Quarterly* 100, no. 1 (July 1996): 64–80.
28 Egan and Hawkes, *Theorizing the Sexual Child*, 46.
29 Edward J. Blum, *Reforging the White Republic: Race, Religion, and American Nationalism 1865–1898* (Louisiana State University, 2005), 9.
30 Bernstein, *Racial Innocence*, 35.
31 Bernstein, *Racial Innocence*, 35.
32 Indeed, by the mid-nineteenth century, many Protestants, even from traditional mainline denominations, considered themselves evangelical. After the Second Great Awakening, evangelicalism grew "rapid and broad." By 1855, the evangelical denominations, Methodist and Baptist, accounted for 55 percent of the U.S.

population. Even those who belonged to "old-line denominations," like the Episcopalians and Presbyterians, gained evangelical branches (David Sehat, *The Myth of American Religious Freedom* [Oxford University Press, 2011], 51–52).

33 Harriet Beecher Stowe, *Uncle Tom's Cabin; or, Life Among the Lowly*, ed. Christopher G. Diller (Broadview Editions, 2009), 45.

34 I have chosen to use the term "slave" to describe Topsy rather than the preferred language of "enslaved people" by contemporary African Americans and antiracist activists. While it is absolutely necessary to recognize enslaved African peoples as full human subjects and agents, Topsy was neither a full subject nor agent in Stowe's imagination. As a character—and caricature—her identity dwells primarily in her enslavement.

35 This is not difficult to ascertain. Stowe writes, "There stood the two children [Eva and Topsy], representations of the two extremes of society. The fair, high-bred child, with her golden head, her deep eyes, her spiritual, noble brow, and prince-like movements; and her black, keen, subtle, cringing, yet acute neighbor. They stood the representatives of their races. The Saxon, born of ages and cultivation, command, education, physical and moral eminence; the Afric, born of ages of oppression, submission, ignorance, toil, and vice!" (*Uncle Tom's Cabin*, 288).

36 Stowe, *Uncle Tom's Cabin*, 189, 280, 287.

Stowe's "dehumanizing" description of Topsy is rightfully critiqued by scholars such as womanist Emilie Townes, who, though understanding Topsy played an important functioning in revealing the wickedness of chattel slavery and its effects on people, still finds Stowe's depiction "troubling" for how it erases Topsy's subjectivity (Emilie M. Townes, *Womanist Ethics and the Cultural Production of Evil* [Palgrave MacMillan, 2006], 140).

It is important to note that within its antebellum context, to suggest that Topsy was fundamentally human but "wicked" due to environmental factors or learned behaviors was becoming a more marginalized position in the South. As different as the girls are, Eva and Topsy come from a common human ancestry (monogenesis), Stowe affirms (Bernstein, *Racial Innocence*, 44), against many of her contemporaries who believed that "nature had permanently fixed the Negro's place, . . . and hence any attempt to alter what was fixed by supposing the inferior types could change their station was misguided" (polygenesis; Kevin Burrell, "Slavery, the Hebrew Bible and the Development of Racial Theories in the Nineteenth Century," *Religions* 12, no. 9 [2021]: 8, https://doi.org/10.3390/rel12090742). Stowe held the long-standing Christian belief that all humans, of all races, were made in the image of God and could be redeemed. Yet the influence of polygenesis was growing in the South and would eventually become a way for slaveholders and their defenders to justify their anti-Black racism (Burrell, "Slavery, the Hebrew Bible," 6).

37 Stowe, *Uncle Tom's Cabin*, 292.

38 Bernstein, *Racial Innocence*, 45.

39 Stowe, *Uncle Tom's Cabin*, 323–324.

40 Bernstein, *Racial Innocence*, 47.
41 Stowe, *Uncle Tom's Cabin*, 471.
42 Bernstein writes of *Uncle Tom's Cabin*: "The refutation of the libel of black insensateness was one of abolitionism's most effective strategies and greatest triumphs" (*Racial Innocence*, 51).
43 See Burrell, "Slavery, the Hebrew Bible."
44 Of course, Native Americans complicated the binary as well and did so prior to the turn of the century. Sally Kitch addresses this in her book *The Specter of Sex* by examining the ways in which Native Americans functioned as "middle bloods" to English settlers, having "special privileges" that Black people did not have and to reiterate the privileges and freedoms that white settlers did have (Sally L. Kitch, *The Specter of Sex: Gendered Foundations of Racial Formation in the United States* [SUNY Press, 2009], 127–128).
45 Owen, *A Queer History of Adolescence*, 45.

The categories of white and black extended beyond the binary as more European immigrants came into the U.S. at the turn of the century. The category of white "Anglo-Saxons" or "Nordics" versus all others became a more favorable category for racial separation and domination. See Brian Donovan, *White Slave Crusaders: Race, Gender, and Anti-Vice Activism, 1887–1917* (University of Illinois Press, 2006), 15. See also Jane Dailey, *White Fright: The Sexual Panic at the Heart of America's Racist History* (Basic Books, 2020), 39.

46 Owen, *A Queer History of Adolescence*, 46.
47 Owen, *A Queer History of Adolescence*, 50.
48 G. Stanley Hall, *Adolescence*, Volume I (D. Appleton and Company, 1904), 649.
49 Owen, *A Queer History of Adolescence*, 53–54.
50 Owen, *A Queer History of Adolescence*, 46.
51 Hall, *Adolescence*, xi.
52 Gail Bederman, *Manliness and Civilization: A Cultural History of Gender and Race in the United States, 1880–1917* (University of Chicago Press, 1996), 86–87.
53 The Boy Scouts of America was founded in 1910.
54 Hall, *Adolescence*, xi; Bederman, *Manliness and Civilization*, 81.

Taking a cue from Sigmund Freud, Hall believed that psychic disorders, like neurasthenia, were rooted in a person's sex life (Hall, *Adolescence*, 285).

55 Blum writes that "American 'civilization' . . . was shorthand for Protestant Christianity, consumer capitalism, and racial hierarchies" (*Reforging the White Republic*, 212). Civilization was certainly gendered as well.
56 The "camp cure" of the great outdoors was sometimes prescribed to women too, though more often they were prescribed bed rest instead (Peter Boag, *Re-Dressing America's Frontier Past* [University of California Press, 2011], 178).
57 Bederman, *Manliness and Civilization*, 103.
58 Boag, *Re-Dressing America's Frontier Past*, 180.
59 Owen, *A Queer History of Adolescence*, 147.

60 Matt Lavietes, "Florida School Districts Removed Roughly 300 Books Last School Year," NBC News, September 12, 2023, www.nbcnews.com; Associated Press, "Texas Pushes Some Textbook Publishers to Remove Material on Fossil Fuels," NPR, November 18, 2023, www.npr.org.

61 Meredith Johnson, "The Dangerous Consequences of Florida's 'Don't Say Gay' Bill on LGBTQ+ Youth in Florida," *Georgetown Journal of Gender and the Law* 23, no. 3 (2020), www.law.georgetown.edu.

62 Derek Thompson, "Why American Teens Are So Sad," *The Atlantic*, April 11, 2022, www.theatlantic.com; Derek Thompson, "America's Teenage Girls Are Not Okay," *The Atlantic*, February 16, 2023, www.theatlantic.com; Ross Douthat, "American Teens Are Really Miserable. Why?," *New York Times*, February 18, 2023, www.nytimes.com; Jean Twenge, interview with Ezra Klein, *The Ezra Klein Show*, podcast audio, May 19, 2023, www.nytimes.com.

63 Feminist ethicist Karen Peterson-Iyer expands on this idea: "Rather than encouraging girls to understand themselves as moral agents and sex as a moral and deliberate choice, purity culture encourages girls to think of themselves as moral children, in need of a father's, or a husband's, sexual protection" (Karen Peterson-Iyer, "Mobile Porn? Teenage Sexting and Justice for Women," *Journal of the Society of Christian Ethics* 33, no. 2 [Fall/Winter 2013]: 100, http://dx.doi.org/10.1353/sce.2013.0036).

64 Christina Reimer, "The Taboo of Virginity: Purity Balls as Negative Rites of Passage," *Arc: The Journal of the Faculty of Religion, McGill University* (2009): 214.

65 Jennifer McGrath, "Pure to Purpose Pipeline: Socializing Purity in White Women's International Aid Work," *Theology and Sexuality* 29, nos. 2–3 (2023): 130–147. https://doi.org/10.1080/13558358.2024.2332979.

66 Reimer, "The Taboo of Virginity," 215.

67 Reimer writes, "Fathers, for pledging girls, are the priestly intermediaries between their daughters and God" ("The Taboo of Virginity," 216). No such intermediary is needed for boys.

68 These are chapter titles in John Eldredge, *Wild at Heart: Discovering the Secret of a Man's Soul*, rev. ed. (Nelson, 2010), 9.

69 Eldredge and his eldest son, Samuel Eldredge, co-wrote a book for young men called *Killing Lions: A Guide Through the Trials Young Men Face*. This book rehearses much of the same themes as *Wild at Heart*, with a younger audience in mind. Beginning in 2018, Eldredge and his sons—Sam, Blaine, and Luke—published an online men's magazine, *And Sons*, described as "a road map for those who want to understand the masculine soul. Adventure, beauty, God, and deep engagement with the world," also for "the young man's soul." See Samuel Eldredge and John Eldredge, *Killing Lions: A Guide Through the Trials Young Men Face* (HarperCollins, 2024) and *And Sons Magazine*, 2023, www.andsonsmagazine.com.

70 Eldredge, *Wild at Heart*, 61, emphasis in original.

71 Eldredge, *Wild at Heart*, 62, emphasis in original.

72 Eldredge, *Wild at Heart*, 8–16, 46.
73 Eldredge, *Wild at Heart*, 4.
74 This is a point made by Philip T. Duncan, that "Eldredge's ideas are dangerous . . . because they are misleading in the way they appeal to biblical authority" (Philip T. Duncan, "Nurturing Voyeurism, Vibrant Sexism, and Violence: Why We Can't [Yet] Afford to Forget About *Wild at Heart*," *Priscilla Papers* 35, no. 1 [Winter 2017]: 6).
75 Eldredge, *Wild at Heart*, 13.
76 See Anneke Stasson, "The Politicization of Family Life: How Headship Became Essential to Evangelical Identity in the Late Twentieth Century," *Religion and American Culture: A Journal of Interpretation* 24, no. 1 (2014): 1052–1151.
77 Cantorna, *Refocusing My Family*, 58.

CHAPTER 3. PURITY PANICS AND YOUNG PEOPLE'S "NATION-SAVING" ROLE IN U.S. SOCIAL HISTORY

1 Michael Hobbes and Sarah Marshall, hosts, "Sexting," *You're Wrong About* (podcast), June 11, 2019.
2 Instances also cited in Steven Angelides, "Sexting," *The Fear of Child Sexuality: Young People, Sex, and Agency* (University of Chicago Press, 2019), 157–177.
3 Quote by Amy Hasinoff on Hobbes and Marshall, "Sexting."
4 See Angelides, *The Fear of Child Sexuality*, chap. 7.
5 Angelides, *The Fear of Child Sexuality*, xxiv.
6 Gilbert Herdt cited in Angelides, *The Fear of Child Sexuality*, xxiv; Angelides, *The Fear of Child Sexuality*, 163.
7 Angelides, *The Fear of Child Sexuality*, 164.
8 Angelides writes of how, in moral/sex panics, the differences between child and teen are "frequently downplayed, collapsed, or ignored within a unified and age-stratified legal category of the Child" (Angelides, *The Fear of Child Sexuality*, xv). Thus, Child encapsulates all of those who fall below the legal age of consent, whether five, twelve, or seventeen years of age.
9 Angelides, *The Fear of Child Sexuality*, xvii; R. Danielle Egan and Gail Hawkes, *Theorizing the Sexual Child in Modernity* (Palgrave MacMillan, 2010); Stevi Jackson and Sue Scott, "A Sociological History of Researching Childhood and Sexuality: Continuities and Discontinuities," in *Children, Sexuality, and Sexualization*, eds. Emma Renold et al. (Palgrave Macmillan, 2015).
10 R. Danielle Egan and Gail L. Hawkes, "Imperiled and Perilous: Exploring the History of Childhood Sexuality," *Journal of Historical Sociology* 21, no. 4 (2008): 365, https://doi.org/10.1111/j.1467-6443.2008.00341.x.
11 Elsewhere, too.
12 Jeremy N. Thomas, "The Development and Deployment of the Idea of Pornography Addiction Within American Evangelicalism," *Sexual Addiction & Compulsivity* 23, no. 2 (2016): 182–195, http://dx.doi.org/10.1080/10720162.2016.1140603.

13 See "Our Daughters Are Having Sex: The Conservative Pushback Against Teen 'Promiscuity'" in J. Shoshanna Ehrlich, *Regulating Desire: From the Virtuous Maiden to the Purity Princess* (SUNY Press, 2014), 111–149.

14 For more on how the child has been deployed for the cause of white supremacy, see Caroline Levander, *Cradle of Liberty: Race, the Child, and National Belonging from Thomas Jefferson to W. E. B. Du Bois* (Duke University Press, 2006).

15 See Peter Boag, *Re-Dressing America's Frontier Past* (University of California Press, 2011); statistic from Brian Donovan, *White Slave Crusaders: Race, Gender, and Anti-Vice Activism, 1887–1917* (University of Illinois Press, 2006), 22.

16 "Now, consumer pleasures and commercial leisure promised men more palpable rewards than Christian self-denial and hard work" (Donovan, *White Slave Crusaders*, 114). See also Gail Bederman, "'The Women Have Had Charge of the Church Work Long Enough': The Men and Religion Forward Movement of 1911–1912 and the Masculinization of Middle-Class Protestantism," in *A Mighty Baptism: Race, Gender, and the Creation of American Protestantism*, eds. Susan Juster and Lisa MacFarlane (Cornell University Press, 1997).

17 John D'Emilio and Estelle B. Freedman, *Intimate Matters: A History of Sexuality in America* (Harper & Row, 1988 [2012]), 172; Edward J. Blum, *Reforging the White Republic: Race, Religion, and American Nationalism 1865–1898* (Louisiana State University, 2005), 211.

18 Ehrlich, *Regulating Desire*, 80.

19 D'Emilio and Freedman, *Intimate Matters*, 158.

20 See "The Emergence of the Social Purity Alliance, 1877–1885" in David J. Pivar, *Purity Crusade: Sexual Morality and Social Control, 1868–1900* (Greenwood Press, 1973), 78–130.

Ehrlich writes, "Reflecting the evangelical fervor of the times, [female moral reformers'] campaign emerged out of a broader moral reform crusade to cleanse the nation of sin, which included an effort to save the souls of fallen women" (*Regulating Desire*, 8).

21 Most nineteenth-century evangelical reformers were postmillennials, meaning they believed that humans could usher in the Second Coming of Jesus by initiating the millennium or the one-thousand-year reign of Christian ethics.

22 D'Emilio and Freedman, *Intimate Matters*, 198.

23 Mark Thomas Connelly, *The Response to Prostitution in the Progressive Era* (University of North Carolina Press, 1980), 56, cited in D'Emilio and Freedman, *Intimate Matters*, 200.

24 This was certainly a fear of Margaret Sanger and the early birth control movement. See R. Marie Griffith, *Moral Combat: How Sex Divided American Christians and Fractured American Politics* (Basic Books, 2017), 1–47.

25 Ehrlich, *Regulating Desire*, 72, 70.

26 Quote from Donovan, *White Slave Crusaders*, 22; Boag, *Re-Dressing America's Frontier Past*, 177.

27 Anti-vice crusaders Clifford Roe and Edwin Sims write specifically of the dangers of the urban environment, turning innocent country girls into (presumably worldly, dirty) city girls. Sims writes, "You feel like saying to every mother in the country: Do not trust any man who pretends to take an interest in your girl if that interest involves her leaving your own roof. Keep her with you. She is far safer in the country than in the big city" (cited in Donovan, *White Slave Crusaders*, 29).

28 Not just novels, but white slavery tracts, plays, and films, too (D'Emilio and Freedman, *Intimate Matters*, 198).

29 Kauffman writes, "She belonged, as has been intimated, to a race in which motherhood is an instinctive passion and an economic necessity, and she was born into a class in which not to marry is socially shameful and materially precarious" (Reginald Wright Kauffman, *The House of Bondage* [Grosset & Dunlap Publishers, 1910], https://archive.org, 10).

30 Kauffman, *The House of Bondage*, 20–21.

31 Kauffman, *The House of Bondage*, 51. The language of "inmate" is from Donovan, *White Slave Crusaders*, 23.

32 The similarity of the names of Madam Rose Légère and the villain slaveholder Simon Legree in Stowe's *Uncle Tom's Cabin* was not lost on critics at the time (Donovan, *White Slave Crusaders*, 36).

33 Donovan, *White Slave Crusaders*, 32.

34 Ehrlich, *Regulating Desire*, 16.

35 Donovan, *White Slave Crusaders*, 26.

36 Likely one thousand Black men and women were lynched between 1889 and 1899. Anti-lynching activist Ida B. Wells estimated that ten thousand were lynched in the period after the Civil War to the turn of the century (Blum, *Reforging the White Republic*, 199). Often interracial relationships, especially between Black men and white women, were perceived to be coerced. See Gail Bederman, "'The White Man's Civilization on Trial': Ida B. Wells, Representations of Lynching, and Northern Middle-Class Manhood," *Manliness and Civilization: A Cultural History of Gender and Race in the United States, 1880–1917* (University of Chicago Press, 1996), 45–76; "'Nobody Knows de Trouble I See': The Cross and the Lynching Tree in the Black Experience" in James H. Cone, *The Cross and the Lynching Tree* (Orbis Books, 2011), 1–29; Jane Dailey, *White Fright: The Sexual Panic at the Heart of America's Racist History* (Basic Books, 2020); Peter Goodwin Heltzel, "Revival, Race, and Reform: The Roots of Modern Evangelical Politics," *Jesus and Justice: Evangelicals, Race, and American Politics* (Yale University Press, 2009), 13–44; Martha Hodes, *White Women, Black Men: Illicit Sex in the Nineteenth Century South* (Yale University Press, 1997).

37 Seth Dowland, *Family Values and the Rise of the Christian Right* (University of Pennsylvania, 2015); Jane Dailey, "Sex, Segregation, and the Sacred After *Brown*," *Journal of American History* 91, no. 1 (June 2004): 119–144.

38 See Dowland's chapters "Christian Schools," "Textbook Politics," and "Home Schools" in *Family Values*.

39 Gary, "The Deep Drone of Unseen Cicadas: Gary's Story," *Homeschoolers Anonymous*, November 24, 2014, https://homeschoolersanonymous.wordpress .com.

40 Joshua Harris, *I Kissed Dating Goodbye: A New Attitude Toward Dating and Relationships* (Multnomah, 1997).

41 Gary, "The Deep Drone," emphasis in original.

42 Dowland, *Family Values*, 14.

43 David O. Moberg, *The Great Reversal: Evangelism Versus Social Concern* (J.B. Lippincott Company, 1972), 28.

44 David Sehat, *The Myth of American Religious Freedom* (Oxford University Press, 2011), 52; Margaret Lamberts Bendroth, *Fundamentalism & Gender, 1875 to the Present* (Yale University Press, 1993), 15.

45 Donovan, *White Slave Crusaders*, 37, 41. See also Ehrlich, *Regulating Desire*, 42.

46 Ehrlich, *Regulating Desire*, 43.

47 Ehrlich, *Regulating Desire*, 44, 48. See also Pivar, *Purity Crusade*.

48 Ehrlich, *Regulating Desire*, 49.

49 Despite these laws' protectionist beginnings, I am not arguing here that age of consent laws ought to be repealed or that age is not an important criterion in evaluating healthy sexual partnerships among youth. As Kate Ott and I have written elsewhere, age of consent alone does not guarantee that a relationship is healthy. We write, "Consent, in its most erotically attuned awareness, demonstrates a mix of emotional maturity, relational awareness, and educational preparation. Consent in this context avoids the pitfalls of many discussions on the topic today, where fixations on birth dates and specific sexual behaviors overshadow more important concerns (we argue) of adolescent thriving" (Kate Ott and Lauren D. Sawyer, "Sexual Practices and Relationships Among Young People," in *The Routledge Handbook of Philosophy of Sex and Sexuality*, eds. Brian D. Earp, Clare Chambers, and Lori Watson [Routledge, 2022], 267–268).

50 Ehrlich, *Regulating Desire*, 56.

51 Blum, *Reforging the White Republic*, 200.

The WCTU's chapters were segregated and functioned independently—at the request of whites who insisted that the Black chapters included the word "colored" in their name to better differentiate them. In 1883, the WCTU founded its "Department of Work Among the Colored People," which was led by African American writer Frances Ellen Watkins Harper, as an attempt to "battle . . . the racisms of the WCTU from within." The department was notoriously underfunded (Blum, *Reforging the White Republic*, 203). Many Black women, like Harper, who were a part of the WCTU were critical of Willard and the organization's refusal to "put its moral authority" toward protecting the civil rights of Black people (Blum, *Reforging the White Republic*, 204).

52 Ehrlich, *Regulating Desire*, 60.

53 Middle-class girls also participated in sexual behaviors, but, as Ehrlich states, "their behavior did not attract the same degree of attention and documentation as that of girls from the 'tenement districts'" (*Regulating Desire*, 70).
54 Ehrlich, *Regulating Desire*, 72–74, 69, 72, 75.
55 D'Emilio and Freedman, *Intimate Matters*, 234, 250.
56 See Griffith, *Moral Combat*, 121–154.
57 D'Emilio and Freedman, *Intimate Matters*, 203–204, quote on 228.
58 D'Emilio and Freedman, *Intimate Matters*, 244, quote on 248.
59 D'Emilio and Freedman, *Intimate Matters*, 274; see also Griffith, *Moral Combat*, 159.
60 Griffith, *Moral Combat*, 58–59.
61 Sara Moslener, *Virgin Nation: Sexual Purity and American Adolescence* (Oxford University Press, 2015), 84.
62 Leo P. Ribuffo, "Family Policy Past as Prologue: Jimmy Carter, the White House Conference on Families, and the Mobilization of the New Christian Right," *Review of Policy Research* 23, no. 2 (2006): 314, https://doi.org/10.1111/j.1541-1338.2006.00203.x.
63 Ribuffo, "Family Policy Past," 315–316.
64 See Elaine Tyler May, *Homeward Bound: American Families in the Cold War Era* (Basic Books, 1988) and Stephanie Coontz, *The Way We Never Were: American Families and the Nostalgia Trap* (Basic Books, 1992).
65 Coontz's work summarized in Dowland, *Family Values*, 149.
66 Dowland, *Family Values*, 9.
67 Griffith writes that the anxiety of the early Cold War era led people to hold tightly to conservative views on gender and sexuality (*Moral Combat*, 121). This was in some ways a reversal of the gains women made in the 1920s with their flapper dresses and bobbed haircuts (both signs of modernity and atheism, as fundamentalists warned).
68 Matthew D. Lassiter, "Inventing Family Values," in *Rightward Bound*, eds. Bruce J. Schulman and Julian E. Zelizer (Harvard University Press, 2008), 14–15.
69 There was also an evangelical feminist movement at the time, which clung to evangelical theologies but believed in women's God-given equality with men. See Pamela H. Cochran, *Evangelical Feminism: A History* (New York University Press, 2005).
70 Dowland, *Family Values*, 157–159.
71 In her history of the race and sex panic in the United States during Jim Crow (1880–1965), Jane Dailey argues that segregation in the South was primarily an effort to prevent interracial sex and marriage, both of which threatened the stability of white supremacy (*White Fright*, 44). In the early years of Jim Crow, laws against miscegenation or interracial marriage were defended in court with rulings like *State of Indiana v. Gibson* and *Pace vs. Alabama*, and in the public sphere, the races were kept separate from social interaction. The underlying racist logic was that "social amalgamation leads to illicit intercourse which leads to intermarriage," which led to biracial children and the dilution of the white race. Though ending sex segregation

was a complicated priority for many Black leaders through the early twentieth century, by the Cold War era, Black activists and groups like the NAACP made the end of sexual segregation one of their chief demands (Dailey, *White Fright*, 57). This all culminated in the 1967 case *Loving v. Virginia*, which declared the remaining anti-miscegenation laws unconstitutional (Dailey, *White Fright*, 9).

72 Dowland, *Family Values*, 7.

73 Lassiter critiques conservatives for not recognizing that their love for free market capitalism was hurting the "traditional family," not helping it ("Inventing Family Values," 28).

74 By the 1970s, there was a break between politically and socially conservative evangelicals and politically and socially liberal (or "apolitical") evangelicals. See Brantley W. Gasaway, *Progressive Evangelicals and the Pursuit of Social Justice* (North Carolina Press, 2014).

75 Dowland, *Family Values*, 2.

76 See James Davison Hunter, *Culture Wars: The Struggle to Control the Family, Art, Education, Law, and Politics in America* (Basic Books, 1991).

77 Jerry Falwell was influenced by Schaeffer in his creation of the Moral Majority (Dowland, *Family Values*, 121).

78 Dowland, *Family Values*, 118, 120.

79 Dowland, *Family Values*, 2.

80 Moslener, *Virgin Nation*, 95–96.

81 Moslener, *Virgin Nation*, 100, 101.

82 There was a surprising new authoritative voice at this time, emphasizing the importance of those traditional family values and sexual purity: the Christian psychologist (Moslener, *Virgin Nation*, 91). Conservative Christianity had had a shaky relationship with the social sciences, as it did with evolutionary biology during the Scopes trial (Griffith, *Moral Combat*, 35–36). This "therapeutic Christianity" would continue to thrive throughout the 1970s, laying groundwork for the proliferation of Christian sex manuals in that decade and evangelical purity culture in the 1990s and 2000s. See Amy DeRogatis, *Saving Sex: Sexuality and Salvation in American Evangelicalism* (Oxford University Press, 2014).

83 Heltzel, *Jesus and Justice*, 105. Such a rubric has a totalizing force, as it whitewashes racial difference and undermines programs and policies that would uplift struggling Black families. Organizations like Focus on the Family remain ignorant to the ways in which white supremacy caused the fracturing of the Black family unit, through chattel slavery, slave auctions, contemporary welfare policies, and the prison industrial complex.

84 Gabrielle Owen, *A Queer History of Adolescence: Developmental Pasts, Relational Futures* (University of Georgia Press, 2020), 124.

85 James C. Dobson, *Preparing for Adolescence* (Vision House, 1978), 9, https://archive.org.

86 Dobson, *Preparing for Adolescence*, 110.

87 See Anneke Stasson, "The Politicization of Family Life: How Headship Became Essential to Evangelical Identity in the Late Twentieth Century," *Religion and American Culture: A Journal of Interpretation* 24, no. 1 (2014): 1052–1151.

88 Moslener, *Virgin Nation*, 102.

89 Moslener, *Virgin Nation*, 96–99, 101–102.

90 Daniel K. Williams, "Sex and the Evangelicals: Gender Issues, the Sexual Revolution, and Abortion in the 1960s," in *American Evangelicals and the 1960s*, ed. Axel R. Schäfer (University of Wisconsin Press, 2013), 99–100.

91 George Gilder quoted in Moslener, *Virgin Nation*, 105.

92 See Larry Eskridge's work on the Jesus People Movement and the evangelical youth subculture that came out of it in chap. 6, "The Jesus Kids," in Larry Eskridge, *God's Forever Family: The Jesus People Movement in America* (Oxford University Press, 2013), 145–178.

93 Heather Hendershot, "Virgins for Jesus: The Gender Politics of Therapeutic Christian Media," in *Shaking the World for Jesus: Media and Conservative Evangelical Culture* (University of Chicago Press, 2004), 91.

94 Regarding the international influence of purity culture, see Linda Kay Klein, *Pure: Inside the Evangelical Movement That Shamed a Generation of Young Women and How I Broke Free* (Touchstone, 2018), 260.

95 Moslener, *Virgin Nation*, 111.

96 According to Moslener, beginning in the 1980s, conservative evangelicals, who believed abstinence-based education would cure the country's ills of teen pregnancy, promiscuity, and abortion, brought programs like True Love Waits out of churches and into the political sphere. True Love Waits transcended religious, organizational, and national boundaries well enough to bring abstinence education to a wide audience (*Virgin Nation*, 113).

97 Moslener, *Virgin Nation*, 109, 111.

98 Denny Pattyn, the founder of the Silver Ring Thing, an abstinence program similar to True Love Waits, "tells his teenage audience that adults have created the sex-obsessed culture that teens now are forced to live in" (Christine J. Gardner, *Making Chastity Sexy* [University of California Press, 2011], 26). He says, "Forgive us, we adults, who have done this to you. . . . I challenge you to be the generation of change" (quoted in Gardner, *Making Chastity Sexy*, 26).

99 Moslener, *Virgin Nation*, 113.

100 Gardner, *Making Chastity Sexy*, 31.

101 Gardner, *Making Chastity Sexy*, 31.

102 Hendershot, "Virgins for Jesus," 93.

103 Eric Tranby and Douglas Hartmann, "Critical Whiteness Theories and the Evangelical 'Race Problems': Extending Emerson and Smith's *Divided by Faith*," *Journal for the Scientific Study of Religion* 47, no. 3 (2008): 347, https://doi.org/10.1111/j.1468-5906.2008.00414.x.

104 Hendershot, "Virgins for Jesus," 105.

105 Donna Freitas, *Sex and the Soul: Juggling Sexuality, Spirituality, Romance, and Religion on America's College Campuses* (Oxford University Press, 2008), 85.
106 Freitas, *Sex and the Soul*, 79.
107 Freitas, *Sex and the Soul*, 82.
108 DeRogatis, *Saving Sex*, 39.
109 Elizabeth Gish, "'Are You a "Trashable" Styrofoam Cup?' Harm and Damage Rhetoric in the Contemporary American Sexual Purity Movement," *Journal of Feminist Studies in Religion* 34, no. 2 (2018): 15, https://doi.org/10.2979/jfemistudreli.34.2.03.
110 It was also, of course, unattainable for those who did wait, as many, many scholars have shown. The wedding night is rarely as magical as the purity literature suggests it will be because of how sex has been presented as an evil in most contexts until suddenly it's not. See Tina Schermer Sellers, *Sex, God, and the Conservative Church: Erasing Shame from Sexual Intimacy* (Routledge, 2017).
111 Described in Moslener, *Virgin Nation*, 165–166.
112 Jay Strack and Diane Strack, *Until You Say I Do*, A True Love Waits Resource (LifeWay Press, 1997), 26–27.
113 Hendershot, "Virgins for Jesus," 101–102.

CHAPTER 4. REIMAGINING ADOLESCENT SEXUALITY AND AGENCY

1 *Spring Awakening* is a 2000s-era Broadway musical that portrays a clash of generations—literally, in how the set, script, and costumes place it in late-nineteenth-century bourgeois Germany—yet when the music kicks in, the actors pull out hand mics and jam out to contemporary rock music. Just as significantly, the musical displays the clash between teenagers and the teachers and parents in their lives.
2 Steven Sater and Duncan Sheik, *Spring Awakening: A New Musical* (Theatre Communications Group, 2007), 59.
3 Sater and Sheik, *Spring Awakening*, x.
4 Sater and Sheik, *Spring Awakening*, 40.
5 Indeed, its original Victorian-era subtitle is "A Children's Tragedy" (Sater and Sheik, *Spring Awakening*, vii).
6 John Wall, "From Childhood Studies to Childism: Reconstructing the Scholarly and Social Imaginations," *Children's Geographies* (2019): 1, https://doi.org/10.1080/14733285.2019.1668912.
7 Sater and Sheik, *Spring Awakening*, 73.
8 Technically this part is sung by Otto, perhaps in the perspective of Otto instead of Melchior; there are several discrepancies between the commentary and the Broadway stage production itself (Sater and Sheik, *Spring Awakening*, x).
9 Sater and Sheik, *Spring Awakening*, 35.
10 [Jack] Halberstam, *The Queer Art of Failure* (Duke University Press, 2011), 12.
11 Kate Ott and Lauren D. Sawyer, "Sexual Practices and Relationships Among Young People," in *The Routledge Handbook of Philosophy of Sex and Sexuality*,

eds. Brian D. Earp et al. (Routledge, 2022). This term was first introduced in Kate Ott, "Orgasmic Failure: A Praxis Ethic for Adolescent Sexuality," in *Theologies of Failure*, eds. Roberto Sirvent and Duncan B. Reyburn (Cascade Books, 2019).

12 Diederik F. Janssen, "Anthropologizing Young/Minor Sexualities," in *Children, Sexuality, and Sexualization*, eds. Emma Renold et al. (Palgrave Macmillan, 2015), 23.

13 Ott and Sawyer, "Sexual Practices and Relationships."

14 Kate Ott, "Re-Thinking Adolescent Sexual Ethics: A Social Justice Obligation to Adolescent Sexual Health," *Journal of Lutheran Ethics* 7, no. 2 (2007): para 11, italics in original.

15 Heather Corinna and Isabella Rotman, *Wait What? A Comic Book Guide to Relationships, Bodies, and Growing Up* (Limerance Press, 2019), 72.

16 Corinna and Rotman, *Wait What?*, 72.

17 Centers for Disease Control and Prevention, "Youth Risk Behavior Survey: Data Summary and Trends Report 2007–2017," accessed February 22, 2025, www.cdc.gov/yrbs/dstr/pdf/trendsreport.pdf.

18 David C. Wiley et al., "Managing Sex Education Controversy Deep in the Heart of Texas: A Case Study of the North East Independent School District (NEISD)," *American Journal of Sexuality Education* 15, no. 1 (2020): 53–81, https://doi.org/10.1080/15546128.2019.1675562.

19 Lindsay M. Shepherd et al., "Comparison of Comprehensive and Abstinence-Only Sexuality Education in Young African American Adolescents," *Journal of Adolescence* 61 (2017): 50–63; and Centers for Disease Control and Prevention, "STDs in Adolescents and Young Adults," *Sexually Transmitted Disease Surveillance 2018*, accessed July 23, 2021, www.cdc.gov/std/stats18/adolescents.htm.

20 Henry J. Kaiser Family Foundation, "Sexual Health of Adolescents and Young Adults in the United States," August 20, 2014, www.kff.org.

21 Articles and studies focused solely on LGBTQ youth present a grim picture as well, as they focus firstly on rates of suicidality and homelessness among queer youth. See Human Rights Campaign, "2018 LGBTQ Youth Report," accessed July 23, 2021, https://assets2.hrc.org; and Ilan H. Meyer et al., "LGBTQ People in the US: Select Findings from the Generations and TransPop Studies," Williams Institute, UCLA School of Law, accessed July 23, 2021, https://williamsinstitute.law.ucla.edu.

22 John S. Santelli et al., "Abstinence-Only-Until-Marriage: An Updated Review of U.S. Policies and Programs and Their Impact," *Journal of Adolescent Health* 61 (2017): 275.

23 According to the Rape, Abuse, Incest National Network (RAINN), "One in 9 girls and 1 in 53 boys under the age of 18 experience sexual abuse or assault at the hands of an adult" and "females ages 16–19 are 4 times more likely than the general population to be victims of rape, attempted rape, or sexual assault" (RAINN, "Children and Teens: Statistics," accessed July 23, 2021, www.rainn.org).

24 Gladys M. Martinez and Joyce C. Abma, "Sexual Activity, Contraceptive Use, and Childbearing of Teenagers Aged 15–19 in the United States," *National Center for Health Statistics NCHS Data Brief* no. 209 (2015): 1, www.cdc.gov/nchs/data/databriefs/db209.pdf.

Rates of STIs among teens, however, are increasing. See Centers for Disease Control, "STDs in Adolescents and Young Adults"; and Prevention and Chelsea L. Shannon and Jeffrey D. Klausner, "The Growing Epidemic of Sexually Transmitted Infections in Adolescents: A Neglected Population," *Current Opinion in Pediatrics* 30, no. 1 (2018): 137–143, https://doi.org/10.1097/MOP.0000000000000578.

25 See Jean M. Twenge, "Have Smartphones Destroyed a Generation?" *The Atlantic*, September 2017, www.theatlantic.com, cited in Gabrielle Owen, *A Queer History of Adolescence: Developmental Pasts, Relational Futures* (University of Georgia Press, 2020), 155.

26 Note that this is contextual, as both Remez and Regnerus argue. Some teenagers claim oral or anal sex to not "count" as sex in order to remain "technical virgins" (Mark D. Regnerus, *Forbidden Fruit: Sex & Religion in the Lives of American Teenagers* [Oxford University Press, 2009], 164). However, others view oral and anal sex under the same broad umbrella as sexual activity. Remez writes, "What young adults consider to be 'sex' also varies by contextual and situational factors, such as who is doing what to whom and whether it leads to orgasm" (Lisa Remez, "Oral Sex Among Adolescents: Is It Sex or Is It Abstinence?" *Family Planning Perspectives* 32, no. 6 [November–December 2000], 301, https://doi.org/10.1363/3229800).

Researchers Steve Clapp, Kristen Leverton Helbert, and Angela Zizak found that teenagers who are religiously affiliated are less likely than their secular peers to have sexual intercourse (31 percent compared to 60 percent); however, they found that evangelical teens were no more likely to postpone sex than those in Protestant mainline traditions, for instance. That is, evangelical teens who sign abstinence pledges are "not any more or less likely" than other religiously affiliated teenagers "to have had sexual intercourse or to have experienced pregnancy or caused a pregnancy" (Steve Clapp et al., *Faith Matters: Teenagers, Religion, and Sexuality* [LifeQuest, 2003], 35).

27 Language from Human Rights Campaign, "2018 LGBTQ Youth Report."

28 R. Danielle Egan and Gail Hawkes, *Theorizing the Sexual Child in Modernity* (Palgrave MacMillan, 2010), 153.

29 Egan and Hawkes, *Theorizing the Sexual Child*, 155.

30 Stevi Jackson and Sue Scott, "A Sociological History of Researching Childhood and Sexuality: Continuities and Discontinuities," in *Children, Sexuality, and Sexualization*, eds. Emma Renold et al. (Palgrave Macmillan, 2015), 43.

31 Barbara Blodgett, *Constructing the Erotic: Sexual Ethics and Adolescent Girls* (Pilgrim Press, 2002), 8.

32 Jackson and Scott, "A Sociological History," 43.

33 Blodgett, *Constructing the Erotic*, 8.
34 Elizabeth Gish, "'Are You a "Trashable" Styrofoam Cup?': Harm and Damage Rhetoric in the Contemporary American Sexual Purity Movement," *Journal of Feminist Studies in Religion* 34, no. 2 (Fall 2018): 19, https://doi.org/10.2979/jfemistudreli.34.2.03.
35 This is similar to how Susan Talburt writes about the construction of queer narratives as intelligible: that the queer child must transition from tragically in the closet and confused to happily out of the closet and confident (Susan Talburt, "Intelligibility and Narrating Queer Youth," in *Youth and Sexualities: Pleasure, Subversion, and Insubordination in and out of Schools*, eds. Mary Louise Rasmussen et al. [Palgrave MacMillan, 2004]).
36 Blodgett, *Constructing the Erotic*, 186.
37 See Sara Moslener, "White Women's Bodies and the Dilemma of Purity Culture Recovery," *The Revealer*, February 7, 2023, https://therevealer.org.
38 Blodgett, *Constructing the Erotic*, 189.
39 Gish, "'Are You a "Trashable" Styrofoam Cup?,'" 19.
40 For liberative Christian sexual ethic, see, for example, Marvin Ellison, *Making Love Just: Sexual Ethics for Perplexing Times* (Fortress Press, 2012); Christine E. Gudorf, *Body, Sex, and Pleasure: Reconstructing Christian Sexual Ethics* (Pilgrim Press, 1996); Ott, "Re-Thinking Adolescent Sexual Ethics"; Cristina L. H. Traina, *Erotic Attunement: Parenthood and the Ethics of Sensuality Between Unequals* (University of Chicago Press, 2011).
41 John Wall, *Ethics in Light of Childhood* (Georgetown University Press, 2010), 71.
42 Immanuel Kant, "What Is Enlightenment?," trans. Mary C. Smith, Columbia University, accessed July 9, 2021, www.columbia.edu.
43 "Kantian autonomy really means obedience to an *internal* authority—not an individual conscience, but a thoroughly impersonal 'agency.' It means submission to the causeless, causally inefficacious, atemporal, inscrutable, and incomprehensible demands of the noumenal [the-thing-in-itself] will" (Robert L. Campbell and John Chambers Christopher, "Moral Development Theory: A Critique of Its Kantian Presuppositions," *Developmental Review* 16, no. 1 [1996]: 6, https://doi.org/10.1006/drev.1996.0001).
44 See, for instance, the utilitarian ethics of Jeremy Bentham and John Stuart Mill.
45 Sally Sedgwick, "Can Kant's Ethic Survive the Feminist Critique?" In *Feminist Interpretations of Immanuel Kant*, ed. Robin May Schott (The Pennsylvania State University, 1997), 79.
46 See Immanuel Kant, *Groundwork of the Metaphysics of Morals*, trans. and ed. Mary Gregor (Cambridge University Press, 1997).
47 Immanuel Kant, *Observations on the Beautiful and the Sublime*, trans. John T. Goldthwait (University of California Press, 1960), 81.
48 See Wall, *Ethics in Light of Childhood*, chaps. 1–4.
49 Immanuel Kant, *On Education*, trans. Annette Churton (Dover Publications, 2003), 108.

50 This individualistic thinking was reflected in early feminist Mary Wollstonecraft's philosophy as well. She argued that if women are given the same educational opportunities as men, they would be just as rational and autonomous as them. See Mary Wollstonecraft, *A Vindication of the Rights of Women*, ed. Eileen Hunt Botting (Yale University Press, 2014).

51 James Samuel Logan, "Immanuel Kant on Categorical Imperative," in *Beyond the Pale: Reading Ethics from the Margins*, eds. Stacey M. Floyd-Thomas and Miguel A. De La Torre (Westminster John Knox, 2011), 75.

52 See Immanuel Kant, "On the Different Races of Man" and "On Natural Characteristics," in *Race and the Enlightenment: A Reader*, ed. Emmanuel Chukwudi Eze (Blackwell Publishing, 1997).

53 Logan argues that though Kant asks his audience to separate their duty from their inclinations (a priori), he himself could not accomplish this. "Even a pure and good will cannot escape this fact, for even to conceive of the a priori, one must dwell in the world of experience" ("Immanuel Kant on Categorical Imperative," 76).

54 For more on the progression between Kantian moral development and developmental psychology, see Campbell and Christopher, "Moral Development Theory: A Critique of Its Kantian Presuppositions"; and David E. Leary, "Immanuel Kant and the Development of Modern Psychology," *The Problematic Science: Psychology in Nineteenth-Century Thought*, eds. William Ray Woodward and Mitchell G. Ash (Praeger, 1982).

55 Wade E. Pickren and Alexandra Rutherford, *A History of Modern Psychology in Context* (John Wiley & Sons, Inc., 2010), 157.

56 Pickren and Rutherford, *A History of Modern Psychology*, 157.

57 Erik Erikson, *Identity: Youth and Crisis* (W. W. Norton & Company, 1968), 96.

58 It's worth noting that Erikson was writing in the 1960s when there was a thriving teen subculture. Prior to the 1920s, there was not a subculture for middle-class white teens to participate in.

59 Erikson, *Identity*, 93.

60 Erikson, *Identity*, 133.

61 Erikson, *Identity*, 141.

62 Carol Gilligan, *In a Different Voice: Psychological Theory and Women's Development* (Harvard University Press, 1993), 12.

63 Erikson, *Identity*, 278.

64 Erikson, *Identity*, 274–275.

65 Moin Syed and Jillian Fish, "Revisiting Erik Erikson's Legacy on Culture, Race, and Ethnicity," *Identity* 18, no. 4. (October 2018): 274–283, https://doi.org/10.1080/15283488.2018.1523729.

66 Syed and Fish, "Revisiting Erik Erikson's Legacy," 278; see Erikson, *Identity*, 302.

67 Gilligan, *In a Different Voice*, xi.

68 Gilligan, *In a Different Voice*, xvii.

69 Wall, *Ethics in Light of Childhood*, 80; Pickren and Rutherford, *A History of Modern Psychology*, 191.

70 Pickren and Rutherford, *A History of Modern Psychology*, 315.
71 Ronald Duska and Mariellen Whelan, *Moral Development: A Guide to Piaget and Kohlberg* (Paulist Press, 1975), 8.
72 Lawrence Kohlberg, *The Philosophy of Moral Development: Moral Stages and the Idea of Justice*. Essays on Moral Development Volume I (Harper & Row, 1981), 409–412.
73 Gilligan, *In a Different Voice*, 18.
74 Gilligan, *In a Different Voice*, 21.
75 Gilligan, *In a Different Voice*, xiv.
76 Wall, *Ethics in Light of Childhood*, 81.
77 Wall, *Ethics in Light of Childhood*, 29.
78 Spyros Spyrou et al., eds., "Introduction: Reimagining Childhood Studies: Connectivities . . . Relationalities . . . Linkages," in *Reimagining Childhood Studies*, eds. Spyros Spyrou et al. (Bloomsbury, 2019), 2.
79 Wall, "From Childhood Studies to Childism," 2.
80 Wall, "From Childhood Studies to Childism," 8.
81 Wall, "From Childhood Studies to Childism," 2.
82 Spyrou et al., "Introduction," 2.
83 Spyrou et al., "Introduction," 4.
84 Spyrou et al., "Introduction," 3.
85 Wall, *Ethics in Light of Childhood*, 24.
86 Wall, *Ethics in Light of Childhood*, 80.
87 Quote from Gilligan, *In a Different Voice*, 23.
88 This term comes from Wall, *Ethics in Light of Childhood*, 81.
89 Nancy Leigh DeMoss and Dannah Gresh, *Lies Young Women Believe* (Moody Publishers, 2008), 85.
90 Alex and Brett are the younger brothers of Joshua Harris, the author of *I Kissed Dating Goodbye*. See chapter 6.
91 I want to thank Rebekah Vickery for drawing my attention to The Rebelution, the Modesty Survey, and the surrounding discourse.
92 The Rebelution, "The Rebelution," accessed February 25, 2024, www.therebelution.com/about.
93 The Rebelution, "The Rebelution."
94 The Rebelution, "Statistical Overview," 2007, web.archive.org.
95 The Rebelution, "Announcement: The Modesty Survey," December 2, 2006, web.archive.org.
96 Shannon Moeller, "The Responsibility of Modesty (Part Two)," The Rebelution, February 6, 2007, www.therebelution.com.
97 This statistic is from a blog post on the pornography blocker website Covenant Eyes. See Luke Gilkerson, "What Do Christian Guys Think About Modesty?," Covenant Eyes, July 27, 2021, www.covenanteyes.com.

The results of the Modesty Survey are no longer accessible through The Rebelution's website or the Wayback Machine.

98 Mahaney was accused of covering up child sex abuse that happened within his network of churches, Sovereign Grace Ministries. See Tiffany Stanley, "The Sex-Abuse Scandal That Devastated a Suburban Megachurch," *Washingtonian*, February 14, 2016, www.washingtonian.com.

99 Egan and Hawkes, *Theorizing the Sexual Child*, 155.

100 Susanne Luhmann cited in Talburt, "Intelligibility and Narrating Queer Youth," 35.

101 Kathryn Bond Stockton, *The Queer Child, or Growing Sideways in the Twentieth Century* (Duke University Press, 2009), 7.

102 Ott and Sawyer, "Sexual Practices and Relationships," 264–265.

103 Stockton, *The Queer Child*, 11; Wall, *Ethics in Light of Childhood*, 29.

104 Dina Georgis quoted in Hannah Dyer, *The Queer Aesthetics of Childhood: Asymmetries of Innocence and the Cultural Politics of Child Development* (Rutgers University Press, 2020), 7.

105 Dyer, *The Queer Child*, 7.

106 See Stockton, *The Queer Child*, 6–7.

107 Wall, *Ethics in Light of Childhood*, 59–60.

108 Language of "interdependent autonomy" is from Spyrou et al., "Introduction," 7.

109 See Wall, *Ethics in Light of Childhood*, 88.

110 Wall, *Ethics in Light of Childhood*, 90.

111 Wall, *Ethics in Light of Childhood*, 108.

112 Wall, *Ethics in Light of Childhood*, 79, 48.

113 Nomy Arpaly cited in Cristina L. H. Traina, "Children and Moral Agency," *Journal of the Society of Christian Ethics*, 29, no. 2 (2009): 23.

114 Traina, "Children and Moral Agency," 22.

115 Traina, "Children and Moral Agency," 23.

116 Traina is careful not to conflate the experiences of a young white child with those of a Black girl or woman. See Katie G. Cannon, *Black Womanist Ethics* (Wipf and Stock, 1988); Nikia Smith Robert, "'Not Meant to Survive': Black Mothers Leading Beyond the Criminal Line," in *Walking Through the Valley: Womanist Explorations in the Spirit of Katie Geneva Cannon*, eds. Emilie M. Townes et al. (Westminster John Knox, 2022); and Traci C. West, *Wounds of the Spirit: Black Women, Violence, and Resistance Ethics* (New York University Press, 1999).

117 Traina, "Children and Moral Agency," 25.

118 See West, *Wounds of the Spirit*.

119 Traina, "Children and Moral Agency," 27.

120 See Jean Twenge cited in Owen, *A Queer History of Adolescence*, 155. See also Amy Adele Hasinoff, *Sexting Panic: Rethinking Criminalization, Privacy, and Consent* (University of Illinois Press, 2015).

121 Ott, "Orgasmic Failure," 111.

122 Lauren Sawyer, "Spring Awakening," *The Sojourn*, Indiana Wesleyan University, March 26, 2009.

CHAPTER 5. READING ADOLESCENT NARRATIVES AGAINST THE NORMS OF PURITY CULTURE

1 Daniel Lavery, "Brio Magazine-Related Branding Opportunities I've Missed," *The Chatner*, March 2, 2021, www.thechatner.com.

2 Daniel M. Lavery, *Something That May Shock and Discredit You* (Simon & Schuster, 2020), 53.

3 Lavery, *Something That May Shock*, 48.

4 John Wall, *Ethics in Light of Childhood* (Georgetown University Press, 2010), 59–60.

5 See Susan Talburt, "Intelligibility and Narrating Queer Youth," in *Youth and Sexualities: Pleasure, Subversion, and Insubordination in and out of Schools*, eds. Mary Louise Rasmussen et al. (Palgrave MacMillan, 2004), 17–39.

6 For this chapter, I narrow the scope of my reading to memoirs and personal narratives from straight women and queer folks of all genders who were born between approximately 1980 and 1990 and participated in the evangelical subculture during their adolescence. This excluded some important memoirs by those in fundamentalist, high-control churches. I felt that their particular experiences were not representative of most evangelical adolescents. All of the personal narratives were written by people who identify as white, who do not mention their race in their account, or whose experiences in purity culture are normative for white adolescents.

7 See Melissa Browning, "Epistemological Privilege and Collaborative Research: A Reflection on Researching as an Outsider," *Practical Matters* 6 (Spring 2013): 1–16.

8 Sandra Harding, "Introduction: Is There a Feminist Method?" in *Feminism & Method* (Indiana University Press, 1987), 6–7.

9 Christian Scharen and Aana Marie Vigen, eds., *Ethnography as Christian Theology and Ethics* (Continuum Books, 2011), 67.

10 Harding, "Introduction," 7.

11 Margaret A. Farley, "The Role of Experience in Moral Discernment," in *Christian Ethics: Problems and Prospects*, ed. Lisa Sowle Cahill and James F. Childress (The Pilgrim Press, 1996), 135.

12 Observable but not fully knowable. See more on intelligibility later.

13 Farley, "The Role of Experience," 135. Also see D. Bruce Hindmarsh, *The Evangelical Conversion Narrative: Spiritual Autobiography in Early Modern England* (Oxford University Press, 2005), 6.

14 Hindmarsh, *The Evangelical Conversion Narrative*, 5.

15 For purposes of this chapter, I use autobiography, memoir, and personal narrative to mean approximately the same thing. Memoir is typically a short section of a person's whole life (autobiography). Personal narrative is an even smaller and shorter section.

16 Hindmarsh citing Charles Taylor (*The Evangelical Conversion Narrative*, 7).

17 See Hindmarsh, *The Evangelical Conversion Narrative*.

18 Linda Kay Klein, *Pure: Inside the Evangelical Movement That Shamed a Generation of Young Women and How I Broke Free* (Touchstone, 2018), 6. Italics in original.
19 Klein, *Pure*, 3, 7.
20 Shannon Ethridge and Stephen Arterburn, *Every Young Woman's Battle: Guarding Your Mind, Heart, and Body in a Sex-Saturated World* (Waterbrook Press, 2009), 37.
21 Klein, *Pure*, 6.
22 Angus Gordon cited in Talburt, "Intelligibility and Narrating Queer Youth," 25.
23 Talburt, "Intelligibility and Narrating Queer Youth," 35.
24 These books were published or republished in the 1990s and 2000s. I find the four primary texts I cite to be representative of the teachings of purity culture. While there were certainly differences in how each author communicates their ideas—some brashly, others with a more paternalistic tone—the ideas were more or less the same among all four of them.
25 I would like to give a special thanks to the online group Purity Culture Anonymous, whose members invited me to speak with them on August 6, 2021, about my research and its intersection with their stories. This group represents international, multiracial, multigendered perspectives and was invaluable to me in writing this chapter.
26 Kathryn Bond Stockton, *The Queer Child, or Growing Sideways in the Twentieth Century* (Duke University Press, 2009), 4.
27 Hannah Dyer, *The Queer Aesthetics of Childhood: Asymmetries of Innocence and the Cultural Politics of Child Development* (Rutgers University Press, 2020), 16.
28 Gabrielle Owen, *A Queer History of Adolescence: Developmental Pasts, Relational Futures* (University of Georgia Press, 2020), 147.
29 Brenda Marie Davies, *On Her Knees: Memoir of a Prayerful Jezebel* (William B. Eerdmans Publishing Company, 2021), 3.
30 Dannah Gresh, *And the Bride Wore White: Seven Secrets to Sexual Purity* (Moody Publishers, 2012), 172.
31 Davies, *On Her Knees*, 6.
32 Nancy Leigh DeMoss and Dannah Gresh, *Lies Young Women Believe* (Moody Publishers, 2008), 92.
33 Davies, *On Her Knees*, 74.
34 See Mark D. Jordan, "Scriptural Authorities," *The Ethics of Sex* (Blackwell Publishing, 2002), 20–46.
35 Heather R. White, "How Paul Became the Straight Word: Protestant Biblicism and the Twentieth-Century Invention of Biblical Heteronormativity," in *Bodies on the Verge: Queering Pauline Epistles*, ed. Joseph A. Marchal (SBL Press, 2019), 290.
36 Shannon Ethridge and Stephen Arterburn write in *Every Young Woman's Battle*, "Lesbian experimentation is not an acceptable form of abstinence. Such goes directly against Scripture (see Leviticus 18:22; Romans 1:24–26) and fuels sexual passions and curiosities to the point that 'just playing around' sexually with another female can become addictive, creating an enormous amount of confusion, guilt, and turmoil in your life" (187).

37 Hayley DiMarco, *Sexy Girls: How Hot Is Too Hot?* (Revell, 2006), 5.

38 "Same-sex attraction," or "SSA," is a term used by those who believe queerness is something that does not define a person—that is, it is a phase, a choice, or alterable. See Davies, *On Her Knees*, 36.

39 This is the argument in *Every Young Woman's Battle* and the more recent texts, Jackie Hill Perry, *Gay Girl Good God: The Story of Who I Was and Who God Has Always Been* (B&H Publishing Group, 2018); and Rachel Joy Welcher, *Talking Back to Purity Culture: Rediscovering Faithful Christian Sexuality* (Intervarsity Press, 2020). For a critique of this shift in purity culture rhetoric, see Lauren D. Sawyer and Victoria Houser, "Purity Culture and the Limits of Queer Evangelicalism," *Theology & Sexuality* 29, no. 2–3 (2024): 200–218, https://doi.org/10.1080/13558358.2024.2332982.

40 Dannah Gresh, *And the Bride Wore White*, 159.

41 Gresh, *And the Bride Wore White*, 27. See also Hayley DiMarco, *Technical Virgin: How Far Is Too Far?* (Revell, 2006), 44.

42 Marvin M. Ellison, *Making Love Just: Sexual Ethics for Perplexing Times* (Fortress Press, 2012), 25.

43 See Jane Dailey, *White Fright: The Sexual Panic at the Heart of America's Racist History* (Basic Books, 2020); and Peter Goodwin Heltzel, *Jesus and Justice: Evangelicals, Race, and American Politics* (Yale University Press, 2009).

44 "If you don't intend to marry him, don't date him" (Gresh, *And the Bride Wore White*, 70).

45 Ethridge and Arterburn differentiate between virginity (holistic purity) and "physical virginity" (*Every Young Woman's Battle*, 97). DiMarco writes of "technical virginity," those who do not have intercourse but have other sexual experiences, like oral sex or mutual masturbation (DiMarco, *Technical Virgin*, 16). In the contemporary purity culture, one can attain "secondary virginity" by recommitting themselves to a life of purity (Mark D. Regnerus, *Forbidden Fruit: Sex & Religion in the Lives of American Teenagers* [Oxford University Press, 2009], 102).

46 Gresh, *And the Bride Wore White*, 160.

47 "Courting" as a Christian alternative to dating was popularized by the book *I Kissed Dating Goodbye* (Joshua Harris, *I Kissed Dating Goodbye: A New Attitude Toward Dating and Relationships* [Multnomah, 1997]). Harris has since renounced this teaching for the harm it caused many young women. See chapter 6.

48 Stevi Jackson and Sue Scott, "A Sociological History of Researching Childhood and Sexuality: Continuities and Discontinuities," in *Children, Sexuality, and Sexualization*, eds. Emma Renold et al. (Palgrave Macmillan, 2015), 50.

49 Zierman writes some of her memoir in second person, perhaps in an attempt to distance herself from beliefs she no longer holds as an adult (Addie Zierman, *When We Were on Fire: A Memoir of Consuming Faith, Tangled Love and Starting Over* [Convergent Books, 2013], 77).

50 Zierman, *When We Were on Fire*, 46.
51 Zierman, *When We Were on Fire*, 58.
52 Zierman, *When We Were on Fire*, 91.
53 Zierman, *When We Were on Fire*, 100–101.
54 Zierman, *When We Were on Fire*, 102.
55 Zierman, *When We Were on Fire*, 46, 42; see also Brandon Wallace, *Straight Face* (Green Bridge Press, 2014), 53.
56 Gresh, *And the Bride Wore White*, 179.
57 Davies, *On Her Knees*, 59.
58 Davies, *On Her Knees*, 90.
59 Klein, *Pure*, 139.
60 Quote from Dyer, *The Queer Aesthetics of Childhood*, 7.
61 See "Sex, Marriage, and Salvation" in Amy DeRogatis, *Saving Sex: Sexuality and Salvation in American Evangelicalism* (Oxford University Press, 2014), 42–70.
62 Klein writes of a half-kiss: "One person might use it to refer to a peck or an otherwise short kiss, another to a kiss that she turned away from, etc. For many, the intention is to keep at least as many purity points as she deserves by not claiming a whole kiss when, for whatever reason, it didn't really feel whole" (*Pure*, 13).
63 Klein, *Pure*, 13.
64 Ethridge and Arterburn, *Every Young Woman's Battle*, 37.
65 Mark Jordan—along with Biblical scholars like David Wheeler-Reed, Jennifer W. Knust, and Dale B. Martin—writes that Paul or Pseudo-Paul does not necessarily use *porneia* to "refer to specific acts or cases." In fact, "Pauline texts may be using *porneia* metaphorically or symbolically, not intending to refer to specific sexual acts at all" (Jordan, *The Ethics of Sex*, 27–28). See David Wheeler-Reed et al., "Can a Man Commit πορνεία with His Wife?" *JBL* 137, no. 2 (2018): 383–398, http://dx.doi.org/10.15699/jbl.
66 Note that all of these books were written specifically to cisgender teen girls.
67 Gresh, *And the Bride Wore White*, 27.
68 Gresh, *And the Bride Wore White*, 99, 87, 101.
69 DiMarco, *Sexy Girls*, 35. DiMarco uses the tragic story of JonBenét Ramsey, the child beauty queen who was murdered in the 1990s, as a cautionary tale for wearing too much makeup: "In her pictures, [JonBenét] looked like a miniature adult—so much so that she turned on some grown men, who created shrines to her and watched every pageant she was in. What mothers and young girls alike don't understand is that too much makeup too soon can make you look so much older that creepy old guys start getting really turned on" (DiMarco, *Sexy Girls*, 34).
70 DiMarco, *Sexy Girls*, 41.
71 DiMarco, *Technical Virgin*, 18–19.
72 DiMarco, *Technical Virgin*, 18–19. Rainbow circles or rainbow parties were "group oral sex parties in which each girl wears a different shade of lipstick, and each guy tries to emerge sporting every one of the various colors" (Tamar Lewin, "Are

These Parties for Real?," *New York Times*, June 30, 2005, www.nytimes.com). Rainbow parties have since been debunked as a moral/sex panic propagated by Oprah Winfrey, among others, in the early 2000s.

73 DiMarco, *Technical Virgin*, 19, 48. Romantic comedies are "female porn" because they are thought to stimulate a woman's romantic desires the way pornography stimulates a man's physical desires.

74 DeMoss and Gresh, *Lies Young Women Believe*, 91.

75 Ethridge and Arterburn, *Every Young Woman's Battle*, 38, 62, 116.

76 See Christine J. Gardner, *Making Chastity Sexy: The Rhetoric of Evangelical Abstinence Campaigns* (University of California Press, 2011).

77 Quoted in Gardner, *Making Chastity Sexy*, 30.

78 Gardner, *Making Chastity Sexy*, 31.

79 DiMarco, *Technical Virgin*, 26–32.

80 DiMarco, *Technical Virgin*, 31.

81 In 2024, the phrase "100%," or "100% white," was added to the American Defamation League's database of hate symbols. The American Defamation League, "100%," 2024, www.adl.org.

82 DiMarco, *Technical Virgin*, 31.

83 See Elizabeth Gish, "'Are You a "Trashable" Styrofoam Cup?' Harm and Damage Rhetoric in the Contemporary American Sexual Purity Movement," *Journal of Feminist Studies in Religion* 34, no. 2 (2018): 5–22, https://doi.org/10.2979/jfemistudreli.34.2.03.

84 Klein, *Pure*, 7.

85 Klein, *Pure*, 195.

86 A similar conversation proliferated in the early 2020s regarding "soaking," the apparently widespread practice among conservative Mormons: "Soaking is when someone inserts their penis into their partner's vagina without thrusting, 'marinating' the penis in vaginal fluid without creating any friction." The practice served as a "loophole," a way for Mormon singles to claim technical virginity (Gita Jackson, "Viral 'Jump Humping' TikTok Teaches the World About Mormon Sex," *Vice*, September 27, 2021, www.vice.com). The practice was met with ridicule and pity on social media, as the preceding article shows. See chapter 6 for a fuller analysis of soaking.

87 [Jack] Halberstam, *The Queer Art of Failure* (Duke University Press, 2011), 119.

88 Klein, *Pure*, 195.

89 Klein, *Pure*, 195.

90 Klein, *Pure*, 125.

91 Interestingly, in his book *Preparing for Adolescence*, Focus on the Family's James Dobson does not condemn masturbation but deems it a gray area (James C. Dobson, *Preparing for Adolescence* [Vision House, 1978], 87, https://archive.org).

92 Klein, *Pure*, 125.

93 Wallace, *Straight Face*, 19.

94 John Eldredge, *Wild at Heart: Discovering the Secret of a Man's Soul*, rev. ed. (Nelson, 2010), 36.

95 Several recent books on evangelical gender roles have spotlighted just how pervasive and damaging this norm is, for men, women, and nonbinary folks alike. See, for instance, Kristen Kobes Du Mez, *Jesus and John Wayne* (Liveright Publishing, 2020); and Beth Allison Barr, *The Making of Biblical Womanhood* (Brazos, 2021). Older texts on the subject include John P. Bartkowski, *Remaking the Godly Marriage: Gender Negotiation in Evangelical Families* (Rutgers University Press, 2001); and DeRogatis, "Sex, Marriage, and Salvation," *Saving Sex*, 42–70.

96 Eldredge borrowed this idea from twentieth-century Christian apologist C. S. Lewis (Mary Stewart Van Leeuwen, *A Sword Between the Sexes? C. S. Lewis and the Gender Debates* [Brazos Press, 2010], 61). Lewis imagines a nonhuman species as gendered masculine and feminine, though they do not have human sexual anatomy. See C. S. Lewis, *Perelandra: A Novel* (Scribner, 2003 [1944]).

97 Augustine, *The City of God*, Book XIV, trans. William Babcock, in *The Works of Saint Augustine: A Translation for the 21st Century*, I/7, 98–137 (New City Press, 2013).

98 Simon Blackburn, *Lust: The Seven Deadly Sins* (Oxford University Press, 2004), 58. Augustine was critical of one's motivation for having sex as well. In his anti-Manichaean treatise, "On Continence," written in 412, Augustine calls it "strange continence!" that this heretical sect would abstain from sex out of hatred for the body (Augustine, "On Continence," cited in Elizabeth A. Clark, *St. Augustine on Marriage and Sexuality* [The Catholic University of America Press, 1996], 36). In *The City of God*, he similarly calls it a sin to only abstain from something God prohibits in fear of punishment (Book XIV).

99 Augustine, *The City of God*, Book XIII, 68–97. See also Rosemary Radford Ruether, "Augustine: Sexuality, Gender, and Women," in *Feminist Interpretations of Augustine*, ed. Judith Chelius Stark (The Pennsylvania State University Press, 2007), 56–57.

100 Ruether, "Augustine," 54.

101 Ruether, "Augustine," 56. Augustine writes that in paradise, humans will be able to control their bodily members via the will. That is, a man can have an erection when he wants to (to procreate) but will not have an erection when he doesn't want to (when aroused). See Augustine, *The City of God*, Book XXII, 536.

102 Ruether, "Augustine," 56.

103 Ethridge and Arterburn, *Every Young Woman's Battle*, 28.

104 Ethridge and Arterburn, *Every Young Woman's Battle*, 31. Gresh writes something similar as well: "While guys often struggle with visual temptation, I find that most of the time you and I are more prone to simple, emotional fantasy" (*And the Bride Wore White*, 64).

105 Ethridge and Arterburn, *Every Young Woman's Battle*, 48.

106 DiMarco, *Technical Virgin*, 59.

107 Ethridge and Arterburn, *Every Young Woman's Battle*, 32.

108 Daniel Oberhaus, "The Biggest-Ever Orgasm Study Tells Us More About How Women Come," *Vice*, September 6, 2017, www.vice.com.

109 "A woman must not wear men's clothing, nor a man wear women's clothing, for the Lord your God detests anyone who does this" (Deuteronomy 22:5, New International Version).

110 DiMarco, *Sexy Girls*, 52.

111 Ethridge and Arterburn, *Every Young Woman's Battle*, 233.

112 Ethridge and Arterburn, *Every Young Woman's Battle*, 234.

113 Ethridge and Arterburn, *Every Young Woman's Battle*, 234–235. In 2012, the then-president of Exodus International, Alan Chambers, denounced conversion therapy at the heels of California's statewide ban of conversion therapy. See Ed Payne, "Group Apologizes to Gay Community, Shuts Down 'Cure' Ministry," *CNN*, July 8, 2013, www.cnn.com.

114 Wallace, *Straight Face*, 18.

115 Wallace, *Straight Face*, 36.

116 Garrard Conley, "Land of Plenty" in *Empty the Pews: Stories of Leaving the Church*, eds. Chrissy Stroop and Lauren O'Neal (Epiphany Publishing, 2019), 35.

117 Katie Cross, "'I Have the Power in My Body to Make People Sin': The Trauma of Purity Culture and the Concept of 'Body Theodicy,'" in *Feminist Trauma Theologies: Body, Scripture & Church in Critical Perspective*, eds. Karen O'Donnell and Katie Cross (SCM Press, 2020), 28.

118 Cross, "'I Have the Power in My Body,'" 28.

119 Cross, "'I Have the Power in My Body,'" 29.

120 This is a reference to Matthew 18:6, NIV: "If anyone causes one of these little ones—those who believe in me—to stumble, it would be better for them to have a large millstone hung around their neck and to be drowned in the depths of the sea." Klein and others point out that this verse is frequently used to shame women for "causing" young men to lust or force their bodies on young women (*Pure*, 3–4). Perhaps a better verse to use, writes Klein, is Matthew 5:29, NIV. "If your right eye causes you to stumble, gouge it out and throw it away. It is better for you to lose one part of your body than for your whole body to be thrown into hell."

121 DiMarco, *Technical Virgin*, 20.

122 DiMarco, *Sexy Girls*, 63.

123 Gresh, *And the Bride Wore White*, 63.

124 I credit this pithy phrase to Chelle Stearns.

125 According to Marlene Winell, "Religious Trauma Syndrome is the condition experienced by people who are struggling with leaving an authoritarian, dogmatic religion and coping with the damage of indoctrination" (Marlene Winell, "Religious Trauma Syndrome," *Cognitive Behavioural Therapy Today*, 39 no. 2 [May 2011]: 17).

126 Cross defines body theodicy as post-traumatic stress disorder unique to purity culture, when "a piece of theology . . . becomes trapped in the body" ("'I Have the Power in My Body,'" 27).

127 Tina Schermer Sellers, *Sex, God, and the Conservative Church: Erasing Shame from Sexual Intimacy* (Routledge, 2017).

128 See Heather Hendershot, "Virgins for Jesus: The Gender Politics of Therapeutic Christian Media," in *Shaking the World for Jesus* (University of Chicago Press, 2004), 87–113. Note that this language was used to describe Black male sexuality as a whole and was used to justify their lynching in the early twentieth century.

129 DiMarco, *Sexy Girls*, 21.

130 Hendershot, "Virgins for Jesus," 93.

131 Jules Woodson, "I Was Assaulted. He Was Applauded." New York Times Opinion, *New York Times*, March 9, 2018, www.nytimes.com.

132 Kristen Leslie calls this the "Myth of the Virgin Mary Survivor," as no woman is a "perfect" victim of abuse (Kristen Leslie, *When Violence Is No Stranger: Pastoral Counseling with Survivors of Acquaintance Rape* [Fortress Press, 2003], 107).

133 See Emily Joy Allison, *#ChurchToo: How Purity Culture Upholds Abuse and How to Find Healing* (Broadleaf Books, 2021); Joanne Carlson Brown and Carol R. Bohn, *Christianity, Patriarchy, and Abuse: A Feminist Critique* (Pilgrim Press, 1989); Marie M. Fortune, *Sexual Violence: The Unmentionable Sin* (The Pilgrim Press, 1983); Kathleen G. Greider et al., "Three Decades of Women Writing for Our Lives," in *Feminist & Womanist Pastoral Theology*, eds. Bonnie Miller-McLemore and Brita L. Gill-Austern (Abingdon Press, 1999); Beverly Mayne Kienzle and Nancy Nienhuis, "Battered Women and the Construction of Sanctity," *Journal of Feminist Studies in Religion* 17, no. 1 (2001): 33–61, www.jstor.org/stable/25002401; Nancy Nason-Clark and Barbara Fisher-Townsend, "Acting Abusively in the Household of Faith," in *Responding to Abuse in Christian Homes*, eds. Nancy Nason-Clark and Barbara Fisher-Townsend (Wipf & Stock, 2011); Christie Cozad Nueger and James Newton Poling, *Men's Work in Preventing Violence Against Women* (Haworth Press, 2002).

134 See Rachel Joy Welcher's book *Talking Back to Purity Culture*, which offers some important critique of purity culture as rape culture while still upholding some of its salient norms, like heteronormativity. See Rachel Joy Welcher, *Talking Back to Purity Culture: Rediscovering Faithful Christian Sexuality* (Intervarsity Press, 2020).

135 See Traci C. West, *Wounds of the Spirit: Black Women, Violence, and Resistance Ethics* (New York University Press, 1999).

136 Ethridge and Arterburn, *Every Young Woman's Battle*, 90.

137 Ethridge and Arterburn, *Every Young Woman's Battle*, 91.

138 Cross, "'I Have the Power in My Body,'" 31.

139 Gresh, *And the Bride Wore White*, 87.

140 DiMarco, *Technical Virgin*, 22.

141 Welcher, *Talking Back to Purity Culture* 103.

142 Cross, "'I Have the Power in My Body,'" 30.

143 Cross, "'I Have the Power in My Body,'" 31.

144 Natalie Ames and Leslie F. Ware, "Latino Protestants: Religion, Culture, and Violence Against Women," in *Religion and Men's Violence Against Women*, ed. Andy J. Johnson (Springer, 2015), 152–153.

145 Psychologist Pete Walker is credited with his addition of the fourth "F," fawn. Those with this physiological response "seek safety by merging with the wishes, needs and demands of others. They act as if they believe that the price of admission to any relationship is the forfeiture of all their needs, rights, preferences and boundaries" (Pete Walker, *Complex PTSD: From Surviving to Thriving* [Azure Coyote Publishing, 2013], 122–123).

146 Hannah Brashers, "How an Evangelical Dating Guide and Purity Culture Gave Me an Anxiety Disorder," *HuffPost*, February 19, 2019, www.huffpost.com.

147 Pamela Cooper-White, *The Cry of Tamar: Violence Against Women and the Church's Response*, 2nd ed. (Fortress Press, 2012), 21.

148 Rebekah Matthews, "A Softer Answer," in *Empty the Pews: Stories of Leaving the Church*, eds. Chrissy Stroop and Lauren O'Neal (Epiphany Publishing, 2019), 67.

149 Matthews, "A Softer Answer," 65.

150 Matthews, "A Softer Answer," 67.

CHAPTER 6. TOWARD A POST-PURITY SEXUAL ETHIC

1 Lyz Lenz, "Lip Gloss, Joshua Harris, and the Woman I Was Supposed to Be," *The Toast*, December 16, 2013, https://the-toast.net.

2 Lenz, "Lip Gloss."

3 Lenz, "Lip Gloss."

4 Lenz, "Lip Gloss."

5 Lenz, "Lip Gloss."

6 See chap. 1, "The Divine Institution and the Segregated Church," in Bjork-James, *The Divine Institution: White Evangelicalism's Politics of the Family* (Rutgers University Press, 2021), 24–43.

7 Lenz, "Lip Gloss."

8 Harris is biracial but passes as white. Harris did not talk about his racial identity as a biracial man until much later in life.

9 Ruth Graham quoted in Sarah McCammon, "Evangelical Writer Who Influenced Purity Culture Announces Separation from Wife," NPR, *All Things Considered*, July 21, 2019, www.npr.org.

10 Joshua Harris, "A Statement on *I Kissed Dating Goodbye*," JoshHarris.com, July 11, 2023, https://joshharris.com.

11 McCammon, "Evangelical Writer."

12 Joshua Harris, "Reframe Your Story," Josh Harris: Reframe Your Story, 2021, https://web.archive.org.

13 For example, Jamie Lee Finch (@JamieLeeFinch), Twitter (now X), August 13, 2021, https://twitter.com/jamieleefinch/status/1426208616290390021.

14 On Twitter, @OnTheOtherHanna writes, "Books are still influencing young Christians, change of heart or not. He is still actively doing damage to Christian

youth" (Hannah Nurrieum [@OnTheOtherHanna], Twitter [now X], July 27, 2019, https://twitter.com/OnTheOtherHanna/status/1155128207487774721). Blogger Corbyjane writes, "Joshua Harris has asked for our forgiveness, and I for one do not give it. [. . .] I hope he *is* sorry. I hope he sits in the realization of the irreparable harm he caused to at least two generations" (Corbyjane Troya, "This Is Not About You: The Joshua Harris Redemption Tour," Medium, August 4, 2019, www.medium.com). Others are more sympathetic, noting that Harris was so young when he was platformed. He was just twenty-two, and single, when he wrote this best-selling book. Writing for a watchdog blog for evangelicalism, Todd Wilhelm speaks of Harris with so much understanding: "I'd venture that most of us look back at experiences in our lives and wish we could go back in time and do things differently" (Todd Wilhelm, "Joshua Harris—The Only Constant in Life Is Change," *The Wartburg Watch*, September 29, 2023, https://thewartburgwatch.com).

15 Cristina L. H. Traina, "Children and Moral Agency," *Journal of the Society of Christian Ethics*, 29, no. 2 (2009): 24.

16 Kate Ott, *Christian Ethics for a Digital Society* (Rowman and Littlefield, 2019), 14.

17 Katelyn Beaty, "Commentary: When the Sexual Prosperity Gospel Doesn't Pan Out," *The Salt Lake Tribune*, July 29, 2019, www.sltrib.com.

18 Julian B. Carter, *The Heart of Whiteness: Normal Sexuality and Race in America, 1880–1940* (Duke University Press, 2007), 31.

19 Carter, *The Heart of Whiteness*, 5.

20 Carter, *The Heart of Whiteness*, 27.

21 Carter, *The Heart of Whiteness*, 9.

22 See Debra Van Ausdale and Joe R. Feagin, *The First R: How Children Learn Race and Racism* (Rowan and Littlefield, 2011).

23 Lawrence A. Hirschfeld, "Children's Developing Conceptions of Race," *Handbook of Race, Racism, and the Developing Child*, eds. Stephen M. Quintana and Clark McKown (John Wiley & Sons, Inc., 2008), 39.

24 Margaret A. Hagerman, *White Kids: Growing Up with Privilege in a Racially Divided America* (New York University Press, 2018), 22.

25 Lorraine Delia Kenny, *Daughters of Suburbia: Growing Up White, Middle Class, and Female* (Rutgers University Press, 2000), 1.

26 Kenny, *Daughters of Suburbia*, 3.

27 See Resmaa Menakem, *My Grandmother's Hands: Racialized Trauma and Pathways to Mending Our Hearts and Bodies* (Central Recovery Press, 2017).

28 Cited in Kenny, *Daughters of Suburbia*, 5.

29 Kenny, *Daughters of Suburbia*, 12, 14.

30 See Kenny's chapter "Justify My Love: The Heterosexuality of Teenage Girlhood," *Daughters of Suburbia*, 78–99.

31 See Kenny's chapter "I Was a Teenage White Supremacist," *Daughters of Suburbia*, 136–166.

32 Kenny, *Daughters of Suburbia*, 137–139.

33 White evangelicals' love of taking photos with Black and Brown children on mission trips is well documented. See Stephanie Drury, "Taking Pictures with Poor Foreign Children During Missions Trips," *Stuff Christian Culture Likes* (blog), March 28, 2011, www.stuffchristianculturelikes.com.

34 Kenny, *Daughters of Suburbia*, 9–10.

35 Hagerman, *White Kids*, 17.

36 Hagerman, *White Kids*, 18.

37 About half of all white women voters, of any religious tradition, voted for Trump in 2016 as well. See Pew Research Center, "An Examination of the 2016 Electorate, Based on Validated Voters," August 9, 2018, www.pewresearch.org.

38 Chrissy Stroop and Lauren O'Neal, "Introduction," in *Empty the Pews: Stories of Leaving the Church*, eds. Chrissy Stroop and Lauren O'Neal (Epiphany Publishing, 2019), xxii.

39 Mihee Kim-Kort, *Outside the Lines: How Embracing Queerness Will Transform Your Faith* (Fortress, 2018), 150.

40 See Gabriel Sherman, "Inside Jerry Falwell Jr.'s Unlikely Rise and Precipitous Fall at Liberty University," *Vanity Fair*, January 24, 2022, www.vanityfair.com.

41 See Sarah Posner, "How the Christian Right Helped Foment Insurrection," *Rolling Stone*, January 31, 2021, www.rollingstone.com.

42 Lisa Tessman, *Burdened Virtues: Virtue Ethics for Liberatory Struggles* (Oxford University Press, 2005), 5.

43 Brandon Wallace, *Straight Face* (Green Bridge Press, 2014).

44 Here I'm borrowing language from John Wall, *Ethics in Light of Childhood* (Georgetown University Press, 2010), 72.

45 Cited in Katie Cross, "'I Have the Power in My Body to Make People Sin': The Trauma of Purity Culture and the Concept of 'Body Theodicy,'" in *Feminist Trauma Theologies: Body, Scripture & Church in Critical Perspective*, eds. Karen O'Donnell and Katie Cross (SCM Press, 2020), 30–32.

46 Cross, "'I Have the Power in My Body,'" 31.

47 Tessman, *Burdened Virtues*, 23.

48 See Kate Ott, "Orgasmic Failure: A Praxis Ethic for Adolescent Sexuality," in *Theologies of Failure*, eds. Roberto Sirvent and Duncan B. Reyburn (Cascade Books, 2019); see also Kate Ott and Lauren D. Sawyer, "Sexual Practices and Relationships Among Young People," in *The Routledge Handbook of Philosophy of Sex and Sexuality*, eds. Brian D. Earp et al. (Routledge, 2022).

49 [Jack] Halberstam, *The Queer Art of Failure* (Duke University Press, 2011), 3.

50 See Gita Jackson, "Viral 'Jump Humping' TikTok Teaches the World About Mormon Sex," *Vice*, September 27, 2021, www.vice.com.

51 See, for example, "Imitation Sex and the New Middle-Class Morality" in Mark D. Regnerus, *Forbidden Fruit: Sex & Religion in the Lives of American Teenagers* (Oxford University Press, 2009), 163–182.

52 Linda Kay Klein, *Pure: Inside the Evangelical Movement that Shamed a Generation of Young Women and How I Broke Free* (Touchstone, 2018), 125.

53 Daniel M. Lavery, *Something That May Shock and Discredit You* (Simon & Schuster, 2020).

54 And, perhaps, teach about other forms of contraceptives and prophylactics like intrauterine devices, diaphragms, dental dams, sponges, patches, and so forth.

55 Marvin M. Ellison, *Making Love Just: Sexual Ethics for Perplexing Times* (Fortress Press, 2012), 162.

56 See Ellison, *Making Love Just*; Kate Ott, "Re-Thinking Adolescent Sexual Ethics: A Social Justice Obligation to Adolescent Sexual Health," *Journal of Lutheran Ethics* 7, no. 2 (2007); Kate Ott, *Sex, Tech & Faith: Ethics for a Digital Age* (Wm. B. Eerdmans, 2022); Kate Ott and Lorien Carter, "ReVisioning Sexuality: Relational Joy and Embodied Flourishing," *Journal of Youth and Theology* 20, no. 1 (March 2021): 1–19, https://doi.org/10.1163/24055093-02001002; Karen Peterson-Iyer, *Reenvisioning Sexual Ethics: A Feminist Christian Account* (Georgetown University Press, 2022); and Margaret A. Farley, *Just Love: A Framework for Christian Sexual Ethics* (Continuum, 2006).

57 Tessman, *Burdened Virtues*, 23.

CONCLUSION

1 Lyz Lenz, "Lip Gloss, Joshua Harris, and the Woman I Was Supposed to Be," *The Toast*, December 16, 2013, https://the-toast.net.

2 From Lorraine Delia Kenny, *Daughters of Suburbia: Growing Up White, Middle Class, and Female* (Rutgers University Press, 2000), 137–138.

3 Hannah Dyer, *The Queer Aesthetics of Childhood: Asymmetries of Innocence and the Cultural Politics of Child Development* (Rutgers University Press, 2020), 16.

4 Dietrich Bonhoeffer, *The Cost of Discipleship* (Touchstone, 1959), 43.

5 See Sheila A. Redmond, "Christian 'Virtues' and Recovery from Child Sexual Abuse," in *Christianity, Patriarchy, and Abuse: A Feminist Critique*, eds. Joanne Carlson Brown and Carol R. Bohn (Pilgrim Press, 1989), 70–88; and Margaret Arms, "When Forgiveness Is Not the Issue in Forgiveness: Religious Complicity in Abuse and Privatized Forgiveness," in *Forgiveness and Abuse: Jewish and Christian Reflections*, eds. Marie M. Fortune and Joretta Marshall (Haworth Pastoral Press, 2003).

6 Michael P. Jaycox, "Payback, Forgiveness, Accountability: Exercising Responsible Agency in the Midst of Structured Racial Harm," *Religions* 10 (2019): 2.

7 For a history of how the language of "cancellation" was appropriated from Black culture, see Clyde McGrady, "The Strange Journey of 'Cancel,' from a Black-Culture Punchline to a White-Grievance Watchword," *Washington Post*, April 2, 2021, www.washingtonpost.com.

8 Tema Okun, "White Supremacy Culture Characteristics," White Supremacy Culture, updated August 2023, www.whitesupremacyculture.info.

9 Mia Mingus, "Dreaming Accountability," *Leaving Evidence* (blog), May 5, 2019, https://leavingevidence.wordpress.com.

10 Mingus, "Dreaming Accountability."

11 Arms, "When Forgiveness Is Not the Issue," 111.

BIBLIOGRAPHY

Abraham, Devi. "It's Back: Purity Culture 2.0, Gen Z Style." *Religious News Service*. December 2, 2021. https://religionnews.com.

Allison, Emily Joy. *#ChurchToo: How Purity Culture Upholds Abuse and How to Find Healing*. Broadleaf Books, 2021.

The American Defamation League. "100%." 2024. www.adl.org.

Ames, Natalie, and Leslie F. Ware. "Latino Protestants: Religion, Culture, and Violence Against Women." In *Religion and Men's Violence Against Women*, edited by Andy J. Johnson. Springer, 2015.

Andrews, Becca. "Sins of Submission." *Mother Jones*. July 26, 2018. www.motherjones.com.

And Sons Magazine. 2023. www.andsonsmagazine.com.

Angelides, Steven. *The Fear of Child Sexuality: Young People, Sex, and Agency*. University of Chicago Press, 2019.

Arms, Margaret. "When Forgiveness Is Not the Issue in Forgiveness: Religious Complicity in Abuse and Privatized Forgiveness." In *Forgiveness and Abuse: Jewish and Christian Reflections*, edited by Marie M. Fortune and Joretta Marshall. Pastoral Press, 2003.

Arterburn, Stephen, and Fred Stoeker. *Every Man's Battle: Winning the War on Sexual Temptation One Victory at a Time*. WaterBrook Press, 2000.

Arterburn, Stephen, and Fred Stoeker. *Every Young Man's Battle: Strategies for Victory in the Real World of Sexual Temptation*. WaterBrook Press, 2002.

Associated Press. "Texas Pushes Some Textbook Publishers to Remove Material on Fossil Fuels." NPR. November 18, 2023. www.npr.org.

Augustine. *St. Augustine Confessions*. Oxford World's Classics. Oxford University Press, 1998.

Augustine. *The Works of Saint Augustine: A Translation for the 21st Century*. Translated by William Babcock. New City Press, 2013.

Ballinger, Jenna (@jennaforeverawkward). "Miss you man #richmullins #religious-trauma." TikTok. July 1, 2024. www.tiktok.com.

Balmer, Randall. *Mine Eyes Have Seen the Glory: A Journey into the Evangelical Subculture in America*. 4th ed. Oxford University Press, 2006.

Barber, Matt, and Brittany Machado. *Give Me Sex Jesus*. 2015. Vimeo. https://vimeo.com.

BarlowGirl. "Average Girl." Recorded February 2004. Track 10 on *BarlowGirl*. Fervent Records, compact disc.

Barr, Beth Allison. *The Making of Biblical Womanhood*. Brazos, 2021.

Bartel, Blaine. *Every Teenager's Little Black Book on Sex and Dating*. Harrison House, 2002.

Bartkowski, John P. *Remaking the Godly Marriage: Gender Negotiation in Evangelical Families*. Rutgers University Press, 2001.

Beaty, Katelyn. "Commentary: When the Sexual Prosperity Gospel Doesn't Pan Out." *The Salt Lake Tribune*. July 29, 2019. www.sltrib.com.

Bederman, Gail. *Manliness and Civilization: A Cultural History of Gender and Race in the United States, 1880–1917*. University of Chicago Press, 1996.

Bederman, Gail. "'The Women Have Had Charge of the Church Work Long Enough': The Men and Religion Forward Movement of 1911–1912 and the Masculinization of Middle-Class Protestantism." In *A Mighty Baptism: Race, Gender, and the Creation of American Protestantism*, edited by Susan Juster and Lisa MacFarlane. Cornell University Press, 1997.

Bendroth, Margaret Lamberts. *Fundamentalism & Gender, 1875 to the Present*. Yale University Press, 1993.

Bernstein, Robin. *Racial Innocence: Performing Childhood and Race from Slavery to Civil Rights*. New York University Press, 2011.

Bjork-James, Sophie. *The Divine Institution: White Evangelicalism's Politics of the Family*. Rutgers University Press, 2021.

Blackburn, Simon. *Lust: The Seven Deadly Sins*. Oxford University Press, 2004.

Blodgett, Barbara. *Constructing the Erotic: Sexual Ethics and Adolescent Girls*. Pilgrim Press, 2002.

Blum, Edward J. *Reforging the White Republic: Race, Religion, and American Nationalism 1865–1898*. Louisiana State University Press, 2005.

Blyth, Caroline. *Rape Culture, Purity Culture, and Coercive Control in Teen Girl Bibles*. Routledge, 2021.

Boag, Peter. *Re-Dressing America's Frontier Past*. University of California Press, 2011.

Bolz-Weber, Nadia. *Shameless: A Sexual Reformation*. Convergent, 2019.

Bonhoeffer, Dietrich. *The Cost of Discipleship*. Touchstone, 1959.

Brashers, Hannah. "How an Evangelical Dating Guide and Purity Culture Gave Me an Anxiety Disorder." *HuffPost*. February 19, 2019. www.huffpost.com.

Brekus, Catherine A. "Children of Wrath, Children of Grace: Jonathan Edwards and the Puritan Culture of Child Rearing." In *The Child in Christian Thought*, edited by Marcia J. Bunge. William B. Eerdmans, 2001.

Brown, Joanne Carlson, and Carol R. Bohn, eds. *Christianity, Patriarchy, and Abuse: A Feminist Critique*. Pilgrim Press, 1989.

Browning, Melissa. "Epistemological Privilege and Collaborative Research: A Reflection on Researching as an Outsider." *Practical Matters* 6 (Spring 2013): 1–16.

Burrell, Kevin. "Slavery, the Hebrew Bible and the Development of Racial Theories in the Nineteenth Century." *Religions* 12, no. 9 (2021): 1–15. https://doi.org/10.3390/rel12090742.

Campbell, Robert L., and John Chambers Christopher. "Moral Development Theory: A Critique of Its Kantian Presuppositions." *Developmental Review* 16, no. 1 (1996): 1–47. https://doi.org/10.1006/drev.1996.0001.

Cannon, Katie G. *Black Womanist Ethics*. Wipf and Stock, 1988.

Cantorna, Amber. *Refocusing My Family: Coming Out, Being Cast Out, and Discovering the True Love of God*. Fortress Press, 2017.

Carter, Julian B. *The Heart of Whiteness: Normal Sexuality and Race in America, 1880–1940*. Duke University Press, 2007.

Centers for Disease Control and Prevention. "STDs in Adolescents and Young Adults." *Sexually Transmitted Disease Surveillance 2018*. Accessed July 23, 2021. www.cdc.gov.

Centers for Disease Control and Prevention. "Youth Risk Behavior Survey: Data Summary and Trends Report 2007–2017." Accessed February 22, 2025. www.cdc.gov/yrbs/dstr/pdf/trendsreport.pdf.

Chang, Heewon. *Autoethnography as Method*. Left Coast Books, 2008.

Chastain, Blake. "'Exvangelical'—A Working Definition." *#Exvangelical*. Podcast. March 2, 2019. https://exvangelicalpodcast.com.

Cills, Hazel. "The Rise and Fall of the Pop Star Purity Ring." *Jezebel*. January 25, 2018. https://jezebel.com.

Clapp, Steve, Kristen Leverton Helbert, and Angela Zizak. *Faith Matters: Teenagers, Religion, and Sexuality*. LifeQuest, 2003.

Clark, Elizabeth A. *St. Augustine on Marriage and Sexuality*. The Catholic University of America Press, 1996.

Cochran, Pamela H. *Evangelical Feminism: A History*. New York University Press, 2005.

Cone, James H. *The Cross and the Lynching Tree*. Orbis Books, 2017.

Conley, Garrard. "Land of Plenty." In *Empty the Pews: Stories of Leaving the Church*, edited by Chrissy Stroop and Lauren O'Neal. Epiphany Publishing, 2019.

Connelly, Mark Thomas. *The Response to Prostitution in the Progressive Era*. University of North Carolina Press, 1980.

Coontz, Stephanie. *The Way We Never Were: American Families and the Nostalgia Trap*. Basic Books, 1992.

Cooper, Brittney. *Eloquent Rage: A Black Feminist Discovers Her Superpower*. New York: St. Martin's Press, 2018.

Cooper, Brittney C., Susanna M. Morris, Robin M. Boylorn. *The Crunk Feminist Collection*. The Feminist Press, 2017.

Cooper-White, Pamela. *The Cry of Tamar: Violence Against Women and the Church's Response*. 2nd ed. Fortress Press, 2012.

Corinna, Heather, and Isabella Rotman. *Wait, What? A Comic Book Guide to Relationships, Bodies, and Growing Up*. Limerence Press, 2019.

Cross, Katie. "'I Have the Power in My Body to Make People Sin': The Trauma of Purity Culture and the Concept of 'Body Theodicy.'" In *Feminist Trauma Theologies: Body, Scripture & Church in Critical Perspective*, edited by Karen O'Donnell and Katie Cross. SCM Press, 2020.

CrunkAsHell. "Single, Saved, and Sexin': The Gospel of Gettin' Your Freak On." Crunk Feminist Collective. February 3, 2011. www.crunkfeministcollective.com.

Crut, Ligia. "I'm Taking Back My Body (The Female Body in the 'Purity' Culture)." *Linguaculture* 12, no. 1 (2021): 117–128. https://doi.org/10.47743/lincu-2021-1-0191.

Dailey, Jane. "Sex, Segregation, and the Sacred After *Brown*." *Journal of American History* 91, no. 1 (June 2004): 119–144.

Dailey, Jane. *White Fright: The Sexual Panic at the Heart of America's Racist History*. Basic Books, 2020.

Daillard, Cynthia. "Sex Education: Politicians, Parents, Teachers and Teens." *The Guttmacher Report on Public Policy*. The Guttmacher Institute. February 2001. www.guttmacher.org.

Davies, Brenda Marie. *On Her Knees: Memoir of a Prayerful Jezebel*. William B. Eerdmans Publishing Company, 2021.

D'Emilio, John, and Estelle B. Freedman. *Intimate Matters: A History of Sexuality in America*. Harper & Row, 1988 (2012).

DeMoss, Nancy Leigh, and Dannah Gresh. *Lies Young Women Believe*. Moody Publishers, 2008.

DeRogatis, Amy. *Saving Sex: Sexuality and Salvation in American Evangelicalism*. Oxford University Press, 2014.

DeVries, Mark, Susie Shellenberger, and Jay Strack, eds. *NIV True Love Waits Youth Bible*. Broadman & Holman Publishers, 1996.

DiMarco, Hayley. *Sexy Girls: How Hot Is Too Hot?* Revell, 2006.

DiMarco, Hayley. *Technical Virgin: How Far Is Too Far?* Revell, 2006.

Dobson, James C. *Preparing for Adolescence*. Vision House, 1978. https://archive.org.

Donovan, Brian. *White Slave Crusaders: Race, Gender, and Anti-Vice Activism, 1887–1917*. University of Illinois Press, 2006.

Douthat, Ross. "American Teens Are Really Miserable. Why?" *New York Times*. February 18, 2023. www.nytimes.com.

Dowland, Seth. *Family Values and the Rise of the Christian Right*. University of Pennsylvania, 2015.

Drury, Stephanie (@StuffCCLikes). Twitter (now X). May 2, 2020. https://twitter.com/StuffCCLikes/status/1256619533017604096.

Drury, Stephanie. "Taking Pictures with Poor Foreign Children During Missions Trips." *Stuff Christian Culture Likes* (blog). March 28, 2011. www.stuffchristianculturelikes.com.

Du Mez, Kristin Kobes. *Jesus and John Wayne: How White Evangelicals Corrupted a Faith and Fractured a Nation*. Liveright Publishing Company, 2020.

Duncan, Philip T. "Nurturing Voyeurism, Vibrant Sexism, and Violence: Why We Can't (Yet) Afford to Forget About *Wild at Heart*." *Priscilla Papers* 35, no. 1 (Winter 2017): 3–8.

Duska, Ronald, and Mariellen Whelan. *Moral Development: A Guide to Piaget and Kohlberg*. Paulist Press, 1975.

Dyer, Hannah. *The Queer Aesthetics of Childhood: Asymmetries of Innocence and the Cultural Politics of Child Development*. Rutgers University Press, 2020.

Egan, R. Danielle, and Gail Hawkes. "Imperiled and Perilous: Exploring the History of Childhood Sexuality." *Journal of Historical Sociology* 21, no. 4 (2008): 355–367. https://doi.org/10.1111/j.1467-6443.2008.00341.x.

Egan, R. Danielle, and Gail Hawkes. *Theorizing the Sexual Child in Modernity*. Palgrave MacMillan, 2010.

Ehrlich, J. Shoshanna. *Regulating Desire: From the Virtuous Maiden to the Purity Princess*. SUNY Press, 2014.

Eldredge, John. *Wild at Heart: Discovering the Secret of a Man's Soul*. Rev. ed. Nelson, 2010.

Eldredge, Samuel, and John Eldredge. *Killing Lions: A Guide Through the Trials Young Men Face*. HarperCollins, 2024.

Ellison, Marvin. *Making Love Just: Sexual Ethics for Perplexing Times*. Fortress Press, 2012.

Erikson, Erik. *Identity: Youth and Crisis*. W. W. Norton & Company, 1968.

Eskridge, Larry. *God's Forever Family: The Jesus People Movement in America*. Oxford University Press, 2013.

Ethridge, Shannon, and Stephen Arterburn. *Every Young Woman's Battle: Guarding Your Mind, Heart, and Body in a Sex-Saturated World*. Waterbrook Press, 2009.

Farley, Audrey Clare. "The Racist Roots of the Southern Baptist Convention's Sex Scandal 'Apocalypse.'" The Soapbox. *New Republic*. May 30, 2022. https://newrepublic.com.

Farley, Margaret A. *Just Love: A Framework for Christian Sexual Ethics*. Continuum, 2006.

Farley, Margaret A. "The Role of Experience in Moral Discernment." In *Christian Ethics: Problems and Prospects*, edited by Lisa Sowle Cahill and James F. Childress. The Pilgrim Press, 1996.

Finch, Jamie Lee (@JamieLeeFinch). Twitter (now X). August 13, 2021. https://twitter.com/jamieleefinch/status/1426208616290390021.

Finch, Jamie Lee. *You Are Your Own: A Reckoning with the Religious Trauma of Evangelical Christianity*. Published by the author, 2019.

Fortune, Marie M. *Sexual Violence: The Unmentionable Sin*. The Pilgrim Press, 1983.

Frankenberg, Ruth. *White Women, Race Matters: The Social Construction of Whiteness*. University of Minnesota Press, 1993.

Freitas, Donna. *Sex and the Soul: Juggling Sexuality, Spirituality, Romance, and Religion on America's College Campuses*. Oxford University Press, 2008.

Garcia, Raphael Tsavkko. "Evangelicals in Brazil Are Stronger Today Than Ever Before." *Aljazeera*. January 7, 2022. www.aljazeera.com.

Gardner, Christine J. *Making Chastity Sexy: The Rhetoric of Evangelical Abstinence Campaigns*. University of California Press, 2011.

Gary. "The Deep Drone of Unseen Cicadas: Gary's Story." *Homeschoolers Anonymous*. November 24, 2014. https://homeschoolersanonymous.wordpress.com.

Gasaway, Brantley W. *Progressive Evangelicals and the Pursuit of Social Justice*. North Carolina Press, 2014.

Gilkerson, Luke. "What Do Christian Guys Think About Modesty?" Covenant Eyes. July 27, 2021. www.covenanteyes.com.

Gilligan, Carol. *In a Different Voice: Psychological Theory and Women's Development*. Harvard University Press, 1993.

Gish, Elizabeth. "'Are You a "Trashable" Styrofoam Cup?' Harm and Damage Rhetoric in the Contemporary American Sexual Purity Movement." *Journal of Feminist Studies in Religion* 34, no. 2 (2018): 5–22. https://doi.org/10.2979/jfemistudreli.34.2.03.

Gish, Elizabeth. "Producing High Priests and Princesses: The Father-Daughter Relationship in the Christian Sexual Purity Movement." *Religions* 7, no. 3 (2016): 1–22. https://doi.org/10.3390/rel7030033.

Glosser, Asaph, Karen Gardiner, and Mike Fishman. "Statutory Rape: A Guide to State Laws and Reporting Requirements." Office of the Assistant Secretary for Planning and Evaluation. December 15, 2004. https://aspe.hhs.gov.

Gordon, Elana. "How Sex Education Changed Under the Obama Administration." Side Effects Public Media. January 23, 2017. www.sideeffectspublicmedia.org.

Greczyn, Alice. "The Photo: How a Girls' Getaway in Joshua Tree Became a Symbol of White Supremacy and Why I'm Not Here to Do Better." *Alice Greczyn*. November 15, 2021. www.alicegreczyn.com.

Greider, Kathleen G., Gloria A. Johnson, and Kristen J. Leslie. "Three Decades of Women Writing for Our Lives." In *Feminist & Womanist Pastoral Theology*, edited by Bonnie Miller-McLemore and Brita L. Gill-Austern. Abingdon Press, 1999.

Gresh, Dannah. *And the Bride Wore White: Seven Secrets to Sexual Purity*. Moody Publishers, 2012.

Griffith, R. Marie. *God's Daughters: Evangelical Women and the Power of Submission*. University of California Press, 2000.

Griffith, R. Marie. *Moral Combat: How Sex Divided American Christians and Fractured American Politics*. Basic Books, 2017.

Gross, Terry. "How the Southern Baptist Convention Covered Up Its Widespread Sexual Abuse Scandal." *Fresh Air*. NPR. June 2, 2022. www.npr.org.

Gubrium, Jaber F., and James A. Holstein, "Chapter 12: Narrative Ethnography." In *Handbook of Emerging Methods*, edited by Sharlene Nagy Hesse-Biber and Patricia Leavy. Guilford Press, 2008.

Gudorf, Christine E. *Body, Sex, and Pleasure: Reconstructing Christian Sexual Ethics*. Pilgrim Press, 1996.

Hagerman, Margaret A. *White Kids: Growing Up with Privilege in a Racially Divided America*. New York University Press, 2018.

Halberstam, [Jack]. *The Queer Art of Failure*. Duke University Press, 2011.

Hall, G. Stanley. *Adolescence*. Volume I. D. Appleton and Company, 1904.

Halperin, David M. *Saint Foucault: Toward a Gay Hagiography*. Oxford University Press, 1997.

Harding, Sandra. *Feminism & Method*. Indiana University Press, 1987.
Harris, Joshua. *I Kissed Dating Goodbye: A New Attitude Toward Dating and Relationships*. Multnomah, 1997.
Harris, Joshua. "Reframe Your Story." Josh Harris: Reframe Your Story. 2021. https://web.archive.org.
Harris, Joshua. "A Statement on *I Kissed Dating Goodbye*." JoshHarris.com. July 11, 2023. https://joshharris.com.
Hasinoff, Amy Adele. *Sexting Panic: Rethinking Criminalization, Privacy, and Consent*. University of Illinois Press, 2015.
Healy, Melissa. "Clinton Frees $250 Million for Sex Abstinence Teaching." *Los Angeles Times*. March 1, 1997. www.latimes.com.
Heltzel, Peter Goodwin. *Jesus and Justice: Evangelicals, Race, and American Politics*. Yale University Press, 2009.
Hendershot, Heather. *Shaking the World for Jesus: Media and Conservative Evangelical Culture*. University of Chicago Press, 2004.
Henry J. Kaiser Family Foundation. "Sexual Health of Adolescents and Young Adults in the United States." August 20, 2014. www.kff.org.
Hindmarsh, D. Bruce. *The Evangelical Conversion Narrative: Spiritual Autobiography in Early Modern England*. Oxford University Press, 2005.
Hirschfeld, Lawrence A. "Children's Developing Conceptions of Race." In *Handbook of Race, Racism, and the Developing Child*, edited by Stephen M. Quintana and Clark McKown. John Wiley & Sons, Inc., 2008.
Hobbes, Michael, and Sarah Marshall, hosts. "Sexting." *You're Wrong About*. Podcast. June 11, 2019.
Hodes, Martha. *White Women, Black Men: Illicit Sex in the Nineteenth Century South*. Yale University Press, 1997.
Hoffman, Jan. "A Girl's Nude Photo, and Altered Lives." *New York Times*. March 26, 2011. www.nytimes.com.
Houser, Victoria. "Crisis Pregnancy Centers: How Evangelical Purity Culture Funded Thousands of Anti-Abortion Clinics." *Canopy Forum*. July 8, 2022. https://canopyforum.org.
Howard, Vicki. "The Courtship Letters of an African-American Couple: Race, Gender, Class and the Cult of True Womanhood." *Southwestern Historical Quarterly* 100, no. 1 (July 1996): 64–80.
Human Rights Campaign. "2018 LGBTQ Youth Report." Accessed July 23, 2021. https://assets2.hrc.org.
Hunter, James Davison. *Culture Wars: The Struggle to Control the Family, Art, Education, Law, and Politics in America*. Basic Books, 1991.
"Indiana State Profile." State Profiles. SIECUS. October 24, 2023. https://siecus.org.
Jackson, Gita. "Viral 'Jump Humping' TikTok Teaches the World About Mormon Sex." *Vice*. September 27, 2021. www.vice.com.
Jackson, Stevi, and Sue Scott. "A Sociological History of Researching Childhood and Sexuality: Continuities and Discontinuities." In *Children, Sexuality, and*

Sexualization, edited by Emma Renold, Jessica Ringrose, and R. Danielle Egan. Palgrave Macmillan, 2015.

Janey the Small (@JaneyTheSmall). Twitter (now X). May 2, 2020. https://twitter.com/JaneyTheSmall/status/1256623141129818114.

Janssen, Diederik F. "Anthropologizing Young/Minor Sexualities." In *Children, Sexuality, and Sexualization*, edited by Emma Renold, Jessica Ringrose, and R. Danielle Egan. Palgrave Macmillan, 2015.

Jaycox, Michael P. "Payback, Forgiveness, Accountability: Exercising Responsible Agency in the Midst of Structured Racial Harm." *Religions* 10 (2019): 1–16.

Johnson, Meredith. "The Dangerous Consequences of Florida's 'Don't Say Gay' Bill on LGBTQ+ Youth in Florida." *Georgetown Journal of Gender and the Law* 23, no. 3 (2020). www.law.georgetown.edu.

Jordan, Mark D. *The Ethics of Sex*. Blackwell Publishing, 2002.

Kant, Immanuel. *Groundwork of the Metaphysics of Morals*. Translated and edited by Mary Gregor. Introduction by Christine M. Korsgaard. Cambridge University Press, 1997.

Kant, Immanuel. *Observations on the Beautiful and the Sublime*. Edited by John T. Goldthwait. University of California Press, 1960.

Kant, Immanuel. *On Education*. Translated by Annette Churton. Dover Publications, 2003.

Kant, Immanuel. *Race and the Enlightenment: A Reader*. Edited by Emmanuel Chukwudi Eze. Blackwell Publishing, 1997.

Kant, Immanuel. "What Is Enlightenment?" Translated by Mary C. Smith. Columbia University. Accessed July 9, 2021. www.columbia.edu.

Kauffman, Reginald Wright. *The House of Bondage*. Grosset & Dunlap Publishers, 1910. https://archive.org.

Kenny, Lorraine Delia. *Daughters of Suburbia: Growing Up White, Middle Class, and Female*. Rutgers University Press, 2000.

Kienzle, Beverly Mayne, and Nancy Nienhuis. "Battered Women and the Construction of Sanctity." *Journal of Feminist Studies in Religion* 17, no. 1 (2001): 33–61. www.jstor.org/stable/25002401.

Kim-Kort, Mihee. *Outside the Lines: How Embracing Queerness Will Transform Your Faith*. Fortress, 2018.

Kitch, Sally L. *The Specter of Sex: Gendered Foundations of Racial Formation in the United States*. SUNY Press, 2009.

Klein, Linda Kay. *Pure: Inside the Evangelical Movement That Shamed a Generation of Young Women and How I Broke Free*. Touchstone, 2018.

Kohlberg, Lawrence. *The Philosophy of Moral Development: Moral Stages and the Idea of Justice*. Essays on Moral Development Volume I. Harper & Row, 1981.

Kuruvilla, Carol. "Youth Ministry Accused of Deceiving Queer Teens with 'Bait and Switch.'" *HuffPost*. August 13, 2020. www.huffpost.com.

Lahr, Angela M. *Millennial Dreams and Apocalyptic Nightmares*. Oxford University Press, 2007.

Lamott, Anne. *Plan B: Further Thoughts on Faith*. Riverhead, 2004.
Lassiter, Matthew D. "Inventing Family Values." In *Rightward Bound*, edited by Bruce J. Schulman and Julian E. Zelizer. Harvard University Press, 2008.
Lavery, Daniel. "Brio Magazine-Related Branding Opportunities I've Missed." *The Chatner*. March 2, 2021. www.thechatner.com.
Lavery, Daniel. *Something That May Shock and Discredit You*. Simon & Schuster, 2020.
Lavietes, Matt. "Florida School Districts Removed Roughly 300 Books Last School Year." NBC News. September 12, 2023. www.nbcnews.com.
Leary, David E. "Immanuel Kant and the Development of Modern Psychology." *The Problematic Science: Psychology in Nineteenth-Century Thought*. Edited by William Ray Woodward and Mitchell G. Ash, 17–42. Praeger, 1982.
Lenz, Lyz. "Lip Gloss, Joshua Harris, and the Woman I Was Supposed to Be." *The Toast*. December 16, 2013. https://the-toast.net.
Leslie, Kristen. *When Violence Is No Stranger: Pastoral Counseling with Survivors of Acquaintance Rape*. Fortress Press, 2003.
Levander, Caroline. *Cradle of Liberty: Race, the Child, and National Belonging from Thomas Jefferson to W. E. B. Du Bois*. Duke University Press, 2006.
Lewin, Tamar. "Are These Parties for Real?" *New York Times*. June 30, 2005. www.nytimes.com.
Lewis, C. S. *Perelandra: A Novel*. Scribner, 2003 (1944).
Logan, James Samuel. "Immanuel Kant on Categorical Imperative." In *Beyond the Pale: Reading Ethics from the Margins*, edited by Stacey M. Floyd-Thomas and Miguel A. De La Torre. Westminster John Knox, 2011.
Lomax, Tamura. *Jezebel Unhinged: Loosing the Black Female Body in Religion and Culture*. Duke University Press, 2018.
Lookadoo, Justin, and Hayley DiMarco. *Dateable: Are You? Are They?* Hungry Planet, 2003.
Lorde, Audre. *Sister Outsider: Essays and Speeches*. Crossing Press, 1984.
Martinez, Gladys M., and Joyce C. Abma. "Sexual Activity, Contraceptive Use, and Childbearing of Teenagers Aged 15–19 in the United States." *National Center for Health Statistics NCHS Data Brief* no. 209 (2015): 1–8. www.cdc.gov.
Martínez, Jessica, and Gregory A. Smith. "How the Faithful Voted: A Preliminary 2016 Analysis." November 9, 2016. Pew Research Institute. www.pewresearch.org.
Matthews, Rebekah. "A Softer Answer." In *Empty the Pews: Stories of Leaving the Church*, edited by Chrissy Stroop and Lauren O'Neal. Epiphany Publishing, 2019.
May, Elaine Tyler. *Homeward Bound: American Families in the Cold War Era*. Basic Books, 1988.
McCammon, Sarah. "Evangelical Writer Who Influenced Purity Culture Announces Separation from Wife." NPR. *All Things Considered*. July 21, 2019. www.npr.org.
McCammon, Sarah. *The Exvangelicals: Loving, Living, and Leaving the White Evangelical Church*. St. Martin's Press, 2024.
McGowin, Emily Hunter. *Quivering Families: The Quiverfull Movement and Evangelical Theology of the Family*. Fortress Press, 2018.

McGrady, Clyde. "The Strange Journey of 'Cancel,' from a Black-Culture Punchline to a White-Grievance Watchword." *Washington Post*. April 2, 2021. www.washingtonpost.com.

McGrath, Jennifer. "Pure to Purpose Pipeline: Socializing Purity in White Women's International Aid Work." *Theology and Sexuality* 29, nos. 2–3 (2023): 130–147. https://doi.org/10.1080/13558358.2024.2332979.

Menakem, Resmaa. *My Grandmother's Hands: Racialized Trauma and Pathways to Mending Our Hearts and Bodies*. Central Recovery Press, 2017.

"#MeToo #ChurchToo." FaithTrust Institute. Accessed January 21, 2024. www.faithtrustinstitute.org.

Meyer, Ilan H., Bianca D. M. Wilson, and Kathryn O'Neill. "LGBTQ People in the US: Select Findings from the Generations and TransPop Studies." Williams Institute. UCLA School of Law. Accessed July 23, 2021. https://williamsinstitute.law.ucla.edu.

Mingus, Mia. "Dreaming Accountability." *Leaving Evidence* (blog). May 5, 2019. https://leavingevidence.wordpress.com.

Moberg, David O. *The Great Reversal: Evangelism Versus Social Concern*. J.B. Lippincott Company, 1972.

Moeller, Shannon. "The Responsibility of Modesty (Part Two)." The Rebelution. February 6, 2007. www.therebelution.com.

Moore, Jina. "How the Atlanta Shooting Shows the Dangers of American Evangelicalism's Trademark 'Purity Culture.'" March 20, 2021. www.businessinsider.com.

Moslener, Sara. *Virgin Nation: Sexual Purity and American Adolescence*. Oxford University Press, 2015.

Moslener, Sara. "White Women's Bodies and the Dilemma of Purity Culture Recovery." *The Revealer*. February 7, 2023. https://therevealer.org.

Moultrie, Monique. *Passionate and Pious, Religious Media and Black Women's Sexuality*. Duke University Press, 2017.

Naps, Sara (@AlsoNamedSara). Twitter (now X). May 2, 2020. https://twitter.com/AlsoNamedSara/status/1256710062975922180.

Nason-Clark, Nancy, and Barbara Fisher-Townsend. "Acting Abusively in the Household of Faith." In *Responding to Abuse in Christian Homes*, edited by Nancy Nason-Clark and Barbara Fisher-Townsend. Wipf & Stock, 2011.

Natarajan, Madison, Kerrie G. Wilkins-Yel, Anushka Sista, Aashika Anantharaman, and Natalie Seils. "Decolonizing Purity Culture: Gendered Racism and White Idealization in Evangelical Christianity." *Psychology of Women Quarterly* 46, no. 3 (2022): 316–336. https://doi.org/10.1177/03616843221091l.

Nueger, Christie Cozad, and James Newton Poling. *Men's Work in Preventing Violence Against Women*. Haworth Press, 2002.

Nurrieum, Hannah (@OnTheOtherHanna). Twitter (now X). July 27, 2019. https://twitter.com/OnTheOtherHanna/status/1155128207487774721.

Oberhaus, Daniel. "The Biggest-Ever Orgasm Study Tells Us More About How Women Come." *Vice*. September 6, 2017. www.vice.com.

O'Brien, Julia M. "The Economics of Family: Changing Biblical Norms." *Biblical Archaeology Review* 36, no. 5 (2010).

Okun, Tema. "White Supremacy Culture Characteristics." White Supremacy Culture. Updated August 2023. www.whitesupremacyculture.info.

Omi, Michael, and Howard Winant. *Racial Formation in the United States*. Routledge, 2014.

Otis, John. "Evangelical Christian Churches Gain Ground in Majority Catholic Brazil." *Morning Edition*. NPR. August 22, 2022. www.npr.org.

Ott, Kate. *Christian Ethics for a Digital Society*. Rowman and Littlefield, 2019.

Ott, Kate. "Orgasmic Failure: A Praxis Ethic for Adolescent Sexuality." In *Theologies of Failure*, edited by Roberto Sirvent and Duncan B. Reyburn. Cascade Books, 2019.

Ott, Kate. "Re-Thinking Adolescent Sexual Ethics: A Social Justice Obligation to Adolescent Sexual Health." *Journal of Lutheran Ethics* 7, no. 2 (2007).

Ott, Kate. *Sex, Tech & Faith: Ethics for a Digital Age*. Wm. B. Eerdmans, 2022.

Ott, Kate, and Lauren D. Sawyer, "Sexual Practices and Relationships Among Young People." In *The Routledge Handbook of Philosophy of Sex and Sexuality*, edited by Brian D. Earp, Clare Chambers, and Lori Watson. Routledge, 2022.

Ott, Kate, and Lorien Carter. "ReVisioning Sexuality: Relational Joy and Embodied Flourishing." *Journal of Youth and Theology* 20, no. 1 (March 2021): 1–19. https://doi.org/10.1163/24055093-02001002.

Owen, Gabrielle. *A Queer History of Adolescence: Developmental Pasts, Relational Futures*. University of Georgia Press, 2020.

Parton, Heather Digby. "The Twisted Fantasy Behind Mike Johnson's 'Purity' Pledge." *Salon*. December 27, 2023. www.salon.com.

Pascoe, Peggy. *What Comes Naturally: Miscegenation and the Making of Race in America*. Oxford University Press, 2009.

Payne, Ed. "Group Apologizes to Gay Community, Shuts Down 'Cure' Ministry." CNN. July 8, 2013. www.cnn.com.

Perry, Jackie Hill. *Gay Girl Good God: The Story of Who I Was and Who God Has Always Been*. B&H Publishing Group, 2018.

Peterson-Iyer, Karen. "Mobile Porn? Teenage Sexting and Justice for Women." *Journal of the Society of Christian Ethics* 33, no. 2 (Fall/Winter 2013): 93–110. http://dx.doi.org/10.1353/sce.2013.0036.

Peterson-Iyer, Karen. *Reenvisioning Sexual Ethics: A Feminist Christian Account*. Georgetown University Press, 2022.

Pew Research Center. "An Examination of the 2016 Electorate, Based on Validated Voters." August 9, 2018. www.pewresearch.org.

Phillips, Amber. "Florida's Law Limiting LGBTQ Discussion in Schools, Explained." *Washington Post*. April 1, 2022. www.washingtonpost.com.

Piaget, Jean, and Bärbel Inhelder. *The Psychology of the Child*. Basic Books, 2000.

Pickren, Wade E., and Alexandra Rutherford. *A History of Modern Psychology in Context*. John Wiley & Sons, Inc., 2010.

Pitkin, Barbara. "'The Heritage of the Lord': Children in the Theology of John Calvin." In *The Child in Christian Thought*, edited by Marcia J. Bunge. William B. Eerdmans, 2001.

Pivar, David J. *Purity Crusade: Sexual Morality and Social Control, 1868–1900*. Greenwood Press, 1973.

Posner, Sarah. "How the Christian Right Helped Foment Insurrection." *Rolling Stone*. January 31, 2021. www.rollingstone.com.

RAINN. "Children and Teens: Statistics." Accessed July 23, 2021. www.rainn.org.

The Rebelution. "Announcement: The Modesty Survey." December 2, 2006. https://web.archive.org.

The Rebelution. "The Rebelution." Accessed February 25, 2024. www.therebelution.com/about.

The Rebelution. "Statistical Overview." 2007. https://web.archive.org.

Redmond, Sheila A. "Christian 'Virtues' and Recovery from Child Sexual Abuse." In *Christianity, Patriarchy, and Abuse: A Feminist Critique*, edited by Joanne Carlson Brown and Carol R. Bohn. Pilgrim Press, 1989.

Regnerus, Mark D. *Forbidden Fruit: Sex & Religion in the Lives of American Teenagers*. Oxford University Press, 2009.

Reimer, Christina. "The Taboo of Virginity: Purity Balls as Negative Rites of Passage." *Arc: The Journal of the Faculty of Religion, McGill University* (2009): 213–222.

Remez, Lisa. "Oral Sex Among Adolescents: Is It Sex or Is It Abstinence?" *Family Planning Perspectives* 32, no. 6. (November–December 2000): 298–304. https://doi.org/10.1363/3229800.

Revolve: The Complete New Testament. Thomas Nelson, 2003.

Ribuffo, Leo P. "Family Policy Past as Prologue: Jimmy Carter, the White House Conference on Families, and the Mobilization of the New Christian Right." *Review of Policy Research* 23, no. 2 (2006): 311–338. https://doi.org/10.1111/j.1541-1338.2006.00203.x.

Robert, Nikia Smith. "'Not Meant to Survive': Black Mothers Leading Beyond the Criminal Line." In *Walking Through the Valley: Womanist Explorations in the Spirit of Katie Geneva Cannon*, edited by Emilie M. Townes, Stacey Floyd-Thomas, Alison P. Guise Johnson, and Angela D. Sims. Westminster John Knox, 2022.

Roden, Renée. "Britney Spears: An Icon for Purity Culture's Wounded Woman." *National Catholic Reporter*. August 31, 2021. www.ncronline.org.

Ruether, Rosemary Radford. "Augustine: Sexuality, Gender, and Women." In *Feminist Interpretations of Augustine*, edited by Judith Chelius Stark. The Pennsylvania State University Press, 2007.

Santelli, John S., Leslie M. Kantor, Stephanie A. Grilo, Ilene S. Speizer, Laura D. Lindberg, Jennifer Heitel, Amy T. Schalet, Maureen E. Lyon, Amanda J. Mason-Jones, Terry McGovern, Craig J. Heck, Jennifer Rogers, and Mary A. Ott. "Abstinence-Only-Until-Marriage: An Updated Review of U.S. Policies and Programs and Their Impact." *Journal of Adolescent Health* 61 (2017): 273–280.

Sater, Steven, and Duncan Sheik. *Spring Awakening: A New Musical.* Theatre Communications Group, 2007.

Sawyer, Lauren. "Spring Awakening." *The Sojourn.* Indiana Wesleyan University. March 26, 2009.

Sawyer, Lauren D., and Victoria Houser. "Purity Culture and the Limits of Queer Evangelicalism." *Theology & Sexuality* 29, no. 2–3 (2024): 200–218. https://doi.org/10.1080/13558358.2024.2332982.

Scanlon, Rachel (@rachelscanloncomedy). "If you sang along, you've also been traumatized Watch my special 'Gay Fantasy', out now! Link in bio!" TikTok. July 1, 2024. www.tiktok.com.

Scharen, Christian, and Aana Marie Vigen, eds. *Ethnography as Christian Theology and Ethics.* Continuum Books, 2011.

Schultz, Olivia Jayne. "Purity Culture's Racist Fruit: Centering the Voices of Black Womanists and Feminists in the Deconstruction of Purity Culture." *Arc: Journal of the School of Religious Studies (McGill University),* 49 (2021): 1–47.

Sedgwick, Sally. "Can Kant's Ethic Survive the Feminist Critique?" In *Feminist Interpretations of Immanuel Kant,* edited by Robin May Schott. The Pennsylvania State University, 1997.

Sehat, David. *The Myth of American Religious Freedom.* Oxford University Press, 2011.

Sellers, Tina Schermer. *Sex, God, and the Conservative Church: Erasing Shame from Sexual Intimacy.* Routledge, 2017.

Shannon, Chelsea L., and Jeffrey D. Klausner. "The Growing Epidemic of Sexually Transmitted Infections in Adolescents: A Neglected Population." *Current Opinion in Pediatrics* 30, no. 1 (2018): 137–143. https://doi.org/10.1097/MOP.0000000000000578.

Sharp, Isaac B. *The Other Evangelicals: A Story of Liberal, Black, Progressive, Feminist, and Gay Christians—and the Movement That Pushed Them Out.* William B. Eerdmans Publishing Company, 2023.

sheologian (@sheologian). Twitter (now X). May 2, 2020. https://twitter.com/sheologian/status/1256620335304249345.

Shepherd, Lindsay M., Kaye F. Sly, and Jeffrey M. Girard. "Comparison of Comprehensive and Abstinence-Only Sexuality Education in Young African American Adolescents." *Journal of Adolescence* 61 (2017): 50–63.

Sherman, Gabriel. "Inside Jerry Falwell Jr.'s Unlikely Rise and Precipitous Fall at Liberty University." *Vanity Fair.* January 24, 2022. www.vanityfair.com.

Silliman, Daniel. "Evangelicals Outgrow Catholics in Central America." *Christianity Today.* February 13, 2023. www.christianitytoday.com.

Simpson, Jessica. *Open Book.* HarperCollins, 2020. Kindle.

Smith, Brent. *Religious Studies and the Goal of Interdisciplinarity.* Routledge, 2019.

Smith, Lillian. *Killers of the Dream.* W.W. Norton & Company, 1949.

Snyder, Gwen. "They Want to Keep Teen Girls Married and Pregnant." *Jezebel.* June 30, 2022. https://jezebel.com.

Spyrou, Spyros, Rachel Rosen, and Daniel Thomas Cook, eds. *Reimagining Childhood Studies*. Bloomsbury, 2019.

Stanley, Tiffany. "The Sex-Abuse Scandal That Devastated a Suburban Megachurch." *Washingtonian*. February 14, 2016. www.washingtonian.com.

Stasson, Anneke. "The Politicization of Family Life: How Headship Became Essential to Evangelical Identity in the Late Twentieth Century." *Religion and American Culture: A Journal of Interpretation* 24, no. 1 (2014): 1052–1151.

Stephano, Christopher (@cjstephanoAITC). Twitter (now X). May 2, 2020. https://twitter.com/cjstephanoAITC/status/1256626216980930566.

Stockton, Kathryn Bond. *The Queer Child, or Growing Sideways in the Twentieth Century*. Duke University Press, 2009.

Stolakis, Kristine. *Pray Away*. Blumhouse Productions, 2021. Netflix.

Stowe, Harriet Beecher. *Uncle Tom's Cabin; or, Life Among the Lowly*. Edited by Christopher G. Diller. Broadview Editions, 2009.

Strack, Jay, and Diane Strack. *Until You Say I Do*. A True Love Waits Resource. LifeWay Press, 1997.

Stroop, Chrissy (@C_Stroop). Twitter (now X). June 9, 2021. https://twitter.com/C_Stroop/status/1402654534518722564?s=20&t=YfVhcLcGAqS-rJyiPgVhow.

Stroop, Chrissy, and Lauren O'Neal. "Introduction." In *Empty the Pews: Stories of Leaving the Church*, edited by Chrissy Stroop and Lauren O'Neal. Epiphany Publishing, 2019.

Sutton, Matthew Avery. *Aimee Semple McPherson and the Resurrection of Christian America*. Harvard University Press, 2009.

Sutton, Matthew Avery. *Jerry Falwell and the Rise of the Religious Right: A Brief History with Documents*. The Bedford Series in History and Culture. Bedford/St. Martin's, 2013.

Swidler, Ann. "Culture in Action: Symbols and Strategies." *American Sociological Review* 51, no. 2 (1986): 273–286.

Syed, Moin, and Jillian Fish. "Revisiting Erik Erikson's Legacy on Culture, Race, and Ethnicity." *Identity* 18, no. 4. (October 2018): 274–283. https://doi.org/10.1080/15283488.2018.1523729.

Talburt, Susan. "Intelligibility and Narrating Queer Youth." In *Youth and Sexualities: Pleasure, Subversion, and Insubordination in and out of Schools*, edited by Mary Louise Rasmussen, Eric Rofes, and Susan Talburt. Palgrave MacMillan, 2004.

Tessman, Lisa. *Burdened Virtues: Virtue Ethics for Liberatory Struggles*. Oxford University Press, 2005.

Thomas, Jeremy N. "The Development and Deployment of the Idea of Pornography Addiction Within American Evangelicalism." *Sexual Addiction & Compulsivity* 23, no. 2 (2016): 182–195. http://dx.doi.org/10.1080/10720162.2016.1140603.

Thompson, Derek. "America's Teenage Girls Are Not Okay." *The Atlantic*. February 16, 2023. www.theatlantic.com.

Thompson, Derek. "Why American Teens Are So Sad." *The Atlantic*. April 11, 2022. www.theatlantic.com.

Townes, Emilie M. *Womanist Ethics and the Cultural Production of Evil*. Palgrave MacMillan, 2006.

Traina, Cristina L. H. "Children and Moral Agency." *Journal of the Society of Christian Ethics* 29, no. 2 (Fall/Winter 2009): 19–37.

Traina, Cristina L. H. *Erotic Attunement: Parenthood and the Ethics of Sensuality Between Unequals*. University of Chicago Press, 2011.

Tranby, Eric and Douglas Hartmann. "Critical Whiteness Theories and the Evangelical 'Race Problems': Extending Emerson and Smith's *Divided by Faith*." *Journal for the Scientific Study of Religion* 47, no. 3 (2008): 341–359. https://doi.org/10.1111/j.1468-5906.2008.00414.x.

Troya, Corbyjane. "This Is Not About You: The Joshua Harris Redemption Tour." Medium. August 4, 2019. https://medium.com.

Twenge, Jean M. "Have Smartphones Destroyed a Generation?" *The Atlantic*. September 2017. www.theatlantic.com.

Twenge, Jean M. Interview with Ezra Klein. *The Ezra Klein Show*. Podcast audio. May 19, 2023. www.nytimes.com.

"Unaltered Ministries." Nonprofit Explorer. ProPublica. January 8, 2024. https://projects.propublica.org.

Vaca, Daniel. *Evangelicals Incorporated: Books and the Business of Religion in America*. Harvard University Press, 2019.

Valenti, Jessica. *The Purity Myth: How America's Obsession with Virginity Is Hurting Young Women*. Seal Press, 2009.

Van Ausdale, Debra, and Joe R. Feagin. *The First R: How Children Learn Race and Racism*. Rowan and Littlefield, 2011.

Van Leeuwen, Mary Stewart. *A Sword Between the Sexes? C. S. Lewis and the Gender Debates*. Brazos Press, 2010.

Walker, Pete. *Complex PTSD: From Surviving to Thriving*. Azure Coyote Publishing, 2013.

Wall, John. *Ethics in Light of Childhood*. Georgetown University Press, 2010.

Wall, John. "From Childhood Studies to Childism: Reconstructing the Scholarly and Social Imaginations." *Children's Geographies* (2019): 1–14. https://doi.org/10.1080/14733285.2019.1668912.

Wallace, Brandon. *Straight Face*. Green Bridge Press, 2014.

Watson, Samuel. "Flexible Gender Roles During the Market Revolution: Family, Friendship, Marriage and Masculinity Among U.S. Army Officers, 1815–1846." *Journal of Social History*, 29, no. 1 (Autumn 1995): 81–106.

Welcher, Rachel Joy. *Talking Back to Purity Culture: Rediscovering Faithful Christian Sexuality*. InterVarsity Press, 2020.

West, Traci C. *Wounds of the Spirit: Black Women, Violence, and Resistance Ethics*. New York University Press, 1999.

Wheeler, Barbara G. "You Who Were Far Off: Religious Divisions and the Role of Religious Research." *Review of Religious Research* 37, no. 4 (June 1996): 289–301. https://doi.org/10.2307/3512010.

Wheeler-Reed, David, Jennifer W. Knust, and Dale B. Martin. "Can a Man Commit πορνεία with His Wife?" *JBL* 137, no. 2 (2018): 383–398. http://dx.doi.org/10.15699/jbl.1372.2018.345030.

White, Heather R. "How Paul Became the Straight Word: Protestant Biblicism and the Twentieth-Century Invention of Biblical Heteronormativity." In *Bodies on the Verge: Queering Pauline Epistles*, edited Joseph A. Marchal. SBL Press, 2019.

"Whiteness." *Talking About Race*. National Museum of African American History and Culture. Smithsonian. Accessed January 24, 2024. https://nmaahc.si.edu.

Wiley, David C., Marina Plesons, Venkataram Chandra-Mouli, and Margarita Ortega. "Managing Sex Education Controversy Deep in the Heart of Texas: A Case Study of the North East Independent School District (NEISD)." *American Journal of Sexuality Education* 15, no. 1 (2020): 53–81. https://doi.org/10.1080/15546128.2019.1675562.

Wilhelm, Todd. "Joshua Harris—The Only Constant in Life Is Change." *The Wartburg Watch*. September 29, 2023. https://thewartburgwatch.com.

Williams, Daniel K. "Sex and the Evangelicals: Gender Issues, the Sexual Revolution, and Abortion in the 1960s." In *American Evangelicals and the 1960s*, edited by Axel R. Schäfer. University of Wisconsin Press, 2013.

Winell, Marlene. "Religious Trauma Syndrome." *Cognitive Behavioural Therapy Today* 39, no. 2 (May 2011): 19–21.

Winter, Meaghan. "The Fastest-Growing Group of American Evangelicals." *The Atlantic*. July 26, 2021. www.theatlantic.com.

Wollstonecraft, Mary. *A Vindication of the Rights of Women*. Edited by Eileen Hunt Botting. Yale University Press, 2014.

Woodson, Jules. "I Was Assaulted. He Was Applauded." New York Times Opinion. *New York Times*. March 9, 2018. www.nytimes.com.

Young, Thelathia "Nikki." *Black Queer Ethics, Family, & Philosophical Imagination*. Palgrave Macmillan, 2016.

Zierman, Addie. *When We Were on Fire: A Memoir of Consuming Faith, Tangled Love and Starting Over*. Convergent Books, 2013.

INDEX

ABOUT THE AUTHOR

Lauren D. Sawyer, PhD, is an ethicist and educator living in Seattle, Washington. She is affiliate faculty at The Seattle School of Theology and Psychology, where she teaches graduate courses in theology and develops trauma-informed curriculum for the Allender Center.